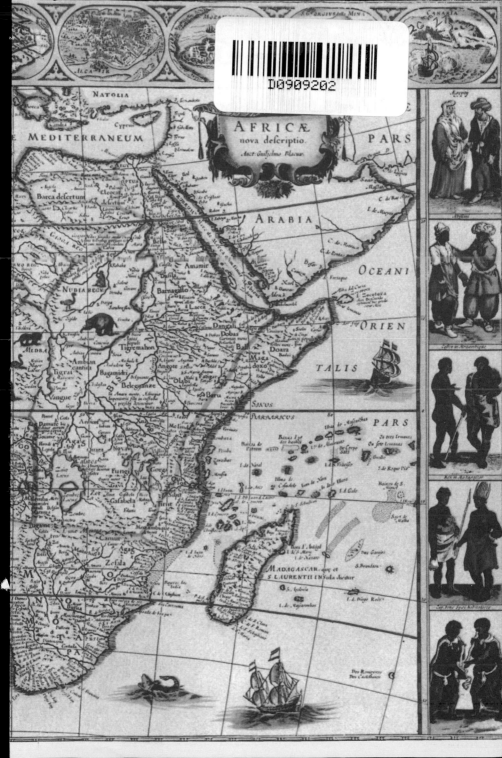

AFRICA'S FUTURE: DARKNESS TO DESTINY

BOOKS BY DUNCAN CLARKE

The Battle for Barrels: Peak Oil Myths and World Oil Futures
Empires of Oil: Corporate Oil in Barbarian Worlds
Africa: Crude Continent – The Struggle for Africa's Oil Prize

Praise for *Africa: Crude Continent*

"A highly accomplished work and must-read on Africa and its political economy of oil … in an epic which illuminates Africa's 'inner worlds' and deftly weaves together the continent's ancient, post-colonial and modern histories … an outstanding work … to delight even old Africa hands in this timely, well-informed and masterful treatise."
Barry Morgan, Africa correspondent, Upstream International, *the international oil and gas newspaper*

"No other writer matches his unique knowledge of the global energy industry and Africa's historical, political and economic oil context. Clarke's insights into contemporary policy, poverty, corporate strategies and African geopolitics make this book required reading for energy industry executives, investment analysts and African policy-makers, diplomats, donor agencies, banks and international lenders. Very good stuff."
Professor Tony Hawkins, Financial Times *correspondent*

"Everyone wants to understand Africa's oil industry, but until now it was hard to know where to start. Now the choice is easy. *Crude Continent* is the most thorough exploration yet of this crucial field."
Robert Guest, former Africa editor, The Economist, *and author of* The Shackled Continent

"If I need to know anything about oil in Africa, I go straight to this book."
Richard Dowden, Director, the Royal African Society

"Clarke's *tour de force* is … brave and bold. Brave in its scope and bold in style, and the odyssey is compelling reading."
Tim Hughes, Programme Head, Governance of Africa's Resources Programme, South African Institute of International Affairs

"Duncan Clarke's *Crude Continent* matches its ambition, tackling a subject that has baffled, frustrated and confused a galaxy of pop stars and super-models, academics and UN experts, aid workers and business leaders, and journalists … informed by an unrivalled knowledge of Africa's oil industry."

Michael Holman, former Africa editor of the Financial Times

"La bible du pétrole African … qui détaille près de quarante ans de bataille pour le pétrole africain, du Cap au Caire. Tel un safari à travers le continent, le récit de Duncan Clarke guide le lecteur dans les coulisses de la conquête du brut africain, avec force détails et anecdotes, tantôt humoristiques."

Jeune Afrique

Africa's Future: Darkness to Destiny

"Duncan Clarke's latest book on Africa sets out to answer tough questions about the continent, often asked but seldom satisfactorily answered: What shaped Africa's economies? What went wrong? And can its recent growth be sustained? The result is rather like travelling around Africa in the company of a knowledgeable and entertaining guide who draws lessons from the past while mapping out the future. Challenging theories and defying conventional wisdom throughout, he knows Africa too well to come up with easy or glib answers and provides a stimulating and thought-provoking journey."
Michael Holman, former Africa editor of the Financial Times

"Duncan Clarke, one of the most astute analysts of Africa – widely read and travelled – writes from the inside about Africa's long history: from the origins of humankind, through slavery and colonialism to the economic dilemmas and difficulties faced today. Enormously stimulating, Clarke boldly rethinks Africa's economic future."
Professor Francis Wilson, School of Economics, University of Cape Town, author of Dinosaurs, Diamonds & Democracy: A Short, Short History of South Africa

"A richly detailed review of Africa's past and what it tells us about the future, providing a sobering view of the realities on the ground. Indispensable for anyone interested in global trends in the 21st century."
Ian Morris, author of Why the West Rules – For Now

"This is a book that exudes an intense love of subject, and regales the reader with exquisite nuances and fascinating insights."
Robert D. Kaplan, author of Monsoon: The Indian Ocean and the Future of American Power

AFRICA'S FUTURE: DARKNESS TO DESTINY

How the past is shaping Africa's economic evolution

Duncan Clarke

P

PROFILE BOOKS

First published in Great Britain in 2012 by
Profile Books Ltd
3A Exmouth House
Pine Street
London EC1R OJH
www.profilebooks.com

A CIP catalogue record for this book is available from the British Library.

ISBN: 978 1 84668 569 9
ebook ISBN: 978 1 84765 799 2

Cartography by Ian Games
Typeset in Times by MacGuru Ltd
info@macguru.org.uk
Printed and bound in Great Britain by
Clays, Bungay, Suffolk

Contents

Maps

The cover map of Africa depicts a modernised image moulded around Africa seen at night, reflecting a huge and luminous continent, surrounded by a world-wide sea of development elsewhere. It portrays an artistic metaphor for the Dark Continent's story, one of gradual emergence towards a more promising but still uncertain set of complex economic destinies.

In memoriam
Desmond Hobart Houghton
Professor of Economics, Rhodes University

In honour
Peter Robson
Emeritus Professor of Economics, University of St Andrews

Preface

What can explain Africa's socioeconomic morphology, its economic growth and its cyclical performance over long spans of time – and are there implications for the future? I could find no satisfactory answer to these questions in economics texts read over many years, nor amid my Africana collection, nor in the prolific output on the economics of Africa from Bretton Woods institutions, banks, think-tanks, writers, analysts or media reporting.

There are profound shortcomings in the vast economics literature on the continent and within modern formalist economics, which, in the last couple of decades, has disconnected from many intellectual achievements of earlier development economics in Africa. This has moved me to consider ideas from the natural sciences, allied to non-linear ideas, to better "explain" Africa's economic saga across space and time during the *longue durée*. Intense worldwide interest in Charles Darwin's centenary stimulated the idea to rethink Africa's economic shape in terms of economic evolution.[1]

Africa's economic drama is best understood in the context of the continent's continuously evolving past. This requires appreciation of old economic modes still shaping the rude realities of subsistence and survival in Africa. Many constructs found today within Africa's economic underbelly are predominantly medieval or pre-capitalist structures. They in part support, or even marry with, Africa's proto-modernity. Here I do not imply any pejorative connotation to the notion of Africa's "underbelly': it is Africa's older world foundations, traditionalism if you like, that act in defence of subsistence economies against the unremitting onslaught of modernity.

While this book weaves an interpretation of the economic evolution of Africa, it is not an economic history of the continent. Still less is it any econometric or quantitative analysis, or political story, or even a text on policy or attempt to "fix Africa". It does not forecast growth for years to come. *Africa's Future: Darkness to Destiny* seeks merely to provide a prism to understand Africa's complex history, giving recognition to its varied economic realities and the evolutionary pathways shaping its socioeconomic conditions.

With a focus on Africa only, I have not tried (except, on occasion, in passing) to draw equivalent comparisons with Europe or elsewhere in this explanation of economic pathways from past to present. Nor does the interpretation seek to address any of the economic questions, choices or trade-offs that so occupy the economics profession. Typically economists raise quite different issues. Their models, as in econometrics, have other aims and are specified typically within narrow, restricted, time-bound limits.

Here any author should assess past "explanations" for Africa's predicament to answer salient questions confronting the continent's economic origins and future growth path: they include shifting demographics, poverty and inequalities, nation-state flaws, institutional deficiencies, conflicts and power struggles, past and incipient balkanisation, the rising middle-income or social class, emerging corporate powerhouses, Africa's shifting place in the world economy, and trajectories within a changed and competitive 21st century.

✸

A word is due on the format, schema, text and ideas in this interpretation of Africa. A number of maps provide visual images of the themes, from the past and present and on the future, discussed in the narrative.

Comments and references to economics literature on Africa are found in the Notes, with suggestions on access to a more detailed bibliography.

In Chapter 1 the origin of Africa's earliest economies is portrayed in images, to illustrate the long roots etched in the past from which the genesis of modernity ultimately sprang. The economic journey has been long and tortuous; it took many pathways before evolution led to the present. It was only many thousands of years after Africa's autochthonous economies were installed that the outer world cast its net across the Dark Continent to understand and map the outline and inner reaches of the continent. This was done slowly, fitfully, with error, and on the basis of imperfect knowledge.

Part I depicts the original nature of economic existence in Africa, its proliferation worldwide and the evolved forms of subsistence that developed within Africa. It sketches pathways to the present. Many mechanisms of subsistence and survival, from ancient times to now, cross-cut by bouts of externally driven exploitative intrusions, make up current economic realities on the ground. Numerous transitions reshaped economic pathways that constructed Africa's story. It is one of complex adaptive process.

To appreciate this evolution key data on Africa's numerics are presented to explain the economic contours. To understand Africa's economies it is important to know its scalar dimensions, economic growth record and comparative performance over time in world terms. I have placed Africa's economies in context from the early common era (CE) to today, posing central questions and indicating lessons to be drawn from this historical experience. Africa has long fallen behind the rest of the world in economic terms. The gap has widened with time as it frequently encountered interrupted economic cycles. Accumulation of wealth and capital has been a fraught process. There has been no quantum leap out of past trajectories, even though economic conditions have been more favourable in the past decade. The ideas of economists and non-economists need to be seen against these economic parameters. Hard-nosed economic measurement allows us to judge contemporary myths that underlie projections or futurology passing for certainty about the decades to come – many based on ambitious linear growth estimates to mid-century, the changing economic matrix and metrics expected in Africa, forecast models used by institutions and development drivers for the future.

In Part 2 the narrative traces historical threads from the Stone Age to Africa's "discovery". It initiated an early wave of continental globalisation. Since mankind's birth in Africa, nature and ecology have played decisive roles across this diverse continent. Hundreds of ecologies have shaped the economic matrix. Nature's constraints continue to have an impact on economies and societies in costs, time, resources, technologies and survival strategies.

In Part 3 we examine the collage of contemporary economic landscapes. Post-colonial Africa was born in an unplanned trauma and with a revised composite of diktat and realpolitik that included a changing of the guard and the demise of the old – including expiry of the imperial mandate with the political rebirth of Africa's nation-states. While strategies, policies and economic approaches differed, the survival fabric of subsistence Africa and its transformed economic shapes remained.

Before looking at Africa's economic future, Part 4 reviews the quest to find out what in the past went wrong. Interpreting knowledge of Africa is a cumulative game. In Chapter 11 I discuss selected earlier works with the aim of developing summate views from leading texts, with no pretension to be exhaustive. Africa's possible economic trajectories are explored in Chapter 12.

When intuiting the economic future there must be no delusion about the naive images and shallow critiques based on Afro-pessimism or its counterpart of equally illusionary Afro-optimism. Both are offered from time to time in place of rigorous, critical thinking. There is no virtue in optimism at the cost of realism. As it was for Machiavelli, ruthless objectivity is our best guide. The state of Africa and its economies today marks the departure point for the future. We know the past has shaped the present: for the future, what do we really know?

I

Finding Africa

Before we examine the present or explore the future, there are images of the past that deserve our attention – notably the matter of survival in Africa and the continent's long history of "discovery". For the outer world this process was long, pieced together incrementally and often accomplished with error.

Genesis

Humankind originated in Africa, so the fossil record reveals, and the "born in Africa" mould touches humanity across the world. The first humans had an economy of sorts. It was from all accounts bare-boned, primitive and crude, essentially survivalist.

Imagine nightfall in the Olduvai Gorge in east Africa's Great Rift Valley 2 million years ago, where a small group of our earliest human ancestors, *Homo erectus*, following millennia of evolution as hominoids, found shelter in Africa's primordial frontier savannah. They were very few and they knew no others. Some decided to seek new pastures further afield. Their material existence was at the most basic level, with survival the daily and ultimate ambition. A parting of the ways took place, initiating exodus to unknown parts of the continent.

There were no geographies or maps known to the émigrés beyond their own limited range of experience. They trekked away from Olduvai, leaving known environs of limited subsistence, to a future unknown elsewhere, starting again as a separate node of the original mode of humanity formed at its earliest inception. Some may have been pushed by shifts in climate and ecologies; others may even have been lured by opportunism or notions about "greener pastures". Much later their descendants reached the shores of the Red Sea and broke out of Africa towards the Levant and in replicated acts of migration and discovery found themselves in new lands as far as the Caucasus, East Asia and elsewhere. Their tools and technologies were primitive. At some point they had captured the knowledge of fire, an engine for further economic evolution. Their skills in hunting slowly improved. These treks "inside Africa" and "out of Africa" shaped the core foundations of local and global economies. Economic modes of survival at raw subsistence were crafted and groups of our human ancestors found opportunities for eking out their living in environments far afield and unknown.

Offshoots from Africa's economic genesis spread from the continent around 700,000 years ago to range over Europe. They diverged in nature and physiology to emerge later as Neanderthals, hunter-gatherers in radically different climes, adapting to cold and austere conditions. Roaming in nomadic bands the Neanderthals sheltered in caves and developed specialised tools for hunting, working wood and living off animals in the forbidding terrain. Innovation and adaptation marked these epic journeys, and while the archaeological and paleoanthropological records may never be finally settled, in these early roots were to be found the origins of modern man's economies. The use of contemporary genetic history enables us to infer that it was in the cradle of Africa that all began, with a common ancestry, an original mode of survival and many varied subsequent nodes of socioeconomic existence. These subsistence forms changed with circumstance and ultimately gave rise to the complex world economy.

In Africa the San peoples dominated south-east central Africa, as hunter-gatherers. Their descendants today have been pushed by the competitive evolutionary cycle into very restricted zones and different ways of living. Understanding their art of tracking, as shown by Louis Liebenberg in a masterful account, provides us rare insight into the San cultures of economic adaptation and innovation.[1]

While the cradle of humanity was Africa, it was a dynamic world replete with progressive advances in toolmaking, hunting techniques, subsistence drawn from the edges of Africa's ocean littoral, and with evidence of cultural evolution, art and symbolism. Adaptation was the essential necessity. The Sahara Desert expanded during Africa's long dry patch, somewhere around 200,000–125,000 years ago, cutting off North Africa, while the Kalahari Desert created another barrier. As the warm period returned, following evolution, so *Homo sapiens* again went "out of Africa", once more through the Levant. The surviving remnants of mankind in Africa had to confront new threats some 75,000 years ago as the savannah dried, cold returned and harsh conditions burdened this epic struggle for survival. Around 60,000 years ago, so we are told, probably only around 5,000 people remained in Africa. It was innovation and adaptation that allowed their survival through reliance on a varied and upgraded set of economic means for existence.[2]

Meanwhile, the outer world retained little residual knowledge of the Africa left behind. It remained like this for many thousands of years. Thereafter the slow accumulation outside the continent of knowledge about Africa was only pieced together bit by bit. By this stage large parts of the rest of the world had moved along different economic paths.

Mapping Africa

I am writing this text in a study at home in front of an enormous original map of Africa by A. Arrowsmith, entitled and produced for *The Committee and Members of the British Association for Discovering Interior parts of Africa*, rendered on 1 December 1802. It is a magnificent cartographic insight as to what the outside world then knew about Africa – not a lot.

The Maghreb littoral is depicted in some detail, the Great Desert less so save for caravan routes, while the Soudan or Nigritia in the Sahel belt shows the segmented arenas of old states and suzerainties that existed. At the bottom of the Sahel on the frontier edges of sub-Saharan Africa, the Kumra or Mountains of the Moon are shown to cross from west to east. Below there are vast spaces of *terra incognita* but for the coastal outposts along the littorals of Guinea and old Congo. The Cape hinterlands are depicted as far north as the Damaras and the country of the Booshuanas, and Madagascar is represented in some detail. On the interior edges are places where the Arabs and Portuguese had established trading bases in south-eastern Africa. Nearby inland, the Mocaranga, west of Sofala and along the southern side of the Zambezi, are found enclosed in their kingdom. Most of sub-Saharan Africa is shown as a vast blank space.

Many maps I have elsewhere, around 30 of different vintages, tell earlier and later tales of the cartography of the times from a wide variety of sources.[3]

The earliest maps appear as rock art "map sketches" in Africa's ancient past over 10,000 years ago, still found in ochre all over the Sahara and central-southern Africa and painted even up to 500 years ago. Egyptians, Greeks and Romans made maps of what they knew as Libya (the term Africa emerging in the late medieval period, derived from the allegorical representation for the south-west wind named *Africus* or *Afer*, after the descendant of Abraham). Partly this might have been to differentiate those around the southern Mediterranean from Ethiopians, those of "burnt face" from further south, towards Kush and Nubia and in the shifting cultures found around ancient Meroe in Sudan below the fifth cataract.[4]

With the Arab conquest of the Maghreb in the 7th century, the coastal region became known in Arabic as *Ifriqiya*. Only around the 15th century, following Portuguese exploration along the coasts, was the term Africa applied to the continent as a whole. Others have argued that Africa was defined as "a paradigm of difference", to serve as an exotic prism through which outsiders, mainly from Europe, might reflect images of the "other". Yet as Malvern van Wyk Smith has demonstrated, the refracted images of Ethiopians and "others" derived much earlier, from Pharaonic Egypt, passing thereafter through into classical times by way of Hellenist Egypt around Alexandria and later Roman Africa.[5] The crucible of slaving from Africa to Arabia and later Atlantic destinations settled the word Africa into the lexicon. Later Africans began to appropriate the idea of Africa, initially so done by those in the diaspora that could perceive "Africa" because of their removal and remoteness from it.

Some believe that Pharaoh Necho II (610–595BCE) commissioned a Phoenician expedition that sailed into the southern hemisphere many centuries before Vasco da Gama rounded the Cape of Storms. This claimed circumnavigation of "Libya" might have been a voyage through the Red Sea down the east coast below the Tropic of Capricorn. It was later to become the foundation of Europe's African mythography for over 2,000 years. Herodotus was one of the first writers to describe Africa from travels and discovery, c.489–425BCE. Arab cartography was equally important, influenced by Ptolemy, and shaped the images of later mapmakers. Al-Idrisi (1100–65), a famous Arab cartographer, produced a map of Africa north of the Sahara desert, identifying cities such as ancient Ghana and Timbuktu and Tecrour on the Senegal River.

There were Chinese maps from the 14th century. One depicts the southern peninsular shape of Africa as drawn by Zu Siben (1273–1397), two centuries before circumnavigation of the Cape by the Portuguese. In 1402 the Korean ambassador presented Zhu Di, the Chinese emperor, with a map of the world that showed Africa depicted in shape but not with accurate proportions. Asia it seems had some fragmentary knowledge of Africa.

Then followed medieval Europe's maps and with the Renaissance came maps invoking more details of discovery by the Portuguese, Dutch, English and French cartographers. Nicolas Germanus (c.1420–90) produced maps of Ptolemy's *Geographia* and in 1486 mapped North Africa quite clearly demarcated. The lands to the south were cited as *terra incognita*, with the east coast described as the Bay of the Barbarians. For the first time c.1489–92 the German Henricus Martellus showed Africa in a world map, mainly North Africa and the western coasts to the Cape, and as far as the Zambezi on the eastern seaboard. Others followed to show the land of mythical Prester John, in Abyssinia, the imagined kingdom that had long fascinated Europe, drawn in 1573. Later maps showed African kingdoms inside the continent. From then on cartography on Africa took off.

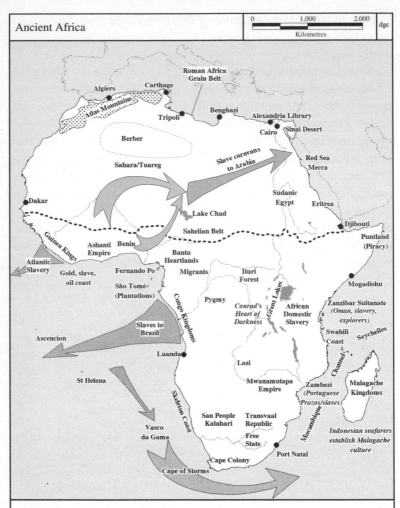

Ancient Africa

0   1,000   2,000
Kilometres

dgc

Roman Africa
Grain Belt

Algiers
Carthage

Atlas Mountains

Tripoli

Benghazi
Alexandria Library

Cairo   Sinai Desert

Berber

Slave caravans
to Arabia

Sahara/Tuareg

Red Sea
Mecca

Dakar

Sudanic
Egypt   Eritrea

Lake Chad

Djibouti

Sahelian Belt

Puntland
(Piracy)

Guinea Kings

Ashanti   Benin
Empire

Bantu
Heartlands

Atlantic
Slavery   Gold, slave,
oil coast

Fernando Po

Migrants

Ituri
Forest

Mogadishu

São Tomé
(Plantations)

Congo Kingdoms

Pygmy

Conrad's
Heart of
Darkness

Great Lakes

African
Domestic
Slavery

Zanzibar Sultanate
(Oman, slavery,
explorers)

Swahili
Coast   Seychelles

Slaves to
Brazil

Ascencion

Luanda

Lozi

Channel

St Helena

Skeleton Coast

Mwanamutapa
Empire

Zambezi
(Portuguese
Prazos/slaves)

Malagache
Kingdoms

San People
Kalahari

Transvaal
Republic

Vasco
da Gama

Free
State

Mocambique

Indonesian seafarers
establish Malagache
culture

Cape of Storms

Cape Colony

Port Natal

Africa's different epochs imprinted the economies of the continent. Romans
and Phoenicians shaped North Africa. Arabs invaded in the 7th century to
establish trans-Saharan trade in slaves and gold. Berber and Tuareg societies
emerged in the Sahara. Migrants from the Bantu heartlands confronted the
San. Omanis controlled Zanzibar. Jan van Riebeeck landed at the Cape in
1652. Portuguese established *prazos* along the Zambezi. West Africa became
known for trading posts and slavery for Atlantic markets.

This all reflected the evolution of knowledge, which advanced in no linear fashion. Accuracy improved as well as detail but early maps were wildly inaccurate, some fantasies, often drawn second-hand or even third-hand from travellers' reports. The art of mapmaking improved in quality over time, as a slow process. The coastline only became well known in the 18th century, and the interiors emptied out, shorn of mythical creatures. Sextants and compasses entered Africa during this age of discovery, while before the age of exploration the continental interior became "Darkest Africa", an empty space. By the end of the 19th century even these areas had been explored and mapped. Modern cartography and space-age mapping finally advanced this revolution in the finest detail.

It was only slowly that Africa became "known" to the outside world in ways it was not known by its inhabitants, except for the detailed knowledge they had long possessed of their own restricted habitats and some adjacent territories.

Part I

Survival in Africa

2

Imagined Africa

The earliest economies in Africa provided the foundation stones for the economies of today with their mix of subsistence and survivalist elements coexistent with modernity. Stone Age Africa was followed by its Iron Age era and the barter or exchange economies that emerged. During this early era various forms of primitive globalisation and accumulation developed under the auspices of African, Arab and Western-managed Atlantic slavery. During the 7th century, Arab incursions in the Maghreb brought new economic patterns. Europe's explorers followed far later across the littoral and coastal reaches, initiating contacts and economic connectivity with Africa's kingdoms and peoples during the epochs from the 15th to 19th centuries. Explorers entered the Dark Continent and penetrated the interior to find a diverse economic base from which to initiate and seek commercial advantage. Breaking into the "Africa House" was not easy, rapid or even initially to great economic benefit. But it set the parameters for the birth of Africa's modern era in the late 19th and 20th centuries. In Africa's long economic history, even before the Greeks or Romans set foot in North Africa, there had already been numerous economic transitions. More came, and more will follow.

Can this complex Africa, its past and present, with one shaping the other, be understood simply and fully over space and time inside the formal models and conventional prisms of the modern macroeconomics so prevalent? I think not. We need to understand why.

Optics

Most economic interpretations of the past and present presume that "Africa is poor". Not true. Africa is not really "poor" as portrayed: it is poorly managed and yet to be developed. Its inherent natural wealth is yet to be fully unlocked, leading many to expect a better future, and there is promise in this direction. Congenital underperformance has been the leitmotif of state management. Nonetheless, Africa has grown despite its politics, illustrating the natural power of its deeply etched economic entities over the political classes and governments that impede them. Existing and vast future potential lies in its abundant natural capital, resource-based industries and the underexploited mineral-energy or oil and gas complexes, while deindustrialisation has taken place over the years, and manufacturing competition today is global. Agrarian failures litter the rural landscapes, but pockets of world-class agribusiness firms invest and produce. There has been no green revolution in Africa, yet. Continental economic transformation could await us in the future. How and when will it manifest?

Once-common debt-driven and aid-reliant strategies have failed lamentably, forcing governments to realign, as they ought to have done decades ago, on sounder models of investment maximisation, expanded trade and commercial engagement outside the decrepit state apparatus. The signal lesson, still not fully learnt in Africa, is that companies trade and invest, countries do not – or if they do so it is typically on weak, inefficient and suboptimal terms. It is no surprise that in this sometimes unrewarding environment, risks abound and investors place most of their funds elsewhere, although more have recently been attracted to Africa. For how long will the currently improved economic cycle last, and on what will it rely? Even now overdimensioned or predatory states, clandestine economies, black economy segments, shadow markets and flawed economic structures remain in Africa's current proto-capitalist model. This matrix reflects immature economic evolution. Consequently, Africa is at some competitive disadvantage to peers elsewhere. Nonetheless, there exists a class of corporate players born in Africa who have emerged, alongside investors from abroad, and these drivers for investment and modernisation will play a more significant part in the future. But will the corporate locomotive prove to be enough?

Post-colony decay in many state organisations, parastatals and publicly funded economic entities is widely found. Will Africa's governments reform sufficiently and rapidly enough to chart a different path from the old ways, and will these initiatives hold? Or is Africa yet to witness another set of failed or failing paradigms that undermine the requirements for transition from economic darkness to different destinies?

First and foremost, the ancient mix of survivalist and allied modern entities constituting Africa's economies, with many state entities, still command the economic space. Conventional economic prisms and macro-models barely capture this collage of adaptive competitive interests and inter-relationships. Without pre-empting any findings here, we all know that Africa's economies are highly heterogeneous, lack efficient central command, reflect differentiation, and display vast wealth and income variances. Future inequalities are more likely than not. Change is afoot, and winners and losers there will be, but who will end up where in this longer-term economic transition?

Presumptive certitudes abound and yet the projections which provide the diet on which many pundits feed form a shifting *à la carte* menu driven by fashion, vested interests, ahistorical knowledge and often weak insight. Likely forms to emerge on the economic stage include many dimensions absent from the past and present: increased technology diffusions, more and larger mega-cities, vast slums within urban conglomerations, more income and wealth inequality, new growth drivers, the continuity of uncertain and unpredictable geopolitics inside Africa and worldwide, more interstate differentiation, wider complexity in the number and connections of economic modes: in short, an evolutionary set of trajectories.

To intuit this economic future – projection and forecast provide little certitude – we might wish to know the answers to a variety of questions: is there any modern limit for the capitalist model in Africa? What implications would there be if so? What curses of economic malaise stalk Africa's future prospects in politics, land tenure, demography and growth rates? If there is no end to Africa's chequered history, it is possible to imagine a more balkanised continent with even ten or more "nation-states" (and in all perhaps 20 or more fragmented de facto zones). What lies down the historical track, and how will our map of Africa look in 2050?

Informalised Africa is large and growing, with more households at or around subsistence level. Poverty is one dominant reality even in South Africa, the most developed economy, with structural unemployment at a minimum of 25% (more like 40% if discouraged workers are counted). Of the 13 million employed, around 3.5 million earn less than $130 a month, two-thirds being farm, domestic or informal workers (60% self-employed, half of them traders). Domestic household workers in paid employment exceed 1 million. Today 2–3 million small trading entities operate as micro-survivalists, with over 1 million found in Gauteng alone. While this off-centre-stage, slow-growth shadow economy presents potential for sources of expansion (within which multiple failures are typical), it is not unique. Together with another 2–3 million small enterprises, they provide over 50% of all jobs. Without this informal mode, most of Africa's economies would collapse. Yet informalisation may not be the growth engine for sub-Saharan Africa even as it becomes the primary mode of survival. Can informalisation accommodate future burgeoning demographics? Does this mean the possible mortgaging of modernity in Africa's economic future?

Unknown geoeconomic shifts may yet bring unwelcome winds of future change in Africa to divert its growth path from established local and foreign sources: shaped around the legacy of investors from the North Atlantic. Competitive threats exist from which Africa cannot be immune. Modern interlopers abound – found in the neo-mercantilist lunge from China, growing Indo-Africa linkages, East Asia's involvements, the "BRICSA" (Brazil, Russia, India, China, South Africa) partnership, intrusions from rising emerging economies, and others. China looms large with its model of *Chinafrique* already an established and growing reality built on centrally managed success pitted against a widely diffused and divided continent.[1] China has no intent to "save Africa" as Sinophiles might believe: it will seek only to balance

Africa's risk, that of a mid-sized Chinese province, with the government's strategic opportunity. For these and other reasons, continental economic differentiation is more than likely, with South Africa's slide expected as Nigeria and others rise. South Africa's political class takes comfort in the country's recent inclusion in the BRICSA nomenclature (for that is all it largely remains) even though all know that its economic weight inside this fictional club will drop daily. Bankers in South Africa wax lyrical about its citation as one of HSBC's self-nominated countries (Colombia, Indonesia, Vietnam, Egypt, Turkey and South Africa) shoe-horned into its "CIVETS" rubric, another largely irrelevant piece of corporate spin. Africa's politicians and bankers seem to love this game of association by artificial naming, as if capturing meaning and economic essence. It is quite possibly a step on the road to delusion.

What expected economic consequences will flow from Africa's geo-strategic posture and current economic condition? While the existing upside in investments adds to likely capital accumulation for the future, this is taking place in the context of the continued scramble for world power, greater control exercised over Africa's economies and a global search for resources. Refashioned economic balances in Africa are expected to flow from this geoeconomic process and its related shifts. What we won't see, I believe, is a coherent economic strategy for Africa or any unified African Union, any realisation of the dream of an African common currency, or any monetary union that matches or has significant long-term beneficial impact on the vast and complex canvas that Africa will remain.

Economic visions

By the end of the first decade of the 21st century, Africa had been cast in new economic shapes, different optics ruled, and economic growth over these years brought the promise of a more bountiful future. Talk of an "African century" was heard, political gurus proclaimed an era of unrestrained secular expansion. It was postulated that the economy of Africa could by 2050 grow to the scale of that of America today. Many politicians dreamt of enhanced power and new riches, their corporate surrogates ready to redesign the future anew.

By this time the modes of economic benefice, commercial sustenance, socioeconomic welfare and household subsistence or survival found across Africa had multiplied. All were progenitors of the original mode of existence found in Africa millions of years before. For most of this time over the last millennium, but for a short phase of very late history, there were no nation-states, applicable international rules, or governments in Africa. There were no grand economic plans or strategies for foreign direct investment. Commitments shaped by interested commercial parties were modest. Africa received no aid, and only later could its states raise public debt. Few corporate firms were found. Yet Africa moved forward, as competitive processes and "natural selection" induced better economic modes adapted to shape Africa's evolution.

Just how far optics had changed was on display at a meeting held by our firm, Global Pacific & Partners, in Cape Town during 2011. Assembled were over 50 high-level speakers and hundreds of corporate and state officials from around Africa to deliberate on the economies of Africa, Cape-to-Cairo. The cognoscenti could envision Africa in its entirety. A bullish mood reigned and there were reasons for optimism. But I detected little appreciation of the past economic historiography of Africa in this meeting, except for a knowledgeable set of insights on South Africa provided by a colleague with an outstanding economic pedigree, Professor Francis Wilson, who pieced together in-depth insights on the long experience of economic change and growth in Africa's most modern economy, noting how the past had distinctively shaped the present.[2] This economic story, covering the centuries, has far wider continental application that bears attention.

What then were the transformative economic pathways followed across the continent's evolution? How did Africa's diverse economies emerge from the time of mankind's evolution in the fossil record? What processes created the complexity and multiplicity of economic forms today that provide sustenance for over a billion people in Africa? What will shape the continent's economies and its economic future?

Prisms on Africa

Evidence on economic survival in Africa has accumulated in a vast body of literature dispersed among various disciplines over time. The challenge remains to develop an explanatory theory adequate to interpreting the historic canvas with its many twists and turns. The search for this economic theory, which has tended to focus on modern history, has engaged hundreds of thinkers, as if it were Africa's hidden Holy Grail.

Any suitable theory needs to be congruent with the economic record, in this case one of extraordinary duration and complexity. Hypotheses should marry with the evidence: they need not coincide with past interpretations, economic ideology, political visions, consensus paradigms, current fashion, morality or modern predilections for "correct" understanding. Most interpretations existing have not been in accord with Africa's long-term economic evolution. It appears most unlikely that the kind of theory required could be merely wrapped in data-driven correlates or econometric models. The latter typically provide simplified abstractions usually judged on their usefulness alone, not their truth. We cannot make Africa conform to the theory. The evidence must lead to adequate explanation, which might then validate the model.

Before elaborating on ideas suggested here, it is advisable to consider some of theories and models that have captured the high ground in past and current analysis of Africa's economies. Some foundation ideas in economics retain their applicability in Africa today, and will for years to come. Part of the analytical and empirical work in my own research on central Africa in the early to mid 1970s was based on evaluation of then conventional economics theories. It is worth briefly revisiting some of these models, ideas and research conducted.[3]

The task was to understand underdevelopment in a central African economy, then Rhodesia. Many had seen this economy in black/white dimensions. Nobel Prize laureate Gary Becker's classic theory of economic discrimination was the most advanced model considered applicable, with allied interpretations by Lester Thurow and Kenneth Arrow – all economic luminaries of the time and since.[4] Their models, based on advanced capitalist societies, were formalist, abstract and rootless. They had no relevance in the socioeconomic circumstances of Africa, where capitalism was important but non-exclusive. Implied in their models was a fully functioning and unrestrained competitive market system, which did not exist in central Africa. None could explain the evident historic realities of underdevelopment.[5]

Many earlier variants of applied models, with specific reference, suffered from the comparable faults.[6] In particular, they posited a dualistic divide between subsistence and market economies. Culture was typically taken as the primary barrier to and explanation for underdevelopment. Economic cleavages resulted, without sufficient explanations of their origins. Institutional realities and history were largely brushed aside. Theorists of economic dualism later sought to address these analytical and empirical deficiencies. They took their lead from the classic work of W. Arthur Lewis, with William Barber the most prominent exponent in central Africa.[7] Lewis's dual economy theory launched a thousand papers. In it the capitalist and subsistence economies developed symbiotically, the latter shrinking, as unlimited labour was absorbed by growth, and accumulation occurred. It was neat – but not applicable.

Lewis's central economic interaction revolved around wage-level relationships in the bifurcated dual economy. Little differentiation was allowed, and simple market-related explanations of nominal economic forms resulted. Africa was more complex than allowed and no account was included of primitive accumulation and the competitive economic struggle that marked Africa's diverse economic pathways. Barber's model, in classical tradition, depicted a dichotomy between monetised and indigenous sectors and saw the traditional family household as the maximising economic unit seeking its own welfare by interaction with monetisation. It suggested a "stages of growth" approach to development. This was woefully inadequate for capturing the complexities of accumulation in Africa's historical process. In both models, the capitalist world became an undifferentiated and ultimately exclusive mode, contrary to abundant evidence around Africa.

It was, then, left to the neo-Marxian tradition to take a crack at "explaining Africa", led by Giovanni Arrighi, writing on central Africa, with many economists in the continent building off this tradition and work.[8] Emphasis shifted to the dynamics of primary accumulation in colonisation, with capitalists exploiting the indigenous peoples. Competitive and often non-synchronistic capitalist penetration into Africa was another feature – as not all "intruders" had similar interests. It equally stressed class struggle, the creation and subordination of the peasantry, and associated wage-labour exploitation for capital accumulation at the edges and periphery of the dominant world economic system, then considered to be imperialist. This clash of liberal and neo-Marxian thought marked economic debates across central-southern Africa at the time, translating into Africa-wide intellectual confrontation.

Arrighi redefined the conceptual template for Africa at the time. This school of thought led to a deeper focus on political economy, economic history, and underdevelopment as a condition beyond the easy analysis of neoclassical economics. Into this mix flowed notions on dependency theory, feudalism, pre-capitalist entities and state formation. It revealed more complex economic forces at work. At the core was the "articulation of modes of production", the neo-Marxian idea to explain the various economic forms found at the interstices of autochthonous Africa and its capitalist intruders. The market was not seen as always central. The essential mechanisms to drive economies forward, accumulation and investment, had numerous non-market features, while variants of capitalism could be found, including settler colonialism, not unique to central Africa.

Even so, these models inadvertently reflected the core ideas of the dualism they sought to critique. One major shortcoming was their failure to recognise the breadth of variety of non-capitalist or extra-market means of survival in place that inhabited Africa's economies; these were far more complex than those depicted in either the liberal tradition or the neo-Marxian school. Centrally, there were many economic modes of subsistence and survival, with diverse mechanisms of accumulation to be considered.

Pioneering historiography has shown that Africa's story needed something else to explain it. Most of my work then concentrated on these different economic modes – plantations, mines, informal and contract workers, the rural/urban nexus, and domestic households of masters and servants, among others. An abiding interest in issues of economic survival continued. In travels across many of Africa's cities and remote rural economies, around its huge rivers, in mountain ranges and on all its seaboards, I encountered many more forms of economic survival. There were historical peculiarities, subsistence anomalies and experiences of the rise and fall of economies and states, which did not fit the conventional theories and contested models of the ivory towers in Africa or elsewhere. This seemed to call for better understanding of diversity in the economic fabric. The economies had emerged inside complex histories, representing varied conditions of subsistence and survival amid rising modernity across the continent. How did this occur, and why?

In the first half of the 1980s, there emerged notions of non-linear economic dynamics and groundbreaking ideas in chaos theory. These struck me as applicable to Africa if placed in the context of its economies, histories and developing environs. Here was a better over-arching concept to explain the volatilities, uncertainties and complexities making up Africa's economic equation, viewed inside the long shifts and turmoil that the passage of time had imposed. The question then coming to mind was how these diverse strands of theory and knowledge could be interwoven to provide better prisms through which to "read" the nature, evolution, structural changes and socioeconomic patterns evident in Africa's dynamic economies. These carried inside them the legacies of the past and the seeds of the future, modernising entities found amid, within or on top of the mix of Africa's ancient economies on which they had been built. Was there some "theory of everything" to decode Africa's economic shifts over time and across its economic space?

There were many economic theses, social science theories and sophisticated econometric models, and multiple suggestive notions, to depict Africa's historic and emerging conditions. But there were few clear principles to follow in seeking to resolve this complex problem. If it was not possible to satisfactorily decode the past, what hope could there be of diagnosing the present, let alone intuiting what had long been an apparent mystery: an applicable way of thinking to "explain" Africa's economic drama? It is not the argument here that the past must be fully explained before we can understand the present – but explanations of the past and present are intimately connected.

I say this notwithstanding the many excellent interpretations that have gone before from knowledgeable economists, historians, writers, thinkers, analysts, Africanists and intellectuals within social science. Maybe most were not concerned with this issue but almost all have struggled to reveal this "hidden variable", or set of principles, which might yield the insight many would wish to find. We should not perhaps be surprised by this apparent weakness in our collective understanding, given Africa's histories, economic riddles and mix of societies which have been and are even now undergoing rapid change.

The scale of the task should not be underestimated. It could be akin to searching for a needle in the African haystack. An acceptable model would need to cope with vast distances in time that span Africa's history, huge variances across myriad economic landscapes, and differential rates and shapes in socioeconomic change. It would need to deal with the multiple economic cycles affecting heterogeneous societies, with economic forms and structures that have varied in typology and evolutionary success, and explain the erosion of older economic shapes by the new.

For millennia and more recent centuries already, Africa's position has greatly altered, sometimes slowly, at other times rapidly, as the continent emerged and interfaced with the many and varied interconnecting world economies that surrounded it. So, does a sufficiently encompassing way of thinking exist to elucidate Africa's past, present and potential future economic realities? If not, why has economics not yet devised such a framework?

Fixations on "fixing" Africa

Development economics on Africa presents many legacies of theory, data, knowledge and interpretation. This discourse has been articulated for well over 50 years.[9] Discussions have tended to be instrumentalist in character or aimed at "solving" problems, like poverty and inequality. This is not our task. Yet it has led economics into politics and ideology (for some to "make poverty history"), even partial and unrestrained advocacy (promoting aid or fixing imbalances). It has often situated the analytic outside the "big picture", and failed to place diagnosis inside the context of the long-term processes of evolutionary change.

A mosaic of theories has since littered intellectual landscapes while shifting lineages of thought have contested the field as rivals to seek primacy, funding and influence on direct policy. A collage of relics can be seen across this battlefield: plans, grand strategies, mooted international economic orders, efforts to provide all with basic needs, attempts to resurrect "the south" (a wholly ambiguous idea), and in modern form philanthropy and bureaucracies to meet messianic millennium development goals. Some ideologies of development have reflected quasi-religious dimensions as the "great and the good" (with anointed economists in tow) have taken to the Herculean task of fixing the great divides between rich and poor within Africa's modernity and its traditional societies. Colonial anthropology sought to define the "problem", commissions of enquiry followed, institutes of development studies formed, scholars roamed far and wide publishing voraciously, and Bretton Woods institutions became the repositories of funding and development research. Political figures (usually once out of office) entered the fray with a plethora of foundations, think-tanks, commissions, books and panels offering unsolicited and presumptively sage advice.

As a result a cacophony of voices has cluttered the Africa stage. There has been much heat, less light. Old ideas have often been recycled in new form like old wine in new bottles. Many worthy economists have become prisoners of discredited, inherited or invented concepts or partial empiricism. A smorgasbord of notions, some clearly detrimental, has been the Africa fare.

Inevitable stages of economic growth were postulated, while critics flocked to views to the contrary proffering emphases on colonial dramas, continuing pauperisation amid capitalist-led exploitation, and selective economic sociologies mooting the virtues of either rapid modernisation or revolution. The proximate causes of underdevelopment were analysed to death, almost. Many a culprit was found, guilt was allocated, and plenty of remedies were suggested. Neo-Marxian thought was linked with dependency theory and those proclaiming the existence of "unequal exchange" between world capitalist centres and the periphery as ideas to explain this drama. Third-worldism arose. Countries were encouraged to adopt autarchy in economic policy, with self-reliance and village collectivisation along state-mandated pathways, and communalism and nationalism as the salvation. Many experiments, as in Tanzania and Guinea-Conakry, ended in grief, along with the Western aid-driven model of upliftment. Modern manifestations continue in the form of calls for "development states", control of the "commanding heights", nationalisation, economic centralism and resource nationalism – all purporting to "fix" poverty. Africa still remains a prisoner to the ideas of many a defunct economist.

The collage of ideas and models for "fixing" poverty and delivering salvation for the poor has engaged more and more economists in a pseudo-race against time, the eternal enemy. In reality, time may exist only so that everything does not happen all at once. Eventually, solidarity in the third world waned as less-developed countries, the "least developed", new industrialising countries and newly emerging market combinations formed and dissolved, to realign nation-states in alliances of political or economic convenience. This is today seen in the infamous BRICs (now BRICSA) formulation, an imaginary cargo cult that will supposedly deliver redemption from the scourges of disadvantaged economic conditions. Others have proclaimed the "end of economics" as a legitimate mechanism to alone solve these wicked travails, preferring instead the hand of politics, governance and sheer will. Rhetoric commanded common sense in many forums. Lessons were provided from those who had ascended the development curve, from the Nordic countries and elsewhere: if only they would "follow our model", all would be set aright.

In the flurry of righteous concern, the tasks of theory took a back seat, advocacy centre-stage. The NGO-world flourished as this self-inflicted, heroic task fragmented into a mosaic of single-issue solutions, each with a cluster of self-appointed champions to take matters forward. Patronage and partiality trumpcd many sound economic lessons drawn from the past as competition between self-serving ideologies supplanted the notions and evidence of economic evolution. Today a slew of pseudo-economic ideas proclaim paradigms for the idealised way forward – sustainable development, climate-responsible growth, equalised globalisation, shared economic futures, human-centred growth (complete with indices to measure all), finite world-driven equity notions – with a multiplicity of interventions to create the "development state" and the emergence of fabricated international collectivities to re-engineer economic balances, even to meet artificial aims embodied in millennium development ambitions. In many senses, economics has been taken over by the uninitiated and the "jacks-of-all-trades" bar that informed by the dismal science.

Into this firmament entered many a view that would discount economics as a discipline with anything to offer. Western and non-Western economic thought was condemned as remiss, often seen as the intellectual engine designed merely to generate inequality and social exclusion. Post-modernist ideas sought to replace the development economics of old, seeking fancy means to manage growth in a romantic and populist style, with moral exhortations founded on allocated guilt, sought-after redemption or financial compensation for past evils. Economics, with development economics, stood accused of a welter of intellectual faults as if it were a post-colonial invention: reductionism, imperialism, desocialisation, dehistoricisation, and more besides.

As an apogee and obituary for economics and its theoretical and empirical crack at understanding underdevelopment, others proclaimed the limits of economics and its obsolescence, with verdicts that, if true, would in principle apply to its manifestations in Africa.[10] But is this really the case? Why should this critique of economics preclude any valid encompassing theory about Africa's economic evolution?

✳

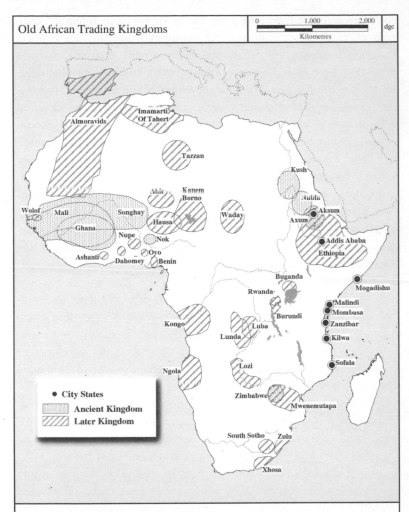

Old African Trading Kingdoms

0   1,000   2.000
Kilometres

dgc

- Almoravids
- Imamarti Of Tahert
- Tazzan
- Kush
- Nubia
- Aksum
- Wolof
- Mali
- Songhay
- Axum
- Ghana
- Air
- Kanem Borno
- Waday
- Ethiopia
- Hausa
- Addis Ababa
- Nupe
- Nok
- Ashanti
- Oyo
- Dahomey
- Benin
- Buganda
- Mogadishu
- Rwanda
- Malindi
- Mombasa
- Burundi
- Zanzibar
- Kongo
- Luba
- Kilwa
- Lunda
- Sofala
- Ngola
- Lozi
- Zimbabwe
- Mwenemutapa
- South Sotho
- Zulu
- Xhosa

- ● City States
- Ancient Kingdom
- Later Kingdom

Before colonisation Africa's autochthonous societies were diverse, some kingdoms and empires. Ancient and later kingdoms came and went with the historical tides in the Sahel and West Africa. Sudanic powers ruled in the Upper Nile and Ethiopian kingdoms lasted centuries. The Kongo succumbed to Portuguese power, the Mwenemutapa to internal discord. City trading entities were established on the eastern seaboard, as interfaces for Arabs and Africans in the interiors. Few kingdoms survived the advent of colonisation.

The approach that I develop here does not seek to deny the significance of social, state and individual agency: that would be ridiculous, a denial of the obvious. But all initiatives, efforts and decisions in Africa's economies have been constrained by nature, the multiple and complex changing ecologies found, and the institutional or economic structures built in and embedded from the past.

The first step is to recognise that Africa, with its constituent economies and states, has had a long history, shaped over millennia. The same longevity has applied to socioeconomic structures inside Africa's diverse space. These economic histories cover hundreds of years during which the dominant outcome has been modest evolution, with slow change to recast the economic foundations. Today, Africa's economies reflect this mix of almost everything: ancient, subsistence, medieval-like, survivalist and shifting modernity. Their evolution has been achieved step by step in multiple processes, isolated or in concert. It has been an epochal saga.

3

Economic modes

Where are the origins of wealth and accumulation making for dynamic growth and economic evolution in Africa found? How did the continent get to its present state and why did economic growth take so long?

Thinking Africa

Africa's present – its varied peoples, economies and states – is a reflection of a huge, complex, evolving system that has adapted over millennia, centuries, decades and years. Evolution has worked its magic over time. But it has been a slow process. The hunter-gatherer economy of 12,000 years ago is estimated to have had an annual per-head "income" of around $90 (1990 prices).[1] Most of Africa's economic growth was recorded since, on an accelerating path in the 20th century and after (in only 0.1% of this time span), to reach contemporary income levels.

In 1900 Africa was materially poor compared with today. Wealth accumulated since then forms the bedrock of most economies while Africa has fared worst among all continents. It became the classic loser in the world's fast-shifting transition to wealth and enhanced income over the last 2,000 years.[2] Yet recent growth has been rapid seen on the larger scale of time. Perhaps economic theory embodying these temporal dimensions can tell us how and why it happened. Any plausible answer must necessarily be one about evolution in practice, to show how the economies in Africa differentiated, were subject to competitive selection and diverged in performance.

This economic evolution was inherently complex and will follow established pathways and unknown designs through trial and error going forward, as Africa's economic algorithm is acted upon by history, natural or market constraints, creativity, technologies and innovation. Though this has Darwinian overtones, we should remember that it was from Thomas Malthus (1766–1834) and classical economics that Charles Darwin took his initial cues. Darwin noted the competitive struggle for survival inherent in Malthus's subsistence world, remarking upon it as "the theory by which to work". [3] To me this model has significance for Africa.

Nonetheless, market equilibrium ideas won the day in intellectual discourse over the course of the last century and a half. One result was that what happened between the snapshot ends of the points of starting and ending equilibria received scant attention in mainstream economics. The profession was transformed through the rise of neoclassical economics, growth theory and later enhanced models built on technology and the knowledge economy. The study of complex adaptive systems emerged far later and elsewhere (in physics), but came back into the fold in the late 20th century via non-linear economics, chaos thinking and complexity theory. In the meantime, a great deal in economics became detached from the real world, its vintage appearing like a throwback to an earlier scientific era. Market models did not explain their origins, were imperfect in practice, became hidebound by perverse assumptions and restrictive rules, seemed to operate outside time and looked mystifying in a straitjacket unattuned to natural economic rhythms. Reality checks found many theoretical edifices wanting. While much-beloved, econometrics and its many practitioners were either unable or unwilling to "explain" the human record, its messy economic worlds, disequilibria and disorder with economic decay, or how the past shaped the present and might influence the future.

For Africa this intellectual detour sidetracked explanation of how its economies grew, varied and selected different economic paths, sometimes ending up in history's cul-de-sac. Natural economic selection continued but was ignored in economics. Some economies and entities advanced, others retreated; some became endangered and confronted semi-terminal decline. All entities – traditional or modern – struggled to sustain their pre-assigned evolutionary economic niches. On this eternal drama, our economic record remains weak. Why? Because the fundamental platforms and constituents in Africa's economies are composed of several thousands, maybe millions, of interconnected elements in complex adaptive systems that cannot be straitjacketed into the neat images of conventional economic theory, canned history or macro-level policy diagnosis. Studies of the nation-state and the economic images liberally bestowed upon them have not imagined Africa this way before. This has been a story long ignored by economics, if not by history. For this reason, we need to rethink Africa and its economic interpretations anew.

Subsistence and survival

The concept of subsistence has a long pedigree in economic thought. It found expression in classical economics and Marxist, then neo-Marxian, thinking. Ferdinand Lassalle (1825–64) argued in the mid-19th century that an iron law of wages at subsistence level applied. Thomas Malthus had already used this idea to explain the forces sustaining basic subsistence for survival: as population expands, it pushes up against the limits of the environment, driving living standards down to subsistence levels. On this view population growth is checked only by war, famine or disease. David Ricardo (1772–1823) refined the idea, explaining that the market and customs could redefine levels of subsistence. Karl Marx (1818–83) believed that capitalists would always push wages towards subsistence levels. Many variants followed in both classical and neo-Marxian interpretations. Subsistence was essential, the basic economic need.

In Africa the Malthusian-style subsistence economy dominated the historical record. Few were better off than their distant ancestors, even by 1900. Many were even poorer. Material welfare did not begin to rise until the late 19th century and then marginally and sporadically. Africa's traditional economies did not participate directly in the industrial revolution that swept Europe. During these times the heavy hand of the past gripped the continent in the constraints of survival at minimal subsistence levels and of income. This more than the politics of empires, ideology or cosmology shaped Africa's economic universe. It took eons for Africa to break away from the chains that imprisoned most of its inhabitants at bare levels of material existence that had been common during the Neolithic era. When foreign technologies and investments arrived from the late 19th century onwards, there were major disruptions in the equation of subsistence. Now societies had to find means of survival amid changed circumstances. Different mechanisms for precarious survival emerged. Divergence took place between these ancient economic practices and the necessities for adaptation to proto-modernity were established across the continent. Competition arose in the economic order and for some the natural economy of subsistence was displaced, forcing partial inclusion in the entities that made up the fabric of the newly installed economic machines of productive capitalism.

The world of "steady state" subsistence buckled under these exogenous and then-locally established conditions. Following what amounted to massive displacement, the task for most communities became increasingly one of how to survive within modified economic constraints. Old economic pathways became redundant or had to adapt. Whether the earlier nexus was built on traditionalism, feudal economies, slavery or older trading networks, all were induced to adjust as monetisation spread and became the necessity for survival. Sustainable consumption at subsistence level based on "own production" was no longer the natural order of the day. The game became survival in fraught or uncertain circumstances. Whereas before subsistence might have been "guaranteed" by the social matrix in existence, the economic modes "elected" for survival provided no such safeguard or guarantee. Subsisting communities had to become surviving ones as changed economic dynamics pushed millions into new conditions for living, some desperate, that had not been encountered before. The continuity of ancient economic practices did not, however, disappear suddenly. They became attached to, even partially integrated in, the emerging fabric of capitalist accumulation. Vastly different levels of wealth, income and status flowed from this redefined pattern of rights, obligations and opportunities that overcame ancient Africa. Today, it can be seen that many different modes of subsistence and survival shape the economic landscape and are deeply embedded in Africa's economic histories.

Behind the formation of pre-modern societies, including empires or nation-states that later emerged, have been economic foundations built on mixtures of subsistence combined with dominant modes of extraction, control and commercial or state monopolies. These allowed ruling elites of different types to extract the available economic surplus. This process enabled investment or accumulation, the basis for economic expansion, to ensure the sustenance of the socioeconomic order over time. Scholars have long depicted pre-capitalist societies in terms of this idea. The radicals of the classical era in economics found this notion a fundamental tool to explain the economic base on which the political architecture held together and evolved.

Lineage-based economic modes characterised the barbarian hordes in Roman times, with ancient practices built on slavery. Later variants transmuted into feudalism with control exercised by feudal-cum-aristocratic lords holding sway over serfs held in penury under local or even wider systems of *etatist* control. An "Asian mode" described the power of despotism over villages and communal producers on the land even while personal servitude equally reigned. These interpretations were an attempt to provide a materialist explanation of historical periods and identify technical relationships within the economies that "articulated" or were connected to social relations found within these societies. Whatever the massive differences in power, wealth, income or status within these older economic formations, there were implicit obligations assumed by those with authority to ensure basic subsistence for serfs, dependants or subjects. When dominant powers were displaced, traditional obligations often withered and the imperatives of survival shifted onto the shoulders of displaced communities and households. Conditions for survival thereby became highly varied and precarious.

In Africa many pre-capitalist and non-market economies, even in so-called stateless societies, acquired surpluses for accumulation by means of authority or control levied on households or different strata. This took place through slavery, trade dominance or power exercised through the mechanisms of force: armies, oppression, punishment, tribute or sanctioned ideologies. This form of accumulation in wealth allowed the local enriched to exercise dominance over their subjects, the impoverished. The evidence of significant prevailing inequalities is etched in Africa's histories across the continent. There were almost no societies that reflected images of communal bliss, romantic Arcadia, or undifferentiated modes of economic survival. As time passed, cleavages were accentuated within and around Africa's pre-capitalist structures, though these were not strictly class divisions in the classic sense.[4] Those with social or economic status, hierarchies, ennobled groups, chiefdoms, royal houses, or nascent aristocracies were found in varying forms of stratification and exerted their rights of power and economic privilege. Economic differentiation was entrenched within rural households based on lineage, family division of labour and control over reproduction, and sometimes through religious status or social identities. Western fascination with this primitive mode, its pseudo-communal image and non-capitalist forms, marked many a report from Africa's explorers, missionaries and early anthropologists. The process of mystification continued in the mindsets of many modern economic saviours seeking to diagnose and reshape Africa's predicament. Yet whatever the limitation of these earlier works on economic modes and their taxonomies, they brought more understanding about the primal foundations of the subsistence economies in Africa.

But the theories so far developed have had serious weaknesses. In almost all cases the economic modes identified, even where useful as historic descriptions, were locked into static thinking around the status quo or point-in-time depictions of socioeconomic structure. Mechanistic methodologies governed accounts of transitions from one mode to another as if such transitions were discrete watersheds in history. The relationship between old and new modes over time was typically presented in terms of dualisms – for example, slavery/feudalism, feudal/ mercantilist, pre-capitalist/capitalist, or peasant/modern. Here the long arc of history was neglected. In reality, many an older modal form found continuity and survival with several others within economic evolution through long periods of time. In dualistic models, older economic forms, however portrayed, were presented as having little lasting imprint on economic structure. Many were typically consigned to the dustbin of history. Usually they were erased from the theoretical equation. Yet it requires only reasonable observation across the economic fabric of Africa to find evidence of the existence of many older forms of subsistence and survival which have continued in presence over lengthy spans of time. For our purposes, this traditional view airbrushed away the hard-wired and complex economic realities on the ground in Africa.

There is no simple definition of an economic mode to be offered. Earlier conceptions formed around capitalist/subsistence, feudal or peasant entities and even socioeconomic classes reflect the idea only at the level of large-scale social or abstract entities. Nonetheless, they may be of some use. However, the notion of modes as employed here requires further disaggregation. We need to capture smaller categories of similar entities within the economy driven by the imperatives of economic interest, subsistence and survival. Yet I am not persuaded that this can be atomised down to the level of the individual, single firm or even the isolated household as conventionally done in classic market theory. The essence of any economic mode is the association within it of entities of the like-minded, even some with competitive interests.

Thus we can think of, say, an industrial, mining, plantation, or oil and gas mode, for instance – though bearing in mind the many entities that compete within them to make up such a collage. This idea should not be confused simply with a "sector" as defined for national accounts: often trade associations reflect such sorts of combined and associated collections of companies and firms; and while economic modes may come in organised forms, many may be unorganised or even disorganised entities and reflect categories of persons in similar situations (say, slum dwellers seeking urban subsistence or means of survival).

Essentially an economic mode seeks its own survival and destiny. These economic forms make up the basic economic fabric. While this conception may not satisfy theoretical purists, it is satisfactory as a

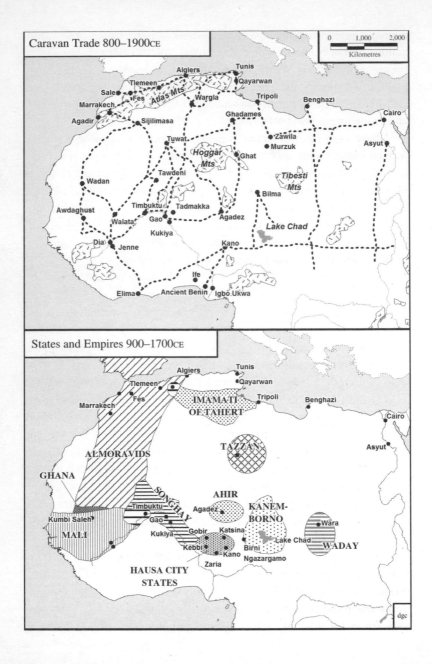

Caravan Trade 800–1900CE

0   1,000   2,000
Kilometres

Algiers Tunis
Tlemeen   Qayarwan
Sale   Fes   Wargla   Tripoli   Benghazi
Marrakech   Cairo
Agadir   Sijilimasa   Ghadames
Atlas Mts   Asyut
Tuwat   Zawila
Hoggar   Murzuk
Mts   Ghat
Wadan   Tawdeni   Tibesti
Mts
Awdaghust   Timbuktu   Tadmakka   Bilma
Walata   Gao   Agadez   Lake Chad
Dia   Kukiya
Jenne   Kano

Ife
Elima   Ancient Benin Igbo Ukwa

States and Empires 900–1700CE

Algiers   Tunis
Tlemeen   Qayarwan
Fes   IMAMATI   Tripoli   Benghazi
Marrakech   OF TAHERT   Cairo
Asyut
TAZZAN
ALMORAVIDS
GHANA   AHIR
Timbuktu   KANEM-
Kumbi Saleh   SONGHAY Agadez   BORNO
Gao
MALI   Kukiya   Gobir   Katsina   Wara
Kebbi   Birni   Lake Chad   WADAY
Zaria   Kano   Ngazargamo
HAUSA CITY
STATES

dgc

38

heuristic device enabling significant understanding of competitive inter-actions within economies that play crucial roles in Africa's long-term economic transitions. We might even think of the economic mode almost as a form of species: the basic unit of classification with taxonomic rank and, like organisms, capable by analogue of proliferating, interbreeding and producing derived offspring.

I have come to this broad concept or model of economic modes formed outside past traditional theories and boundaries. It allows us better insight into the deeper fabric that connects with Africa's complex histories where economic evolution is central to interpreting the past and the present. By way of crude analogy the mode, as in statistics, may be taken as the element that occurs most dominantly in the economic dataset, like the economy. A focus on the mode allows us to define the specific entities that form the socioeconomic composite.

Competitive entities

Within any socioeconomic form, industry or zone of survival can be found further differentiated smaller entities that search for competitive space within the mode of their primal existence. This is as true in rural as in modern Africa. In agro-allied industry, for instance, are found large plantations, small producers, peasants and individual cultivators, even urban households partially reliant on rural forms of subsistence. We can refer to economic entities at this level as "nodes" (as denoted in Latin: *nodus*, or knot) − connecting points fixed around survival within the mode or as subsets of the economic topology of the mode. The notion of nodes is set at a more micro-level than the economic mode (rather like neutrons within the atom), as a lower-level component of the economic universe. Typically, many nodes constitute any discrete mode.

The fate of nodes within any mode − for example, a firm inside an industry, maybe a mining company or oil/gas venture, or a collectivity of households − is often linked to the destiny of its own economic habitat. Economic policies or market movements might aid or compromise any industry and so affect the status and survival or success of nodes within the industry concerned. Some nodes, such as entities, households or firms, seek economic survival only within a specific mode, whether agrarian, industrial, commercial, resource-based or other. Others may transition out of their past locus into new or different arenas as they adapt to the rigours of survival in evolving competitive landscapes.[5] For instance, as the terms of trade in rural economies deteriorated across Africa in past decades, many households sought survival in informal trading and nascent economies found within slums and urban centres.

Specific nodes may have economic relationships built with others inside different modes, say in the form of economic networks, as one means for survival. Typically, peasant households may be agrarian producers and simultaneously participate in migrant labour markets or even in the sale of goods or services within non-agrarian industries such as crafts and tourism. Some entities may straddle one or more economic zones, in a strategy of diversity designed for survival. But all have the same aim: continuity and replication over time. In rarer cases, specific nodes may break out of their natural world to establish what might become another economic mode altogether.

These changes are continuous and adaptive. Modes and nodes encounter dynamic transmutation in often unplanned or unpredictable ways. In this sense economic modes in Africa are in continuous adjustment. Their nodes or constituent entities within them may split away, or even straddle them – as do some rural/urban migrants – seeking to maximise survival chances, incomes or wealth, as if operating in allied or separated economic worlds. Each has the same aim: self-calculated survival with the aim of meeting subsistence needs, including social and economic wealth retention, if possible accumulation, and continuous replication over time.

Our understanding of Africa would be more complete if we also allowed for appendages that hang onto the wider continental economies and economic modes within them, as "external modes". They include economic entities externalised, as it were, inside the continent but situated away from their normal means of subsistence, or even hosted abroad, for reasons of survival. In the first case we might think of a mix of displaced peoples, refugees, or those who escaped their conventional subsistence boundaries to live another day. Africa is greatly plagued by this economic condition. External modes abroad may be found in different forms, for instance in the African diaspora, exiles and overseas refugees. They may also include firms and individuals holding corporate cash stashes outside Africa, even overseas subsidiaries or dual listings, state offshore accounts, holding companies based as many are in the Seychelles or Mauritius, and possibly companies that are incorporated abroad though with their main focus for commercial survival targeted in Africa.

Taken together, the economic modes found in Africa have grown significantly in number with time. So have their constituent nodes. As a whole, these elemental parts of the economic universe reflect the core base of the underlying socioeconomic fabric in complex collages within and outside the nation-states. While states, governments and political arrangements come and go, the economic modes and nodal forms tend to exhibit much longer life spans.

The hand of history

With our concept of economic modes as key entities in Africa's economic evolution, we can rethink the continent's economic story from Olduvai and the original journeys towards "inner Africa" and "out of Africa". Before these wanderings took place, there was a single mode of existence or survival. Thereafter more economic modes gained ascendance in the long march of human and economic evolution, through many different epochs. Africa's "great trek" from Olduvai set in train a multiplicity of mechanisms of survival, from the Stone Age through the Iron Age and onwards to the pre-modern era. By then there were a multitude of discrete economic modes found across Africa's economic landscape – in hunting and gathering, subsistence agriculture, iron working, cattle cultures and agrarian settlements – with probably hundreds and then thousands of economic nodes within them. Here I am depicting survivalist sets of households or social communities as one separate mode. They were initially different in locus from others, since many communities operated in isolation. Only later was economic interconnectivity achieved through barter, trade, warfare, social interaction and the like. This was well before the outside world "discovered" Africa's coastal reaches, mainland and vast hinterlands.

Roman Africa had built a flourishing Mediterranean economy. The later collapse of this empire, the infusion of Vandals and subsequent altered interfaces with Berbers and Tuareg in the Sahara initiated changed economic circumstances, even while the Nile Valley economies came under duress in this era. The Arab incursions into Africa in the 7th century brought changes to subsistence and survival interfaces in the Maghreb and altered economic ways of living. In the continent there had long been evolution in modal patterns since local economies were never merely static. While Arab intrusion in the Maghreb resulted in advanced forms of trading and slaving, there were other penetrations below the Sahel. Later Arabian links to the eastern seaboard through the Omani sultanate established separate trading posts and slaving ventures there, with bases in Zanzibar. Cross-oceanic connections to India and Asian markets were another. Then Portugal's caravels went down the west coast, round the Cape and along the south-eastern littoral, bringing competitive trading and slaving with mercantilist connections to once-isolated communities on the coasts and in the interior.

It was around Africa penetrated from outside along its coasts that the oldest of the more modern modes we now encounter were first established. These bases were enhanced by the great powers of Europe in the form of different state and private intrusions from the Dutch, Scandinavians and British, among others. Thereafter was born the Atlantic slave trade, later legitimated commerce, the finale being the partition of Africa (1884–85) and a subsequent scramble for land and imperial control. From this arose nation-states in which several thousands of African polities, mostly subsistence-oriented, were constrained and subsequently transformed. If each of these autochthonous societies had had 20 or so different modes of survival within them – from rulers to subjects, agrarian production to craft works, iron working and mining for gold or metals, salt production or products for trade and slaving, as well as tribute labour for agriculture, among others – then many more differentiated economic modes would have been found across Africa well before colonialism.

The insertion of capitalist ventures into Africa varied in originating forms: through missionaries, trading posts, ports, interior barter, mines, towns and commercial hubs, farms and plantations. Later there emerged the structured nation-state edifices to add considerable complexity to Africa's economic fabric. The sublimation of rural households inside Africa's old domains, and the creation of the peasantry and migrant-labour system that eventually replaced slavery, took place over long periods of time. This led to vast fragmentation in ancient socioeconomic fabrics: in villages, kraals and self-subsistence households. By 1913, on the eve of the First World War, the scramble for Africa and the fixing of 40 states controlled from abroad was complete, even if statehood evolved again soon thereafter and more significantly again in the 20th century. Quite feasibly by 1913 there could well have been hundreds of different economic modes of subsistence, some proto-modern in character. Inside them would have been many more thousands of nodes of economic survival.

This conceptual journey takes us a long way from the "out of Africa" economic scenario. It reflected evolutionary dynamism, greater complexity, inner connectivity, new pathways and changed foundations for Africa's economic growth. The last 100 years to the present accel-erated this differentiation in and across Africa. More states emerged, economic growth took on varied trajectories, companies and investors came from abroad, Africa's own societies found new niches and the economies grew. Hence new sites of modernity emerged alongside older and ancient orders of subsistence. Some older modes transmuted, differ-entiated and even modernised. Others succumbed and perished.

For example, in the distant past, elephants were killed with spears in traditional fashion. Organised hunting with firearms followed. Now Africa has a well-developed system of concessionary game manage-ment, allied to safari operations with animal-viewing tourism drawn from home and abroad. There is in parallel widespread poaching and illicit traffic in game, hides, ivory, rhino horns and game products. The sequence of connectivity can be traced back centuries.

Early missionaries established the ecclesiastical pathways for churches and even commercial ventures. This endeavour was allied later to related would-be saviours in the form of the international and private aid business, with non-governmental organisations (NGOs) creating charities to offer economic salvation or welfare provision, the task even taken up in some of Africa's states. By some counts the "aid business" today engages thousands of projects and entities in Africa. Even at the birth of South Sudan in July 2011 there were over 380 NGOs in Juba, while the Ministry of Finance was largely run by 60 advisers: as one state official put it, "young kids, and undergraduates or interns, supposedly called experts".

Trading posts on coastal fringes ended up growing into ports and in some cases became the bases for chartered companies, which occupied and traded with Africa's hinterlands. Old routes for the trans-shipment of traded goods and products by foot and porter or caravans, and down the eastern coast by dhows, were joined and in most cases overtaken by modern roads, railways, shipping and airlines. Yet still dhows sail East Africa's littoral. Trading in Africa is today highly dynamic, complex and based on an enormous evolved lattice of personal, corporate and commercial connections Africa-wide and with the world.

The search for gold, ancient in origin within Africa, merged into metal prospecting, with many later claimants: small workers, mining houses, corporate behemoths and even state mining firms. The iron workings of the past were replaced by modern mining, with the import of modern machinery, and metals industries. Modern technologies replaced much of the old, though not everywhere. Indeed, new technologies entering Africa mostly evolved inside specific modes or industries. Some have even graduated to world-class status providing opportunities for export, as with gas-to-liquids technologies.

Old Africa's rural societies were reshaped into peasantries and gravitated under economic incentive or duress into wage labour in plantations, farms, mines and to the urban centres that sprang up as slums and *bidonvilles* around many rapidly growing cities. This partly replaced the locus of subsistence and survival once found in older rural habitats, kraals and bush homesteads. Subsistence dependence is now far more complicated

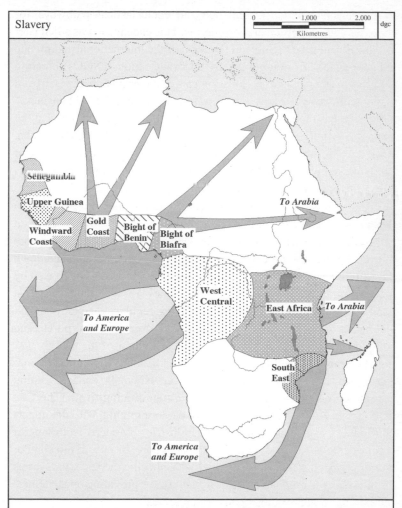

Slavery

0 · 1.000 2.000
Kilometres

dgc

Senegambia

Upper Guinea

Gold Coast

Windward Coast

Bight of Benin

Bight of Biafra

To Arabia

West Central

East Africa

To Arabia

To America and Europe

South East

To America and Europe

The scourge of slavery marked Africa's economies from Roman times, and nominally ended only in the early 20th century, with new forms practised even today. Millions were captured, sold or inducted into slavery from the 7th century onwards by Arabs for slave markets in Arabia. Various types of domestic slavery flourished in most of Africa's ethnic societies. Atlantic slavery controlled by Europe's maritime powers accounted for around 12 million slaves taken to the Americas, notably Brazil.

in nature than ever before. Continuous economic evolution transformed these landscapes of survival and subsistence in Africa, bringing differentiation and many more modes into the picture. Consequently the economic fabric has been radically reshaped, and continues to evolve.[6]

※

This way of envisioning Africa is not the standard image of nation-states or discrete economies. It does not conform to the metrics of orthodox economics with which all are familiar, commonly used as the taxonomy for understanding and calculating economic status and growth in Africa.[7] Ours is a bottom-up perspective looking into Africa's deeper economic fabric. It is based on the roots of survival and evolution of subsistence that have been the true drama within Africa and which forged its economic histories.[8] In this appreciation of the core economic fabric of Africa, it is by no means clear that the pervasive models of economics, macroeconomic analysis or orthodox growth theory have had sufficiently deep meaning or any realistic application.

Our vision of economic modes in Africa suggests that a far more complex subsistence and survival world is found. This collage has grown within Africa despite the many vicissitudes of political upheaval, coups d'état, state crises, conflict and social turmoil that marked Africa's economic road through the 20th and 21st centuries. It articulates Africa in large measure as driven by its own realities. This view suggests considerable expansion in the foundations of Africa's economic universe and presents an image of magnified spatial spread notwithstanding the huge historical drama of Africa's troubled past. Perhaps this can tell us something else about Africa's economies: and maybe suggest new insights on its economic future

Our ideas about economic modes and nodes fit with Africa's historiography. Such a model holds several virtues as a prism through which to interpret Africa's economies. The notion meshes the micro with the macro in ways not normally treated. The model is in essence deeply empirical: it requires us to follow the threads and pathways of economic history as they have evolved, thereby avoiding the traps of static analysis or the crudity of economic dualism. It can, I think, help sketch the long road from the past to modernity. Our interpretation of economic modes stays close to the deep-level economic architecture of Africa's socioeconomic complexities. Identifying this economic fabric enables the visioning of the fundamental and hard-wired structures that define subsistence and survival among different economies, ecologies and social spaces. It offers ground-level insights with which to view evolution in Africa's economic histories while remaining inherently dynamic in interpretation.

Equally important, the idea of shifting and competitive modes and nodes allows for an understanding of the *longue durée* in Africa's complex past. Here epochs are not treated as discrete, as if without influence on later eras. The prism of economic evolution permits identification of the essential drivers in Africa's economic saga by abstracting away from the simpler and very recent notions of the nation-state and its alter ego, conventional macroeconomics. Africa's economic fabric is far more nuanced than those conventional ideas suggest.

Africa unimagined before

The origins and evolution of economic modes and nodes in Africa have been largely constructed from differentiation combined with competitive selection. Government and central direction have not been the single operative drivers, even where they shaped, or impeded survival, or changed the terms of trade or subsistence existence between economic modes and their nodal subsets. In our model, the emphasis is on the non-macro worlds that form the fabric of Africa's economies. In this manner it is possible to appreciate the deeper-level economic realities that evolve with time and competitive circumstance, in the fundamental aim of all: the search for subsistence and continuous survival.

Subsistence economies and adaptations adopted for survival all encountered problematic passages in the transitions of Africa's economies. Much of this drama appears often to be missed in economic orthodoxy. These entities make up the sources of Africa's fragmentation:

like uncounted economic silos, proverbial black holes, and unconnected entities that do not enter into the calculus of national accounts or macro-economic evaluation. Most economics done on Africa and held in high regard is constructed around limited data at this nation-state level, and even that may often be found wanting. Yet these *etatist* artefacts in Africa with histories of 100 years or usually much less are often only as fundamental and "real" as in the mind's eye.

National accounts are somewhat flawed composites, aggregations with "sector" definition, capturing mainly the modern economies. They are typically based on assumptions of implied uniformity as if the elements constituting them were uncompetitive and harmonious, and can be reduced to the common denominator: monetary value. Indeed, national accounting convention has been to attach arbitrary monetary value to the amount that subsistence households produce (assumed as consumption too). Then the value for subsistence economies is deduced by multiplying this amount by the numbers of so-defined households found in that economy. This conventional "rule of thumb" may cope with the formalism of "accounting", but it does not depict any economic realities: for instance, known surpluses, differentiations, connections outside "subsistence" worlds, or changing levels of material subsistence over time. It is questionable whether this macro-conventional framework can lead us to a deeper knowledge and understanding of Africa's economies and their transitions.[9]

Many of the elements (modes and nodes) in economic evolution have not been the focus of economics or econometrics undertaken on Africa, maybe because of lack of data, perhaps because theories used have been absent in this regard too. There are few if any "afrometrics" found on economic modes yet. Limited historical or contemporary economic portraits exist for these complexities in the economies of Africa. Nor has orthodox economics developed any identification or measurement of economic modes over space and time: the sort of "dynamic geoeconomics" or evolutionary economic mapping needed that perhaps awaits future theoretical or empirical research.

It is worth setting out some of the differences in our way of thinking with typical consensus models on economics as widely used on Africa.

Importantly, our concept does not square with the macro-images and state metrics on Africa portrayed by the leading institutions that model, measure, estimate and provide economic guidance on the continent's welfare and trajectories, such as the Economic Commission for Africa (ECA), African Development Bank (AfDB), and entities like the World Bank and IMF. These bodies generate streams of reports and extensive data in the orthodox manner, but the reports provided often come without satisfactory exposure at ground level of the many economic modes found or their condition and evolution over time.

The corporate world often latches onto such analyses and seeks to make sense for its own interests of the commercial meanings involved. Companies want to know how economic trends, data and estimates might affect their own survival and growth. Many remain confused, and operate against the implied results, since their game is sheer corporate survival whatever the spin portrayed about success. Risks indicated are often discounted and typically managed within their own portfolio set or experience-based "biased" judgements. This is often at variance with the "advice" implied in institutional macro-analysis. For most companies the ruminations of Bretton Woods institutions are irrelevant to the game of commercial survival.

Modern advisory bodies, allied to corporate entities – large advisory firms, accounting behemoths, and the like – often work off these basic data and models of economic futures so derived, in a partial understanding of Africa's modes and economic complexities. Typically, their approach is one of unrestricted ahistoricism. Much business school "thinking" and typical spin on Africa travels similar paths, demonstrating a predilection for economic "sound bites" in preference to deeper-level economic analysis. The superficial economics found diffused in most media and reportage on the continent is likewise episodic in nature and lacks normal historical or analytical depth. But here the media have a different remit: desire for populism and natural deadline urgency. In contemporary social science, as practised in many institutes and academic institutions, the understanding and use of inherited development economics is often unknown or merely absent. Comprehension of the wide variety of economic modes of existence across Africa is thus typically weak or non-existent. In most of these cases, stylised economics commands the stage.

✳

Economic theories typically seek to be useful, and exist or hold validity for the intention required. What then might constitute a valid theory on economic evolution for Africa to match the economic realities of multiple modes and the transitions discussed?

Suitably robust theory needs to mimic empirical histories and evidence over long time periods across different milieux. It should account for paradigm changes in Africa's economies. At the limit it ought to be able to explain the phenomenon of multiple modes of subsistence and survival: ancient and pre-capitalist, slave models and mercantilist to feudal modes, incipient or fragmented capitalism, and even selective post-modern economic forms. The model should recognise both the modes and the nodes underlying Africa's macroeconomic world, and portray the continent's deep-level economic architecture. It should depict the hard-wired economic fabric and complex economic base to reflect (like a growing evolutionary tree) the branches and economic connections found that develop in a competitive organic relationship. As a system of complex adaptation, the composite elements need to be shown in an evolving and dynamic economic universe that portrays the competitive selection process and the pathways taken.

As growth depends on the initial conditions found, could there be some "natural growth rate" derived from economic pathways that exist and cannot easily change? Growth projections are usually constructed on extrapolated macro-data, typically based on technical coefficients or presumed rates of change, which are in effect fictions of convenience in which cyclicity and turbulence have been "squeezed out". Most linear projections operate this way. Yet past long-term growth-rate cycles might provide better indicators for shaping future trend lines, especially for periods looking forward as long as 30–40 years.

In the past economic retardation has been evidenced in Africa, perhaps even as a partly natural process, and in several instances the

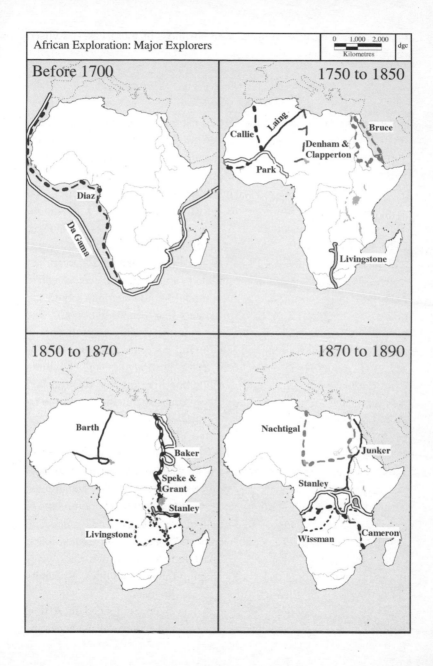

African Exploration: Major Explorers

wrong evolutionary paths have been selected. More of the same may await us down the track. The economic fabric of the nation-states could come under more pressure, and may wilt in certain locales. This may lead to fragmentation and balkanisation, or even breakdown into the failed state economic mode. It seems wishful thinking to envision Africa's future as one of level playing fields, especially when the economic landscapes have been, remain and most likely will still demonstrate continued dynamic instabilities, conflict and turbulence. The political configuration in Africa is an unsettled one and a huge variety of state types contest the terrain for longevity and survival.

We need equally to keep in mind the boundaries and evidence of Africa's economic numerics and metrics. Careful consideration may show up the fallacies of many overoptimistic and facile forecasts. Africa's economics cannot be left to the non-complex or mere econometric number-crunching that so dominates most analyses and applied economics. The remapping and rethinking of Africa's future economic growth story would be essential if even part of this, let alone all, were to be true.

Economic modes form the basis of Africa's economic histories and "make" or shape the economic landscape. In their economic relationships they form a vast tableau like a giant input/output matrix. The collage is ever changing, increasingly interfaced, and adapting anew to altered economic and socio-political circumstances. This totality forms an evolutionary economic chain stretched across the ages. It offers a view of primordial economies based on bare subsistence in transition to contemporary modernity. Understanding this history offers us images rarely seen before, at least in the interpretation of the economics of Africa. How then did this *Tableau Africain* come about?

4

Africa's evolution

Let us consider Africa's economic mosaic and some elemental pieces of the historical puzzle. Epochs have come and gone. Economies have moved forwards and backwards. The inexorable machine of time marches on as the modal input/output parameters and relationships change. Generally, economic shifts in Africa rarely seem sufficient to deviate much or for long from the trajectories written into Africa's inherited "natural rate of growth", by which is meant the long-cycle trend. While outside economic forces have partly shaped Africa, we might surmise that there are significant organic or endogenous drivers rooted within Africa and its economies. These seem deeply entrenched in the economic architecture, even if they slowly evolve, dissipate, or adapt to perform new roles in the long term.

Some periods and conditions of transition may be slow, others more rapid and transformative, as with the intrusion of capitalist modes over the last century, operating alongside ancient economies. The socio-economic and institutional fabric of "old Africa" reflected pre-market economic architecture. In numerous instances exogenously driven events or technologies acted upon the original templates of Africa's old economies, but have yet to wholly displace this non-capitalist foundation. The dynamics of modernity take a long time to fully install.

One of the principal drivers worldwide in the ascent from under-development to competitive modernity has been technological and technical progress. Undoubtedly many of Africa's societies have a higher level of technology embedded in their economies than ever before, including in capital stock and skills, even where these assets and knowledge sets may lag those of competitors abroad. Technologies in Africa evolved – today's complex mix reflects both old and new. Hundreds of millions of Africans still rely on walking for getting around, in both rural and urban areas. Traditionally, bicycles have been the first step up the transport technology ladder. Today there might be anywhere up to 10 million bicycles in sub-Saharan Africa. There are growing numbers of motor scooters too, perhaps 1–2 million. Fleets of cars, trucks and buses – from dilapidated vehicles to the most modern – clog the highways and urban centres, with perhaps around 10 million found across the continent. Yet many in Africa do not own any means of transport. Most commuters rely on buses and taxis, and rail, shipping and airline networks are proliferating.

Many technologies have followed similar evolutionary paths: from illiteracy to functional literacy and computer literacy, rudimentary construction of dwellings in basic mud and grass materials to urban sophistication based on high-tech engineering know-how, and so on. But advanced technical capacities in Africa have often been trapped within a mass of debilitating conditions, many of local origin, that impede their full exploitation: in flawed states, through mismanaged industrial strategies, as the result of outdated or inward-looking economic policies, via blockages to the flow of ideas and innovation, as a result of restrictive regulations, and through limits or controls placed on foreign investment.

Thus the economic modes from the past will continue to exist and adapt, even when reliant on thwarted technologies, if they can find new niches for survival within the evolving economic structures. Some modes of existence will suffer erosion, even to the point of extinction where they are unable to meet competitive threats. Others adapt to changed circumstances and opportunities: witness the Somali pirates in Puntland and their economic practices adapted for plunder in the modern era.

Long arc of history

Some lessons about ancient Africa continuity can be drawn if a long-backward look is taken of the continent's formation and evolution.[1] By 200CE around 20 million people lived in Africa, half in North Africa and the fertile Nile Valley developed in Pharaonic times and then later part of the Roman Empire. By 1500 numbers had reached 47 million. Today 1 billion live scattered and concentrated with varied economic arrangements across this enormous space. Climate changes restricted the original locus of humanity, from where began the "out of Africa" trek, to a tiny space within the land mass (less than 0.1 % of the continent according to the fossil record). Thereafter movements within Africa took place. At this time the sub-Saharan region was controlled by local peoples only.

One millennium ago waves of migrants from the Gulf of Guinea heartlands swept south to displace the widely spread San peoples. As agrarians and pastoralists their economies and technologies had advanced beyond the mode of the hunter-gatherers. The ancestral economies of the San gave way to this powerful influx, but they were no "affluent society", as some postulated. Their world was Hobbesian in nature. As the Cro-Magnon overran the Neanderthals in Europe, so the Bantu societies displaced San economies and cultures. In the south-eastern zones, the residual San later encountered feudal and capitalist economic forces that eclipsed them and dispersed them in territories a fraction of the size of those of their ancestors. Small Khoisan remnants today are but a constrained, microscopic shadow of their former ancestral numbers. These Bushmen now constitute an underclass, ringed in by ranching, farming, the desert and game parks, and often controlled by Africa's governments for which their votes and voice count for little. Evolutionary tides have marginalised their social existence, today one of modest survival.

Agrarian and pastoral practice before colonisation, with the development of iron-smelting technologies, facilitated the dispersal of Africa's populace. This brought new means of existence into play, initially most advanced along the banks of the Nile, with exploitative intrusions of pillage in the Maghreb and targeted into Sudanic Africa. Economic modes of survival built on even older regimes arose along the shores of the Mediterranean, Nubia and Ethiopia. In time the economies in and around the Niger and Niger Delta developed kingdoms and empires of temporary substance based on hierarchies of subsistence, in central-ised states within the Sahel. These societies had local trading networks, crops and cattle, gold and salt, and encountered Arabs and caravans to the east on routes that carried Sahelian slaves to markets inside the continent and abroad.

In sub-Saharan Africa primitive subsistence economies prevailed. A few powerful kingdoms dominated local communities and spaces. Warfare was widespread over many centuries. Contrary to romantic notions, this was no idyllic world: life was raw, social realities fearsome, slavery commonplace and bare subsistence conditions normal for most. This servile order was governed by traditional rights. Wide economic inequalities prevailed. Many of the poorest gravitated towards enslave-ment in one form or another. Men commanded women and children in deeply rooted gerontocratic hierarchies, allowing for chiefs, headmen and "Big Men" to dominate economic imperatives.

Foreign influence arrived at Africa's shores in various guises. Africa became shackled to Europe and via this umbilical cord to many new economic forms of existence, not least slavery, mediated by Africa's elites at the time. This eventually led to widening commerce that created coastal outposts and inspired pre-colonial intrusions into the hinter-lands, and later colonisation. The transformation of Africa had begun, and it has continued. First explorers and traders, then settler economies, commercial enclaves, mining and plantations, followed by farms and towns, with industry and much more, all brought new economic means of survival and rupture to ancient ways.

Rudimentary and synoptic, this epic story depicts the brief history of the many modes of subsistence from and into which Africa's economies evolved. The rapidity of these latter changes was dynamic, disruptive and led to newly competitive parts of the economic fabric that displaced or anchored the old and ancient economies in their orbits. The ancient and modern would come to coexist and cohabit in the common economic space.

Big picture

A few general observations, applicable to Africa, deserve mention and appreciation in this big picture view. Except during the era of origins of mankind and the surge out of Africa, the continent has never occupied a central position in the global economic universe. As a continental entity, Africa has been adaptive towards or reliant on changing world economic structures and dynamics.

No nation states in Africa, pre-modern or of recent vintage, have alone determined the entire economic complex found within or around them. All have been significantly configured by their economic modes. Political architecture has exhibited a shorter lifespan than the constituents of the economic fabric. This record attests to the power, durability and longevity of fundamental economic structures, including economic forms antecedent to them. Typically, competitive modes survived beyond the end-date of their various connected nation-state formations. Economics here trumps politics. Contemporary nation-states mostly lack deep-rooted, long-term historicity or connectivity within Africa's longer-term economic transitions.

Africa's contemporary century state formations are often still fluid, many unsettled, some contested, and most have been or typically remain a target for periodic control or capture by narrow polities or elites within them. Some may not survive the longer tests of time. The evidence of unstable states, failing states, some failed, is part of this record of discord and fragmentation. It is less the evidence of nation-state continuity that marks Africa's past or contemporary political economy; rather it is the endurance and longevity of its economic modes or forms of survival, subsistence existence and competitive capitalist dominance that has longer prevailed. Thus politicians, organised parties and their policies appear in this historiography as transient, replaceable, even disposable, and not essentially decisive in shaping the economic foundations that fix the enduring relationships between economic modes, their survival or success. The various economic combinations found in Africa and inside different states are the outcomes of far longer and deeper processes of natural and competitive selection flowing from continuing adaptive circumstances. Their origins, interfaces and dynamics should be the focus for understanding the basic fabric of Africa's economies, rather than the nation-state artefacts that typically receive most attention.

The economic foundations of survival and competition in Africa can be traced from the past to present forms. This bedrock of the economies underpins markets and development trajectories. The fabric cannot be easily re-engineered by the architects of ideology or economic policy, whether these tools are used by local politicians or by foreign institutions. The essential raison d'être for any economic mode – subsistence formation or even capitalist entity – is basic survival, and the necessity to acquire the means for continuous existence in form or newly adapted shape. Self-sustained accumulation is inherent in this long-term process. Focus on economic success in Africa, and periodic failure to achieve it, has often led to misunderstanding of these fundamental survivalist requirements shaped around evolutionary necessity. The process implies profound but highly uncertain notions of non-teleological economic growth, which may be unfathomable in essence. Elected pathways and modal logic dictate subsistence and survival to form the backbone of Africa's "wicked materialism" in history and economic evolution.[2]

Hands of destiny

To not fall prey to the idea that Africa's economic destinies have been written in the stars, or that mankind plays no role in an unknown and unknowable economic future, some caveats are needed. It is essential to allow space for human agency: but within limits so as not to allow an overdetermining role. Therefore it is suggested as prudent to consider here an inverted application of Pareto's 80/20 principle, which states, in essence, that typically 80% of effects derive from 20% of the causes.[3] Our template, in contrast, argues that the largest slice (ie, 80%) of economic determinants shaping current and future trajectories derives from the presence, configuration and survival of economic modes. The balance of growth (the residual 20%) may be regarded as left to combinations of chance, intervention or human decision. The mode may thus shape some of its own history but not necessarily the conditions of its own choosing.

In the original Olduvai mode of existence there might have been no discretion about survival and no 80/20 rule (even inverted). Pure survival would have been determined entirely by austere natural conditions. With the passage of time and the emergence of competitive entities, and later the state, economic discretion would have emerged, and the mode's subsistence options and control would have become reliant in part on many decisions by others.

Here it is suggested as an analogue that perhaps around 80% or so of Africa's economies are already hard-wired from the past and by the constraints of the present. The latitude for manoeuvre in structure is restricted. Growth may be improved or damaged by human agency in the form of dynamic and inverted Pareto-style balances constructed over time. This should be taken as a metaphor, rather than any strict numeric rule. It allows us to account for historical precedent, if you like the facts on the ground, and both the human hand and the so-called "invisible hand" of the market. The primary keys to economic survival and evolution are thereby located in decisions taken on resource allocation, investment and accumulation at the level of the economic modes in existence.

Economic modes in Africa

The econo-materialistic template applied here – centred on the evolution of economic modes – is derived from a range of perspectives: history, economics, non-linear economics and competitive survival notions based on natural sciences as might be applied to Africa's economies. Rapid change in the last 50 years or so has been more significant than before. Interpretive models of the past appear wanting in capturing the essence of Africa's evolutionary dynamics.

At the origin of its history, Africa had but one mode. It is now composed of probably hundreds of distinctive economic modes with many thousands of nodes within them, all of varied vintage and composition. Competitive adaptation has marked this passage of time.

Economic modes and constituents have lineage, as well as history, embodied in their forms: parts of ancient agrarian Africa evolved to peasant economies, some became pre-capitalist market-driven entities, and inhabitants of others emerged as wage-labourers on plantations, or became subsistence dwellers in urban shanties, many as informal traders, while others "escaped" into capitalist Africa's demi-monde or modern economies. Lineage shifts were crafted by history and eco-geography under the competitive pressures of continuous and unstoppable economic change. This provides a far richer view of Africa than that offered in conventional models.

As one example in Africa of profound intermodal displacement over time, consider the long periodicity and drama that accompanied the displacement of the San peoples of sub-Saharan Africa following the great Bantu migrations below the Equator.[4] This deconstruction of San economies was followed by the settler colonial presence, with policies of ethnocide adopted in and beyond the Cape hinterland hundreds of years ago. Hunter-gatherer subsistence gave way to agrarianism, feudalism, pre-modern capitalism, market economies and ultimately to modernity itself as this transition was accomplished over a long period of time.

Looking at Africa's economic emergence this way yields other questions: what are the mechanisms of fundamental change embedded in Africa's economic evolution; are there some basic drivers that can be found applicable; what in the end erodes the original subsistence mode and its derivatives; has it really just been a case of frontier or modern capitalism triumphing over poorly organised subsistence entities? Clearly, the evident features of survivalist economies play major roles along with all the usual checks and constraints on evolutionary growth: demographics, impoverishment, wealth and income differentiation, and capital accumulation spread unevenly among branches of the economies. It would seem to me that this rich tapestry of Africa's economic historiography has been far more complex than that presented in the classic dualist models of orthodox economics, which reduces the drama to a struggle between capitalism and the world of subsistence. There have been various modal transitions, some overlapping and all locked inside the game of competitive survival.

In the competitive struggle between various modes, hereditary origins in the economies' forms typically persist but give way in due course to reweighting in relative significance as dominant modes reshape the landscape, making it easier for some and harder for others to keep ancient economic practices in place. This is akin to what Joseph Schumpeter (1883–1950) called "creative destruction" (the process by which innovations disrupt and displace previous patterns), typically manifested inside long-term economic cycles. Evolution drives this process, as some economic modes are fractured, compromised or "culled" from the landscape.

There have been many deficient, flawed or failed economic pathways taken in Africa's cycle-shaped and multiphase economic evolution.[5] Some end in economic paralysis or cul-de-sac; others in conflicts with damaging costs. Deficient economic pathways can still be found in Africa's economies today. In a few countries they have led to secession or irredentism, in others implosive economies or even revolution. Many an economic pathway has yielded beggary or stagnation. Unviable pathways travelled for a decade or more can significantly block, slow or even reverse economic gains earlier made: for instance, in many of Africa's Marxist or militarised states in the 1970s–80s, from Mobutu Sese Seko's drive for authenticity and kleptocracy to Julius Nyerere's *ujaama* strategy, following several import substitution models; in states that forsook monetary sanity; or in some that overrelied on single-commodity dependence as in Zambia under Kenneth Kaunda's humanism; and in countries where elites sought ethnic spoils before economic stability.

Today we find evident candidates for false roadways chosen for the future: states riddled with bureaucracy or even kleptocracy, many with low savings models, countries with poor investment records yet profligate conspicuous consumption predilections exercised by elites and political leaderships – and let us not forget Robert Mugabe's confiscatory and larcenous regime.[6] Pathways to relative decline or ruin may be emerging in some economies with the hallmarks of uncompetitive management, with resource nationalism too, and in the self-serving fictions of the "development state", an idea lauded in South Africa with its heavily overdimensioned governmental structures and poor economic growth performance over the years. In many cases governments have chosen what amounted to "anti-growth" strategies, placing the virtues of short-term redistributive economics ahead of long-term expansion.

In South Africa the economic policy of selective empowerment has cost an estimated $100 billion since 1994, with limited – if any – benefits accrued in terms of net economic growth. More is on the cards; at this rate potentially $300 billion is likely to be consumed before the mid-century. With the antiquated South African Communist Party as a member of the tripartite alliance that governs the state, South Africa may be the only country in Africa retaining the fossilised artefacts and ideologies of old communist regimes guiding important components of economic policy. Here cultivated nostalgia runs deep, with many in the governmental complex forever harking back to the evils of the distant past as an excuse to cover for the economic failures of the present: as if any "look backwards" strategy could serve any purpose at all. Perhaps more important has been the deep corruption and inefficiency pervading the state complex, with a rapid decline in the quality of public service and the erosion of capacity and competence allied to the lowering of productivity, despite increased resources and funds taken by the state apparatus out of the fiscus and economy. As with Zimbabwe, the continuing and costly exercise of dubious "liberation economics" holds potential risks by paving an economic pathway to underperformance, if not ruin. This model resembles the proverbial frog in the saucepan of water: eventually the water boils, and the economy asphyxiates.[7] The costs to "growth lost" from defective pathways can be considerable when viewed over the long term, even though they may suit their advocates and beneficiaries at the time.[8]

The primary mechanisms of evolution in Africa are socioeconomic, more than merely political, as various modes of existence are reformed in linkages to the wider economy, in geospatial hierarchy, along with their shifting balance of strength and ability to survive and replicate. Part of this mutation relates to the emergence of investment capacity, the key to continuity and growth, as the capital/labour ratios modify as new technologies give the advantaged a competitive edge. The process may take decades or generations to be accomplished. The long-term cycle of consistent economic growth, however, brings about enlargement of the capital stock, added wealth with income variances and limits to levels of viable reinvestment, so establishing new boundaries to warranted consumption. In this competition, economic entities have unequal chances of survival. Typically, the prospects of economic survival and growth for any mode rest on the initial conditions prevailing at the moment of competitive engagement with others. Some will be inherently disadvantaged in the long run. In the long span that development takes, the economic universe plays its inherited cards as the capital-accumulation and investment process, less so the policies of nation-states, directs the struggle for survival in the emerging market and more complex economy.

The seeds of success, often long planted, appear to be typically embedded inside the new modal forms that supersede the old, ancient patterns adapted to earlier epochs. In Africa's economic history the emergence of different economic taxonomies is evidence of economic selection through time. Few modes register immutability: all appear to change in some manner or another. There are cases where changes were derived from catastrophism, major events that shook the economic foundations. Yet the larger picture is that of evolutionary economic transition.

Every mode across the continent today arrived in time and space shaped by other preceding and contemporary modes, some highly competitive, others perhaps complementary. Here are the echoes of divergence, which today appear deeply embedded in the faster-moving economic landscape, even where some modes had common origins. Those capable of adapting best, fitting in to new conditions and reinventing their strategies for survival, have been the ones that have had success in the competitive game of economic selection. Around 100 years ago some 10,000 polities in Africa, each with several modes within, were reshaped inside and controlled by newly established nation-states. They encountered wider generic competition for survival. The economic game became more dramatic given Africa's multiplying commercial engagements with the world at large, thereby requiring competition with all. This multivariate economic evolution mirrors the natural competitive process of pathway selection underpinning Africa's economies. There will remain in future the inescapable dimensions of ruthless competition, accumulation, predation and parasitism, which mark the drama of this continent's economies as they move from different phases of underdevelopment towards an imperfect modernity.

The economies of Africa cannot at any one time accommodate all modes at the same level of capital stock, investment and household income or consumption. Hence wealth and income differentiations develop. More can be expected. Even while changes have occurred in wealth and income disparities, notably in the last decade, to broadly restore the status quo before around 1970 or so, this differentiation may not necessarily be much further reduced this century, let alone ordained by fiat, mandated by economic policies or installed by political ideology. Africa's economic habitat is finite at any point in time, and an endless competition has selected the modes that might inhabit scalar niches within the economic space. Yet with economic growth the limits of habitat may expand over time and allow for more variance within them. But as the historical record shows, some modes will still fail the test of longevity because of acute competition with others. Even where different modes command a relative equality of economic status at any stage, their capacities for adaptation may be unequal and so growth rates enjoyed by each will often vary. Thereby, over long periods of time, huge divergences can appear, as a result of the inexorable power of differential and compound economic growth.

Competitive selection accentuates diversity almost spontaneously, alongside resistance to dislocation, although state interventions may modify trajectories, if perhaps only temporarily. This makes it harder to presume that state economic policies will have equal impacts. Indeed, some modes inevitably adapt better than others. Is there then evidence of this economic evolution and selection in Africa's historical process? I believe so.[9]

5

Subsistence pathways

The exodus from Olduvai towards the modern economies in Africa was accomplished only in an extremely long transition. It took thousands of years for most peoples in Africa to overcome raw subsistence; even now many remain at low material levels. This may tell us something about the durability of the scourge of those surviving in poverty.

We know that economic modes, like species, have exponentially multiplied over the years from Olduvai to now. This is the case even in highly centralised states. The numeric frequency of modes in existence grows exponentially and the gap with the static number of nation-states widens with time. The intermodal connections in Africa have expanded profusely with time and circumstance. The primary forms of competition have been between different modes of subsistence and the artifices of modernity. Most fundamental survival-based or critical decisions on investment and accumulation for subsistence or growth have been taken by and at the mode level. But economic entities can be crushed by competition or technologies deployed by peers or even by fiat exercised by the state through controls, regulation or mismanagement. This dynamic metamorphosis does not deny the role of the human or invisible hand. Economic survival remains the eternal quest.

Transformations in existence

Let me sketch out a few economic pathways from the past to the present, looking at some of Africa's survivalist constituents as their economic forms changed over history, or in some cases were revolutionised by the progress of time. From this emerges a view not always fully appreciated of the dynamic and interconnected circuitry and networks forming the subsistence wiring of the economic fabric found within Africa.

Slavery was long practised and widely found in Pharaonic Egypt and even in Kush and Nubia in those days. It carried on in Roman times across North Africa. This economic art was no stranger to Sahelian and sub-Saharan communities from the earliest times. Given that slavery was a domestic mode in Africa at the outset, it is not surprising that it was further developed by Arab slavers into a cross-Saharan trading network involving probably around 8 million people over the centuries it was conducted. The Omani and East African mode of slavery too was grafted onto a local set of inland slave markets and connections with Arabia and the east. Atlantic slavery, a specialisation of Europe's maritime powers, drew probably around 13 million slaves from the hinterlands of the Gulf of Guinea, Niger Delta, Angola and even as far afield as Madagascar at times. In the Cape of Good Hope, slavery and then indentured labour was a mode of economic dependence for the early settlements around Cape Town and within its inland feudal economies for a couple of centuries, with many slaves brought from Indonesia, and from around the east coast, joined by those locally entrapped. This widespread economic practice caught Africa in a vice-like grip of human traffic under austere conditions for over two millennia, continuing after its nominal abolition in the early 19th century. Records of sporadic slavery mark the 20th century and the feudal backwaters of some of Africa's economies even today.

Plantations using slaves were established in Fernando Po, Rio Muni and São Tomé. Slavery became a feature of Mauritius and Réunion, as well as the Comoros, and the Portuguese established the *prazos* system with forced labour early on in the Zambezi valley and areas now part of Moçambique.[1] From these ventures arose many of the plantation agrarian structures found today. The common post-slave mode of exploitation emerged in feudal form, and some practices of this type can still be found in Africa. The wide variety of economic practices that followed slavery transmuted into a mix of forms that created new means of subsistence and survival: feudal tenancies with serfs, agrarian labour tenants, in time wage labour, contract and migrant labour through Wenela (primarily for South Africa's mines in and around the Witwatersrand) and regional labour supply networks (such as the Rhodesian Native Labour Supply Commission). Ultimately, the process led to widely diffused and commercial forms of modern employment. Informalisation arose from the incapacity of Africa's economies to absorb its demographic progeny.

As elsewhere, traditional powers in Africa engaged in forced labour, tribute labour and slavery, as well as captured peoples for local armies and for tillage of the land. In time, following colonisation, these practices became illegitimate if not illegal, even if not uncommon. In the emergence of many modern states, chiefs, headmen and kraal heads were given authority to command local economic space, and were even encouraged to enter modern bureaucracies under the aegis of "indirect rule" or by fiat of central governments. The traditional agrarian modes in Africa wilted significantly under the impact of the late 19th and 20th century search for cheap or migrant wage labour. Measures were introduced (hut tax, poll tax and compulsion) to generate a class of peasants and low-cost rural workers on plantations, mines and farms, as well as supply domestic servants and others for urban jobs. Millions found their existence in worlds entirely different from what had governed economic life before.

Some of the earliest venturers into Africa before colonisation were missionaries, who spread into Southern and Eastern Africa as well as other regions. From these ecclesiastical missions of "investment" emerged a host of God's modes of economic activity, with the spread of churches and charities, and later, but no less important, thousands of branches and even more projects run by NGOs. Today, there are additionally probably thousands of separate but centrally managed company projects of social goodwill – in schools, clinics, self-help schemes, rural ventures and others – financed as "corporate social investment", and spread across the entire African economic landscape. It is one long-established mode or engagement in Africa outside normal commercial endeavours.

These changes, installed and managed by the agents of benefice, arose partly because of the breakdown of ancient economic structures in the rural economies, as well as poverty in the towns and townships of an urbanising Africa. The ancient certitudes of rural old-age subsistence, in some cases even survival, could no longer be taken for granted. Welfare societies were one manifestation, co-operatives another, and in time these initiatives set down the philosophies that crafted incipient mechanisms for pensions or gratuities at the end of employment, ultimately leading to welfare states in a few African countries.

Africa's mining industry today, founded on the rich mineral geologies that traverse the continent's landscapes, has long antecedent roots. It did not just implant itself as it is found now. There had been mining on a small, non-industrial scale by the ancients, a widening set of metals worked across Africa from the first millennium, and old workings that were the source of gold and iron from long past. From this early and ancient mining followed independent small workers, later larger capitalist mines, with company mining investments in remote areas. Today there is a mix of corporate, conglomerate, private, local, foreign and state firms, and even many thousands of illicit miners, who plough Africa's soils in search of their El Dorado.

Coastal landings by early seafarers, explorers and commercial mercantilists, as well as prominent slavers, on the west and east coasts, from the Gold Coast to the Niger and the Cape, as well as Zanzibar, Delagoa Bay and Sofala, set down the coastal routes and shipping patterns that established the ports of many of Africa's littoral states. These became the early gateways to the hinterlands and far-flung interiors. From these small initial forays, trading outposts and networks followed up the rivers and inland deltas, while explorers developed knowledge of the Great Lakes and inland river basins that served as commercial arteries then and now. On the North African littoral the seaports of Tripoli, Alexandria, Algiers and others had already experienced longer economic histories; this is one reason North Africa built wider and deeper networks across the Mediterranean and into the Levant.

As with China, Africa was first opened to the world from the outside. Before that its interiors were the almost exclusive domain of autochthonous polities (there were no "Africans" then), with Berbers and Tuareg interfaced in the north with Arabs, and in time locked into conflicts over the means of subsistence. Many dramatic economic changes and powerful technologies entered through these portals of first entry – "Africa's door of no return" – and many followed to build the continent's global trading and commercial networks, shipping fleets, tanker routes, seaborne fishing ventures, naval bases and oceanic networks that date back to the pre-Roman era. Dhows, caravels, sailing boats and in time steamships able to enter ports, river estuaries, fragmented deltas, protected inlets, safe harbours and sheltered coastlines provided a radical realignment in Africa's economics and fortunes. The ocean mode connected the inner recesses of the Dark Continent to the wider commerce of Europe, Asia and even other parts of Africa with which it had never been engaged. Comprador ventures were established with local chiefdoms and traditional powers scattered along the littoral, and commercial piracy flourished in and around the Mascarenes. To witness the power of these early footprints we need only to consider the earliest consequences of Jan van Riebek's arrival at the Cape in 1652, and what that meant in time for South Africa, following Dutch settlement. It was the origin of wineries and the industry that came after, and sowed the economic seeds for the emergence of modern South Africa.

The traditional fishing communities of Africa had been established across the littoral, along coastal reaches and Africa's many rivers and inland lakes well before the advent of colonisation, with some later overtaken by the modern technologies of fishing fleets, foreign trawlers, the use of more hardy nets and aquaculture practices, including trout farms, the spread of dams and cultivated commercial fishing. Today, Africa's fishing industry is large and modern, with Nile perch flown from Lake Victoria by Antonov planes to markets in eastern Europe, and deep-sea fishing a sport widely practised off Africa's coasts. All these modes of existence and survival continue to operate alongside one another, in competition for fish resources and access to productive marine areas.

Many ancient means of survival have likewise been reconfigured and in turn transformed Africa. In Central Africa, when David Livingstone made epic marches across the continent, the "mode of elephant hunting" was encountered and vividly described in his diaries.[2] Hunters followed the known elephant trails, selected the highest overhanging trees, ascended them, and armed with spears would drive these weapons into the backs of passing elephants, following in pursuit for the eventual kill, for meat and sustenance and eventually for the ivory trade. New technologies and weapons in the form of guns allowed Fredrick Courtney Selous and legions of independent hunters (Henry Hartley among them) to decimate the elephant herds on the central African savannah, and in time the flourishing African ivory trade had expanded. Thereafter game parks were established, later private conservatories for animals, and a vast tourism industry arose, with culling one means of placing value on animals killed in organised and commercial ways. Of course, in times of conflict many elephants were slaughtered by state and private militia and even official armies, and illegal hunting never stopped – the rhino poaching encountered in South Africa in the past few years as an example. Villagers across Africa have long regarded elephants as a menace and threat to economic survival and crops, as well as the flora essential to their well-being, while some even argue that this giant of the savannah acts as a serious impediment to agrarian development in many parts of sub-tropical Africa.

These old modes of subsistence have been at the root of economic evolution in Africa, notably as capitalist economies of various types found new techniques, technologies and capital to displace, develop or expand beyond the capacities of ancient economic practices. This has created a highly diffused and differentiated economic world, in which competitive modes overtook those unattuned to the requirements of survival inside Africa's economies.

From rudimentary agriculture practised in traditional societies, key to survival, and its relative displacement by both arable and pastoral newcomers, sprang more viable types of farming across a wide range of commercial models following the insertion of private property markets into the rural landscapes. Cattle cultures have continued to this day in Botswana and South Sudan (including pastoralists like the Dinka Ngok, for instance), and nomads in the Sahara still follow ancient pastoral practices. Sahelians, Tuareg and others traverse vast open spaces and base many of their economic modes on what worked before. Even as Africa is still largely rural or with peasant economies prevalent, the majority of sub-Saharans rely on rural or agrarian endeavours. Many sophisticated agro-allied industries stand alongside these old modes of existence, both in competition and in cases with complementary activities. Even so, rural Africa has gone from breadbasket to basket case in the recent past and still awaits any green revolution. This fraught condition involves around 75 million smallholders of varied sorts. Around 62% of people in sub-Saharan Africa depend on agriculture for survival (33% in North Africa). Around 85% of Africa's farms are smaller than 2 hectares, most held under traditional title. Without major agrarian improvements and reform, the US Department of Agriculture has warned that by 2020 the "food insecure" in sub-Saharan Africa consuming below 2,100 calories daily will exceed more than 500 million (more than 50% of all Africans then). More recently, Africa has adopted the land-lease model of agrarian allocation to foreign companies and governments for their specific needs.

While many an African kingdom or empire acted as the arbiter of external and long-distance trade in the past, colonisation brought in new rulers, with their corporate houses or chartered companies, small firms and merchants houses that evolved into conglomerates, large companies, and even Africa-born and -owned multinationals. Some local firms today stretch across Africa's widening commercial markets and abroad to take advantage of the expanding opportunities afforded by globalisation.

Small-scale craftworks and industries from Africa continue to be widely found, as they were over the past few centuries, but the arrival of imported technologies allowed the nascent industrial and manufacturing complexes to become the core of Africa's industrialisation. The industrialisation process accelerated after the Second World War. In the past 20 years Africa's industries have succumbed to considerable pressure from new competitors in the form of low-cost consumer goods and industrial imports from the East, China most of all. Africa is deindustrialising today. It may struggle to ever reclaim its lost position in world manufacturing.

Likewise, modern service industries evolved in Africa to meet the needs of the modernising economies that emerged in the 20th century and since. Located in its towns and cities, also elsewhere, today they offer a full range of skills and services that were absent in these economies before they encountered the vicissitudes of colonial development. In Mauritius and selected locales elsewhere, this model has gone further to offer world-class tourism, outsourcing, offshore banking and related legal or accounting services, making Africa's economies quite unrecognisable from what they had been 100 years ago.

Today, the many thousands of hotels, guest houses, small hostels and lodges spread around Africa offer one-to-five-star lodging experiences in capital cities and on many remote and exotic islands, which before were largely neglected except for occasional visitors, adventurers, even pirates in some cases. The Africa-wide tourism industry did not exist in the distant past. Arabs and early explorers were probably the first to avail themselves of local African hospitality. This industry is expected to grow substantially given that Africa's share of the world tourism market is still small.

While rural Africa was the domain nexus for subsistence at the time of Africa's encounter with Europe, it became displaced, modified and transmuted by the onslaught of modernity. The migrant exodus from thousands of villages, homesteads and kraals was towards not only mines and commercial farms but also towns and cities. Urban Africa flourished, expanded and grew in some cases into megalopolises. Recently Africa has been urbanising faster. A noticeable economic element of this social transfer from village to town has been the relocation of subsistence as economic modes shifted. This forced people to adapt to once-unknown circumstances, as needed for survival, in economic conditions like those that prevailed during the Industrial Revolution. Towns, cities, peri-urban zones, townships or slums, with

squatter settlements, have become the loci for most of the informalisation found in Africa's economies, in one way or another. They have
equally provided a place for the neglected strata of societies that have
been displaced by economic circumstance, conflict or rural impoverishment. In some cases people who once inhabited Africa's forests and
mountains eke out quite different modes of urban or rural existence,
including those from the Ituri forest and elsewhere, like the Kalahari
Khoisan or so-called Bushmen. Many displaced social entities find their
living, often at the bottom of the economic rung, in this often chaotic
milieu, an experience not necessarily unique to Africa. Today in Africa
many millions are homeless – one mode of survival both prevalent and
growing, Africa's cities teem with the marginalised and beggars, a class
of survivors caught in the interstices between the medieval and modern.
Street traders numbering in the millions are ubiquitous and often live
from day to day. Criminal gangs in economic centres are likewise not
uncommon, the urban equivalent of rebels and larger militias that find
economic satisfaction mainly in rural areas as practitioners and architects of continuing multiple acts of predation.

Outside the main urban conurbations dwell large and growing
numbers of people who seek economic survival around Africa's
many border posts and crossings from one country to another. Africa
has several hundred separate land borders and many more formal or
informal crossing points along these often-uncontrolled frontiers around
which have grown hundreds of border trading complexes.[3] Up and down
Africa's main arterial routes – roads, shipping routes and railway interconnections from one part of Africa to another – many people live, work
and survive in thousands of quasi-villages complete with small traders,
tiny shops and economic activities as mechanisms deployed for survival
and basic subsistence. These ventures, which were not there before,
continue to multiply, and they are likely to become more significant.

In Africa today, more so than ever before, "subsistence has many
faces" and exhibits multifaceted portraits for survival. This complex
and rapidly evolving economic world – Africa's survivalist underbelly,
often largely pre-modern and sometimes quasi-market-oriented in
nature – will need transformation before any fully fledged economic

destiny around modernity might be reached. It will be a gargantuan task.

Achilles' heel

There are some well-managed and improving state systems with viable economic edifices in Africa but not as many as there should be. Some state firms manage to make profits and improve their balance sheets. A few even compete on the regional and world stage. But Africa is woefully behind the best-in-class and competitive performance as a whole. Most of all, many state structures in effect act against what could be seen as the public interest.

The often weak and incompetent measures that have been applied by many nation-states to remedy Africa's historic dilemmas of low rates of long-term growth and pervasive poverty are well known. Many of these economic conditions and flaws originated in the scale and inflation of the state apparatus all over the continent. It is Africa's own, self-inflicted Achilles' heel.

Errors in state organisation, fiscal funding, the management of state firms, economic policy and commercial strategy continue to be made. State economic modes, as repositories of revenues and taxes, have been built in post-colonial Africa from the relics or remnants left by the colonial exodus. Africa's inheritors, its political classes, have sought to manage these structures of administration and parastatal complexes with varied strategies, aims, ambitions and usually many more personnel. It has not always been a smooth transition.

Civil servants and politicians in Africa have become a large and expanding category inside the economic universe, as one specific mode of economic survival that cannot be ignored. The size of Africa's governments, with ministers and their minions, presidents and their cabinets, foreign dignitaries and diplomatic staff, state officials, thousands of parastatals, commissions, government boards, quasi-official quangos, city municipalities, different tiers of federal and local control, and associated committees and bodies, replete with support staff – and vastly inflated cost – has expanded everywhere. Rare is it for any government in Africa to downsize, or even consider doing so. There is even an African Parliament that sits in Midrand in South Africa, replete with its own bureaucratic edifice, and an expanded African Union installed in Addis Ababa to be accounted for. Both grow in size each year and perform in underwhelming fashion. In Africa's bureaucracies productivity varies but is often abysmal. Many are employed in Africa's state bureaucracies; fewer work for them. This gigantic *etatist* complex and drain on scarce resources, finances, public capital and markets in Africa is one of the causal origins of its poor historic performance and bedevilled contemporary malaise.

Africa's state firms cross almost all industries. Not all focus on their balance sheet. Many offer subsidies under political pressure, in electricity and services, compromising their viability. Inside this quasi-state and semi-capitalist world, insiders have long been the profiteers of public resources, the outsiders paying in higher taxes, bribes and thwarted service quality and delivery. Many of the upper echelons in parastatals vote on their own inflated salaries and benefits without public scrutiny. Theirs is often a world of "other people's money". Politicians with their expansionary and aggrandising agendas, some with autarchic policies – still prevalent in Africa, seeking nationalisation, resource nationalism and new edits of regulation – encourage this tax-draining burden and negative economic dynamic. There is no shortage of instances to be recounted.

Stability and rising efficiency have been hard to achieve, let alone sustain, inside Africa's state collage. Only as the pre-colonial gave way to the colonial – following long periods before that witnessed an array of empires, local kingdoms, trusteeships, protectorates and internationally mandated vassal states – emerged the foundation stones for post-colony state structures. Few nation-state edifices found today have been wholly stable for the duration of independence; some have become more disorganised, and others been constipated by ever-expanding or less competent bureaucracy. South Sudan has but a momentary vintage, starting from ground zero. Libya too must now begin anew.

The economic fabric and many modes of economic sustenance

in Africa have often been rocked, undermined, neglected, or directly impeded by these parts of the economic architecture. It should be little surprise that this has been the case given the variety of state types found in Africa's past, notably the past 50 years. Similar throwbacks still command many parts of this economic terrain. An unsettled collage of ideologies and political regimes has defined this state economic universe over the course of the past 100 years: slave and settler states, those beholden to the trekboer cultures, the apartheid edifice in South Africa and its replacement alter ego, the Congo Free State, a multitude of one-party states of diverse type, "states within states" that have been at times in the hands of the militarised, warlords and rebels or separatists, states as hermitic enclaves (Eritrea still), contested states (Western Sahara for over 40 years), many continuing micro-states (some fiefdoms or akin to family-run businesses), and areas abandoned within states taken over or in the hands or control of nomadic or irredentist groups. Many states in Africa – I would estimate today around 30 – endure the discreet and undiluted charms of Big Man rule, whatever their nominal claims to modernity.

The list of de facto faulty forms of state practice in Africa's recent past and contemporary record is long: with failed and failing states, political dynasties and monarchies, feudal and quasi-capitalist entities, some states under military control, federations of temporal convenience that have come and gone, others that have been resurrected or mixed in with disadvantaged states bereft of funds, or those landlocked by history and punished by geography. The predatory or quasi-criminal government has been no exception over long periods of Africa's state history; some are still in this mode. In only a few cases has there been a long tradition of stable and efficient state order, which many hoped might emerge at independence or later when democracy, as an idea, swept into Africa in the 1990s. Most states reverted to type and lapsed into authoritarianism while another variant became the much-beloved continental version of the nominally democratic or pseudo-democratic state, with a growing number run by governments of questionable inclusive "unity" pulling in different directions.

You might wonder how Africa's more preponderant and survivalist economic modes managed to overcome this continuing legacy and enabled the continent to expand its economies and grow. On the balance of any evidence, this has occurred not because of the states and governments they have endured, but probably despite them. It has been an accomplishment and signal triumph that needs our attention.

Economic contours, past and present

While Africa has many economic modes to underpin its existence, and these have endured tumultuous transitions over the last few decades, even before, it is because the economic and commercial infrastructure has been spider-web like, adaptive, interwoven intricately far and wide, shaped in a lattice of connections, that there has been competitive survival and even economic growth. Displacement, differentiation and competitive selection have governed this process – for example, from the early 20th century, the Zeederberg coach in roughshod form was the main means of transport in central Africa, eventually giving way to modern transport by road, rail and air. All transport modes have adapted. In what way has this process shaped Africa's macroeconomic contours?

Capitalist modernity brought Africa its formative economic infrastructure, electricity networks, the unlocking of its rich natural resources in minerals, oil and gas, commercial farming and eventually industrialisation. Economies are now hard-wired with telephony, sea cables, mobile phones and satellite services, which today serve subsistence and modern economies alike, whether formal or informal in constitution, however unequally these structures and services may be spread.[4] While a new future waits, as more will be done to improve basic infrastructure and benefit more of the populace in time, it has been a long road.

What is the significance today of the economic modes depicted within Africa? How did their economic evolution take place, and at what speed over the long spans of time? Why has Africa's long-term economic growth been sporadic, cyclical, at times uneven, and lamentably lagging the rest of world? Here we need to interrogate economic history and available data in the search for preliminary insights and answers. Let us begin with the question of economic modes, the core units for subsistence and survival in the past, which can still be found widely spread in Africa.

I cannot claim that there is any simple methodology to accomplish this task. We shall need to use crude but I hope indicative measures to intuit this economic growth in Africa's economies. Here the demographic record found in Africa and the related data on GDP and income per head for the last 2,000 years crafted by Angus Maddison are widely considered to be the best source on the period starting from ICE.[5]

If Olduvai was an original mode of existence, can we estimate today, even roughly, the growth, shape and numbers of economic entities in Africa?

Remember that at Olduvai there was no formal state machine, government or system with which all are now familiar. It was a unique human condition from which all else followed down the years. A "state of nature" prevailed, even if this group at our origins might have acted on shared social rules and consensual existence for subsistence. A few émigrés split from the Olduvai base camp, moved north and south, and began the proliferation of similar and then later many diversified economic modes in Africa in a sort of factorial numeric that multiplied profusely and became more complex. By the time humans had breached the Red Sea to Eurasia there would have been many more isolated social entities seeking their economic survival within Africa. Human numbers and proto-economies expanded during the Stone Age and Iron Age in Africa following agrarian development beyond the primitive and wide-ranging social migrations across sub-Saharan Africa, to the west and elsewhere. Separate entities of subsistence would have proliferated.

The economic practices, both Roman and Berber, found and developed on the southern shores of the Mediterranean and into the Sahel grew with intercity trade, multiple crafts, agrarian practices, shipping and a host of commercial activities that had made this world the heart of civilisation. When the Romans commanded the northern shores of Africa in the 1st century CE, Maddison estimates Africa's population at 17 million (out of a world population of 225 million). It took 1,000 years for Africa's population to nearly double, reaching 32.3

million by 1000, and another 500 years for it to rise to 46.6 million. All this suggests that tough times, indeed Malthusian subsistence realities, prevailed during these long intervening years. Between 1 and 1500 the population growth rate was barely 0.06% annually. Primitive and stagnant economies, with the lack of endogenous technology growth and austere conditions for survival, marked this historical epoch.

From the 7th century onwards the Arabs came to dominate the interior Maghreb and Sahara, bringing with them trade, goods and technologies to open up this inland sea of sand. Economic modes multiplied in the wake of this formidable transformation of the Sahara and Sahel. Later, perhaps more than 1,000 years ago, emigrants swept south from their heartlands on the west coast towards the Cape and its hinterlands, to encounter the widespread hunter-gatherer peoples. By this time the many independent Bantu societies below the Sahara must have counted thousands of separate economic modes in one form or another between them, as they typically lived in small collectivities of households, often isolated in separate kinship groups.

From 1500 onwards Africa was a continent of interest to Europe, and Leo Africanus (aka the Moor) had brought knowledge of its cultures, economies and interiors to the courts of Italy and the Holy See. An Andalusian-born explorer from Granada (known as Al-Hasan, born Muhammad al-Fasi) and later a writer, Leo Africanus became a household name among Europe's medieval elite. His knowledge and learning, transmitted to the papacy, helped shape Europe's cartography and geography of Africa for almost three centuries. Leo was unanimously respected as the most authoritative source on the political and social domains known as the Barbary Coast and Sudanic Africa. This effort pre-dated the onset of Europe's exploration and expansion into Africa. An important reason for Leo's fame – maybe Africa's first celebrity – was that no competing sources on the Maghreb were available to Europe. Leo's revelations were to shape Europe's interest in Africa's famed gold, economic riches and empires. One feudal mode here recognised another.

Meanwhile, the era of exploration and navigation around Africa's western coastlines by sea was beginning, implanting new economic ventures in and across the continent, eventually on both coasts. By 1652 the demography of Africa was around 57 million strong. By the time British settlers came to South Africa from 1820 onwards, Africa had only 74 million people, a population half of Nigeria's today. Before the turn of the century in 1900 the Africa census count would have stood at around 110 million, about 10% of the 1 billion people on the continent today. Africa's subsequent explosive demography has been a product of only 110 years or so.

Taking an average village for current purposes at, say, 1,000 people, there would have been around 110,000 socioeconomic units of one sort and another in 1900 – probably a large underestimate. There could have been many more. Following historical texts in which it has been reported that a wide range of distinctive economic activities could be found in these subsistence communities, with a guesstimate of perhaps 50 or so each, our estimate of separate economic nodes would be in the range of 500,000. Thousands of African polities, large entities based on ethnolinguistic and cultural shape or differentiations, had been in existence at the time of the 1884–85 Berlin Conference when Europe carved out nation-states in the scramble for Africa to set down boundaries superimposed on the societies in place. By 1910 there were 40 states in Africa (only Liberia and Ethiopia were excluded from imperial fiat), with more complexities in the economies installed. Over the next century, during the early years of which imperial Europe "stitched up" its colonial structures, Africa's nation-states evolved to the present 55 countries (excluding statelets and de facto zones of contested separatism with quasi-independence). From this set of circumstances and with an eye on the likelihood that the more complex economies in Africa, in all comprising 1 billion people, might have many economic modes of survival and subsistence today, the numbers of nodes constituting the basic economic fabric would be potentially in the vicinity of 1 million or more.

These are of course rough, even crude estimates. Neither national accounts nor census data are designed to answer these questions. Historians have not made the attempt. The actual number of self-dependent forms is not here the main issue, which is rather to recognise that economic modes have evolved and multiplied, grown formidably in number, and substantially altered in type and mix, as well as in commercial relationships. They have become increasingly differentiated as competitive selection has worked its magic to reshape Africa's economic fabric over the millennia. While this process was somewhat slow at first, it became an accelerating phenomenon.

Another approach is to guess the numbers of known modes and connected entities that make up Africa's economic fabric today. There are huge numbers of subsistence families and households, rural homesteads and kraals or villages with chiefs and headmen, informal traders, people living on subsistence at or below, say, $1.25 a day, the unemployed and underemployed, companies and listed corporations, state complexes with politicians, officials, bureaucrats and parastatals, small micro-businesses, slum dwellers and millions of small shops (known as *spaza* in South Africa). There are also numerous armed militia and rebels, large official armies, independent taxi and bus operators, operating mines, farms, and oil or gas ventures upstream and downstream, as well as thousands of entities and projects found across varied industries, game parks and safari lodges, hotels of any sort, NGOs and their affiliates, fishing villages with owner-boats, people surviving on Africa's rivers, lakes and coastal fringes and in its forests, extensive mountain ranges and desert environs, and a large and growing number of small towns and larger cities with diverse informal commercial activities dotted over Africa's landscape. The point is that these segmented entities often go unrecognised. Indeed, many seek to "escape" the writ and grip of their states, some of which are regarded as predatory, yet their existence has led to Africa's complex evolutionary economic pattern.

The idea that Africa's governments, or perhaps international bodies, might somehow wholly or simply rearrange this complex economic architecture through liberal moral suasion or intensified regulation seems fatuous. It flies in the face of powerful historical tides, abundant evidence and common sense. Africa's modern economic world was grafted onto the immense collage of continent-wide survivalist economies; it grew within them, mostly around their edges at the outset, in the end reaching the present state through lengthy phases of expansion and development. In recent decades, the modern industries of Africa have spread far and wide – the flourishing oil and gas industry is just one.[6] Yet it was not always this way. Africa took eons to grow its economies to their present position.

Metrics and myths

The doyen of those who have sought to record historic economic trends for the last 2,000 years is Angus Maddison, whose work presents data on Africa's economies and demographics that enable us to measure growth and GDP per head in comparable terms, shown in real dollars on 1990 baseline estimates, all the way from the 1st century CE to the 21st century up to 2008.[7] I have used these data and updated the numerics for Africa to 2010, using the latest official data, appreciating the original source data and caveats applicable to these estimates, as explained by Maddison.

In the 1st century the annual per head income of Africa was put by Maddison at $472, and by 1000 the level had fallen to $425. By 1500 income per head was even lower at $414. The long Malthusian night commanded the economic stage, with a real subsistence-income decline recorded. The inference of the economic record is that most of Africa went backwards for a period of 1,500 years – a salutary lesson in ultra-long-cycle stagnation and chronic decline.

In this era Africa remained for the most part unaffected by the technological advances slowly achieved and embedded elsewhere. Egypt experienced technological regression. Elsewhere, technologies across Africa were basically frozen. It has taken over five centuries for modern technologies to be adopted in Africa and for segments within its modern economies to move closer to world standards; yet even today large parts of Africa live with technologies encountered in the distant past, some typical during Roman times.

Even while Africa as a whole backslid for 1,500 years, average measures can conceal inner trends. The Roman era had brought an economic upside, and in time imperial jurisdiction fell apart and succumbed to the ravages of Vandals, establishing in Carthage, and bringing conflict and new socioeconomic realities that long plagued North Africa. The Saharan domains from the 7th century onwards had been in initial turmoil under Arab penetration but later would expand in economic terms before again encountering difficulties prior to the intrusion of the Ottomans. The region north of the Sahara had a different economic history from sub-Sahelian economies. It experienced higher income and greater urbanisation, and the seashores and ports had brought commercial contacts with more developed southern Europe and the Levant economies. But it too in time encountered long-term stagnation. In the 1st century, North Africa's income per head was $460, compared with $400 in the rest of Africa. By 1820 North Africa was in the same sinking boat, at $447, below levels found in Roman times, while sub-Saharans had per-head incomes of only $415.

Despite the commercial benefits of sitting on the edge of the "Roman lake", plague had bedevilled Egypt from the 6th century onwards though it did not seem to cross the Sahara. There was sedentary agriculture around the Nile Valley and its delta which gained from cropping and new technologies, while the region had a substantially monetised economy backed by an organised state, harking back to Pharaonic days. From early times the Pharaohs and the Ptolemies had created economic surpluses, but these were eventually appropriated by the Romans, then later by the Ottomans. By 1516 Egypt had become an economic backwater, paying tribute to the Ottoman sultan. Links with Europe were cut and the glories that were once Hellenist and later Roman-controlled Alexandria were no more. As a sign of serious economic decline, Egypt's population between 1000 and 1500 fell by 20% to 4 million.

Until the 7th century North Africa's economies were controlled by Romans, Carthaginians, Phoenicians and Greeks. Seaborne trade flourished. Egypt was richest and income levels declined moving west towards Morocco and Mauritania. In the Maghreb outside Egypt, Roman settlement was found mainly on the littoral and rarely went far inland, except in Tunisia for access to the granaries drawn from irrigated lands. Arab conquest in the 7th century severed North Africa's connections with Europe. Muslim powers took over Egypt from 639 onwards and the Arab invasions were completed across the Maghreb inside 60 years, as the Berbers succumbed. Until the Arab arrival and the 8th century, there had been hardly any contact across the Sahara from north to south. The revolutionary technology of the camel caravans changed everything. These ships of the desert broke open trans-Saharan trade, notably in gold and slaves. Islamisation facilitated the organisational capacities of the Sahel's local ruling elites. In terms of Africa, this was akin to the discovery of the New World.

From the earliest Roman times, slavery practised in North Africa had been common. The exploitation of slaves, captured or forced, enabled the empire to function. It was a traffic that grew to huge dimensions with and after the Arab invasion of the Maghreb. From 650 to 1900 around 8 million slaves were exported in this trans-Sahara commerce. It was an immense forced human exodus, the more so given the population size of the time, making it probably proportionately more significant than the Atlantic slave trade as it was limited to only one arena. Gold and slaves were exchanged for horses and weapons, technologies that underpinned some of the empires established in the Sahel at the time.

In Sudanic Africa, implying black Africa, the agrarian mode was extremely weak and technologies were very primitive. There were no landed property rights. Boat technologies on the seashores or on major rivers did not match those of Muslim Africa. Meanwhile, climate and ancient technologies imposed harsh rigour on life under the kinship systems that prevailed south of the Sahara. Nor was this a generally literate set of societies and knowledge transmission relied on oral traditions.

From around 1500 to 1820 Africa's economies flatlined more or less overall, and by that stage GDP per head stood at around $420 (while the population grew to 74 million). More of the continental economy after 1700 became concentrated in the south, around the Cape, with growth poles too found in the continent's far north. Economic living levels in tropical Africa's rural interiors were probably much worse. In those zones there were no trappings of proto-modernity, little competitive technology, an absence of productive central taxation, no security of private property, and no instruments to raise investable public debt or guarantee continuous accumulation and sustained capital formation. Revealed preferences indicated consumption as the priority. Nor was Africa extensively monetised at this time. Barter was still prevalent. This was mostly an era of unremitting stasis in terms of income levels, raising the question of exactly how Africa cut the Gordian knot of entrapment in material misery. External implants and foreign investment allied to incipient globalisation would take much of the credit.

Uplift in economic growth came from modern investments and capitalisation already installed in the few locales on the scattered edges of the continent. Primitive and primary accumulation was part of this story. From 1820 to 1870 Africa began to notch up economic growth in real GDP per head, at an average annual rate of 0.58% over that 50-year period; from 1500 to 1870 the growth rate had only been an inconsequential 0.05% annually. This was almost the first growth ever recorded on a long-run cycle, reaching an average income standard of $500 per year by 1870. While this added a paltry 6% to the average real income from the $472 baseline in the 1st century, it reflected recovery from 1500 when levels had been only $414 per head.

Africa's long-run growth cycle, while marginally positive, was still chronically abysmal. Again the distributional effects would have favoured the far south and far north as established growth poles. But overall the scale of this growth was quite modest. Tough economic conditions prevailed across most of traditional Africa. At this time Africa's demography continued to expand, to 90 million by 1870 and 110 million by the turn of the century in 1900, placing downward pressure on average real income per head and growth dynamics.

It is perhaps appropriate to envision the era from 1500 onwards as one of Africa's continuous replication of subsistence, apart from a few isolated growth poles. Abundant land, relative underpopulation, slow demographic transition, gradual social expansion across the rural landscapes, nomadic pastoralism and some out-migration, and perhaps the lure of more benign ecologies, enabled the real subsistence world to continue under austere conditions. Eventually all this was fractured, and the storyline for these ancient largely barebones economies became one of disruption with relative disintegration. Yet the entrenched impact of more than 1,000 years of embedded subsistence economies, while certainly shocked and ruptured by late 19th-century colonialism, did not crumble entirely. Nor did the advent of early modernism herald any crossing of the Rubicon or quantum shift in economic progress. But the old and new had now to cohabit Africa's economic space. This fateful inner schism would become the drama of the century to follow, and remains so today.

The opening of Africa to the world economy saw real income per head reach $601 in 1900 and $637 by 1913, before the advent of the First World War. Growth per head now stood at higher levels and annual GDP grew by 0.61% over 1870–1900, and 0.46% for the first 13 years of the 20th century, during which time the population had grown faster, to around 125 million. Compared with the 1820 baseline there had been growth of over 50% in income per head by 1913. Still, long-term cyclical growth was slow, recorded at only 0.6% per annum for the 30 years to 1900. This was presaged by the fundamental switch from rural subsistence dominance in Africa's GDP to more mixture in the overall economic foundations and sources of economic growth.

Colonisation over the years 1913–50 witnessed major changes in Africa. Demographic upside was one of them. It was an era of major capital investment. By 1950, even with 228 million living on the continent, income per head had grown rapidly to $889, and hence over the 37-year period at an annual rate of 0.91%. This meant a significant relative shift in growth rates and income standards overall. But it took place with substantial shocks to the traditional economies and in so doing etched new patterns of wealth, capital and income differentiations into economic landscapes. The lifestyles of the rich far outranked those of the preponderant poor. Even the middle classes, small in number, attained income standards that even Africa's potentates had not enjoyed before. This became Africa's first real period of solid long-run economic growth, of a significant magnitude, which continued thereafter. Many important economic institutions and technical advances produced elsewhere – capital markets, companies, factories, literacy, electricity, railways, infrastructure and organisational capabilities – were brought into Africa, so radically changing its economic destiny.

It was only around 1960 that Africa's GDP per head reached the $1,055 mark, with a population then of 285 million. Investment was still sizeable and had a major economic impact. Growth had been achieved from large capital inflows, domestic investment, infrastructure spread, economic linkages built inside Africa and with the world outside, and from technologies and investments to augment the scale and efficiency of the capital stock. Capital/output ratios had risen, while more land had been made commercially viable, so technical coefficients and productive efficiencies improved. Pre-market economies became smaller within GDP measures. Demographics and land surpluses became less significant in the wider capital asset base. Urban-industrial and skilled workforces enabled rising productivity, even export manufactures. By any comparison, this amounted to a revolution in innovation across Africa. More transactions than ever before were conducted in monetised form tethered to or generated inside the market economy. Africa became extensively connected to the world economies of the time. Goods and people could travel more quickly than ever before across Africa, and from its hinterlands and ports to outside world markets. Huge and previously unimaginable volumes of commodities traversed its rail and road networks. World markets were brought closer in time to Africa's shores as commercial shipping routes circumnavigated the vast littoral weaving a web of oceanic and commercial connections. Whatever the merits or otherwise of imperialism, it had induced a degree of industrialisation in Africa that reconfigured many of its nascent and previously backward economies. Yet Africa's winds of change blew again.

So began decolonisation. It brought abrupt changes in regime. There was a flurry of political expectation and much-vaunted ambition across Africa, and the demand for raw commodities and economic expansion worldwide was fortuitous. This watershed too was marked by major disruption across Africa, with ultimate decay in many state institutions and in some of its economies (notably Congo). Still, the early years of independence coincident with a global economic boom allowed Africa to grow too.

Income per head levels and most economies expanded, and GDP per head rose to $1,181 in 1965, $1,335 in 1970 and $1,515 in 1980. On the long-term cycle, economic growth rates of around 1.8% annually had been achieved for 1960–80, this modest score being dampened by the rapid rise in population. In this phase, the demographic transition began to matter more as time passed. Employment growth rarely matched the numbers coming into Africa's labour markets and the phenomenon of structural unemployment reared its head; informalisation was used as a strategic buffer against the weakening capacity of the traditional economies to provide subsistence. For many, survival was all. It required forced and fragile adaptation with economic strategies previously unknown. From the original scramble for Africa eventually emerged, with an interregnum of about 70 years, the struggle for survival: the survival of the fittest, fattest, fastest and favoured.

By this time and during the turbulent 1980s the mistakes of newly emerged nation-states in the management of their economies, with multiple civil conflicts and wars and post-war struggles for political control during the Cold War, were taking a heavy toll on living standards and economic growth. Africa went through an economic downside in the 1980s, so that by 1990 GDP per head had slipped down to $1,425 (dropping $90 per head: the same level of subsistence income attributed to hunter-gatherers 12,000 years ago) while the continent's population shot up to 633 million. Here the hand of demography weighed heavily. It took another ten years from 1990 for recovery to transcend the expanding demographic realities and break above the GDP per head level of 1990 to reach $1,447 in 2000 (still below the 1980 real level). In effect, Africa experienced 20 years of economic trauma with eventual recovery, leaving two lost decades of forgone growth and a generation of backsliding. The impact on the long-run cycle was costly: the three decades 1980–2010 yielded only 0.7% in annual growth. The distributional impact was worst in sub-Saharan Africa.

Only in the first decade of the 21st century did Africa show its economic mettle. From 2000 to 2010 Africa experienced its most productive period, allied to the world commodity boom and global bull market. By 2010 real income per head was around $1,870 (using 5% annual growth in GDP for 2009–10, perhaps slightly generous given world economic recession effects). Africa then sat with its GDP around

$1.9 trillion or so, but with a population of 1.05 billion as well, and it could be seen that the growth rate in income per head for 2000–10 was approximately 2.36% per annum. While longer-run cycle growth rates had improved, this was for a shorter duration than the 20-, 30- and 50-year cycles measured before. This positive achievement was no economic miracle or stellar performance; it still left Africa in 2010 with an average income per head of only $5.12 per day. The gaps widened between those at the top and the majority living with much less, while great and expanding divergences emerged between Africa vis-à-vis the rest of the world.

From 1960 to 2010, during Africa's post-colony era, annual GDP had expanded from $300 million to over six times that size, with an annual average compound growth rate of 3.78%. Yet this allowed per head incomes to rise by only 1.15% annually over this 50-year period. These facts give the lie to the notion that Africa's demographic explosion generated growth. It did not. Those who argue that the projected 1 billion increase in Africa's population to 2050 will be a key growth driver need to acknowledge this inconvenient truth in the historical track record. It was not a launch pad for economic nirvana just as it will not be so in future. The GDP and income per head growth rates for this golden decade, however, trumped that recorded in Africa's problematic early years before the colonial experience, and during its early and most difficult post-colonial phases. But only much higher and more sustained economic growth will offset the pessimistic claims of Malthus, whose shadow still looms large across Africa's future landscape.

With knowledge of this past, some questions come to mind. Was Africa's growth rate somehow naturally inhibited, at some ceiling of small expanding increments over time? Are there upper limits to future growth, and over what period? The big-picture question remains: what long-run cycle economic growth rate can Africa expect from today to 2050?

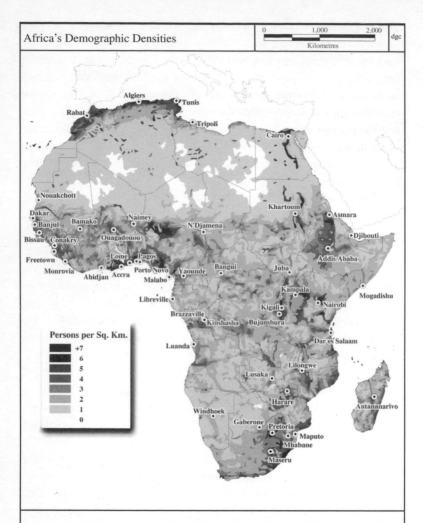

Over one billion people inhabit Africa today, with two billion expected by mid-century. Sub-Sahara is growing fastest, with heavy concentrations found in the Gulf of Guinea, Ethiopia, Rift Valleys, along the Nile, on the Niger, and in south-eastern Africa. In the North, densities are greatest along the littoral and cities of the Maghreb. Vast spaces of the Sahara and Sahel are home to over fifty million, while many open terrains elsewhere have low demographic densities.

Hard lessons

Perhaps a few lessons can be drawn from this historical record and long-term growth experience. They may offer images for reflection on the economic future. Among such lessons would be that Africa has required high and continuous growth rates on a secular basis to lift historic income standards. The longer this has endured the better it has been for income per head. For the future, growth will be needed at solid rates for generations. Great cost can be incurred by a lost decade or more, undermining the future scale of GDP and incomes per head in the continental economy. Cyclicity in long-run growth has been a profound problem in Africa. The rising tide tends to lift all boats, or more so than otherwise. Commodity markets and world economic conditions have played a significant role in Africa, as has the capacity of the continent's increasing number of economic modes, navigating what have typically been turbulent political waters. Notwithstanding acute conditions in the political economy, in some cases even catastrophe, these economic modes have managed to secure growth for Africa over its worst political periods, and continue to be the economic bedrock of basic survival and subsistence.

To date there have been many false starts, interrupted economic cycles or pathways blocked. There has been as yet no quantum leap out of the slow and gradual emergence from the modern past. This raises important questions about the future. The exogenous impacts of foreign markets and commodity booms have at times been of huge benefit. Yet cyclical downturns have taken an enormous economic toll. It would be unwise to expect a future inscribed with high, linear-like secular economic growth rates to prevail for decades, other than in unexpected or exceptional conditions. Large parts of Africa's growth resilience at the very outset appear to have been endogenously driven from its many economic modes, with basic survival increasingly determined within the continent. Then emerged growth induced by exogenous investment inputs. This marriage of both will be an important part of the foundation on which the future will rely.

The sub-Saharan economy did not perform as well as the rest of the continent over this long period, given the earlier economic start and higher incomes with substantial advantages in North Africa until recently. It is amid the large population milieu around and below the Equator that the most profound challenges of underdevelopment will be found.

It is estimated that the population in Africa will reach 1.5 billion by 2030 and grow to 2 billion by or before 2050. It might be suggestive therefore to note a few observations on economic growth rates in future, using the same real income data measures so far applied. For Africa in 2030 to retain the same income per head in real terms as in 2010, GDP would need to be $2.85 trillion, and by 2050 $3.74 trillion. GDP growth in each year, without any fallback, would need to be at least 2.0% in real annual terms for the next 20 years, or at 1.7% annual real growth for the coming 40 years, respectively. This would be enough just to stand still in real per head terms. Even these growth rates, however, appear a challenge on the basis of the long-run cycles recorded so far. This sets out the bare minimum economic task to retain average standards of living as a whole and accommodate the inevitable doubling in population, before any net improvement in GDP per head is banked. In 2011, dramatic reversals in North African economies (notably Libya, Egypt and Tunisia) partially compromised Africa's future trajectory. These events are signal reminders of the deep-seated fragilities existing within Africa. If similar implosions took place in sub-Saharan Africa at some point, the future would be even more problematic.

Is there any "natural growth rate" for Africa to guide economic expectations to be derived from past long-term trend data, with their episodic, patchy, long-run cyclic periods and even occasional reversals? Some observers, unwilling to recognise the past, caution against "looking back", especially in today's climate of bullish optimism. Yet the past has shaped the present as all know. Why not the future? Over the most recent two decades of growth, probably the best in Africa's history, including the economic recovery of the 1990s and the significant upside over 2000–10, the average African GDP growth rate was 3.8% annual in real terms. Even if this 3.8% growth rate applied for the 40 years to 2050, it has been shown that 1.7% would be required just to stand still in terms of income per head, thus mortgaging a large amount of future net economic growth in GDP to cope with emerging demographic necessity. Africa will need to do much better to lift its economies out of underdevelopment.

Left behind

In the long night of worldwide economic growth from the extreme economic minimalism of the hunter-gathers to Africa's early and modern links with globalisation, there is a story to be explained about Africa's relative economic backwardness and the widening of GDP or income per head lags with the rest of the world. On Maddison's calculations, Africa's GDP in the 1st century was $7 billion – around 7% of world GDP then. Two thousand years later GDP was around 3.1% of world income – reflecting a significantly diminished position, a trend that has barely changed since. Africa's income per head measure compared with the rest of the world fell significantly over this time and income gaps widened enormously. While Africa had a slightly higher GDP per head in the 1st century, $472 compared with the world average of $467, by 2010 it was $1,870 compared with the world average of around $8,000 – that is, about 23% of the world level. Africa had entirely lost the plot.

The rise of the West from 1500, and in recent times of the East, and Africa's centuries of flatlining and then troubled economic growth, encapsulates this economic story. It is one masterfully recounted, in relation to the West/East shifting axis and the rise of China, by Ian Morris in *Why The West Rules – For Now*.[8] This is a fascinating epic, not least (paradoxically) because it has little to say about Africa's demise or its economic future; in effect, Africa just did not count for much. Despite contemporary hype, this is still very much the case in terms of world income.

Much of Africa's economic delinquency related to technologies and energy usage, as well as the "late" discovery of Africa after the New World was opened up. For a few centuries Africa found itself outside the core zones of the world trading system – except for slavery. The continent, apart from the economic fringes of the Maghreb and the Cape, became marginal to the emerging shape of global history. Multiple Malthusian checks held Africa back and made it a tough continent to explore and arduous to open. Its locus in world economic cartography, argues Morris, was highly unfavourable. Geography mattered. Africa had little to offer at the time. India and the East appeared more lucrative. There was no Silk Road in the savannah.

While mankind had first ventured out of Africa there had been for eons no return. In the lucky latitudes for growth over the millennia, only North Africa and Egypt featured within the emerging world economy, initially based around the Mediterranean. Except for the Nile Valley, Africa lost out in the development of critical agrarian technologies that found root elsewhere. The systemic domestication of animals and crops came much later into the rest of Africa. In many spheres – energy and urbanisation, technologies, information processing and even the capacity to make modern war – Africa remained over many centuries a simple set of societies, while rising complexity was of the essence for economic growth. Moreover, growth elsewhere was continuous, cumulative and occurred in sequences of incremental steps that did not find any analogue across sub-Saharan Africa. Differentiation went ahead much faster outside the continent, where societies created greater wealth, as did formal state formation with the development of efficient bureaucracies. Geography realigned the world in patterns that largely excluded Africa until it encountered the mixed blessings of colonisation. The record suggests strongly that if it had not, it would have lagged even further behind.

Whatever the global causes, Africa's economies drifted behind the world for more than 1,500 years. Indeed, they have done so for over 2,000 years to date. The long-run catch-up game implied serious competitive disadvantage. Africa's Horsemen of the Apocalypse counted as well: economic deprivation, famine, disease, wars and conflict, along with a host of natural impediments. While geography helped to determine world economic growth, in time growth influenced geography. The horses of development elsewhere had left the stable, while the Africa horse did not.

There was little shift in Africa from its traditional and kinship-based economic societies to statehood and modernity until very late in the day. The move from economies built on plunder to those sustained by taxation followed a similar course. Today, many of Africa's states still suffer from various forms of private and state-orchestrated excess or plunder while the formal tax bases often remain weak. Even in South Africa, around 5 million taxpayers are juxtaposed with a large and growing welfare state, which provides subsidies and grants for 15 million recipients and needs to support 50 million people. Here many an older mode has long floundered and the state has elected to sustain subsistence and survival by means of subsidy in a modern welfare format.

One further lesson for Africa and its "friends" is that, evidently, economic growth has typically been the precursor of democracy, not the other way around. The latter view is nominally lauded nowadays across the continent, promoted by Western politicians, advocated by NGOs and often mooted as the silver bullet that will somehow fix all. It is most unlikely.

Rising phoenix

With little reliance on economics at all, Vijay Mahajan's *Africa Rising* tells a modern tale of the economic dynamism found today in Africa.[9] As a newly arrived political scientist from abroad, Mahajan travelled to a few parts of the continent before providing a business school take on the evolving markets of opportunity, evoked as an antithesis of the gloom that had clouded many minds, with pessimists and concerned cognoscenti reflecting on the past. This was a consumer safari on which Mahajan found new markets rising in Africa, most having emerged off the back of growth over the last decade.

Africa, he says, offers a veritable Aladdin's cave of corporate and consumer *richesse*. There is much surprise and overt pleasure recorded about dynamism and development across a wide range of countries, markets and industries, and the author's discovery of Africa is recounted in interesting anecdotal detail. Africa is found to exude oil

95

and diamonds; Irish beer is sold by the bucket in Nigeria; and with a new gold rush of incoming money from the East, entrepreneurs almost everywhere are looking for a deal. There is evidence of the shift to trade and a decline in aid, rising optimism, cell phones galore, opportunities in retail, medicine, distribution, branding, transport, infrastructure, education, water and sanitation, even golf clubs and tourism, a range of prospects in sports, broadcasting, media and technology, as well as charity. Bank assets have ballooned and, of course, there are many more financiers setting up shop for the banked, mobile unbanked and potentially bankable, to capture the capital and financial flows in the African economy that is said to be the "10th largest in the world" – except that it is not. There is in fact no such thing as "Africa's economy" *per se*, only many fragmented and often competitive ones. No one country trades significantly with every other. No one state has companies invested Africa-wide. Few commonalities in economic architecture exist. The only common currencies used are foreign. The "African economy" is a popular myth and figment of the outsider's imagination, the litany repeated nowadays even within the continent, and an easily sellable fiction readily recycled *ad nauseam* in the media and the sound bites emanating from some of Africa's business schools.

Mahajan's expose nonetheless has felt Africa's modern economic pulse. The economic body is alive and in better shape than before. Yes, there are growing numbers of crocodiles farmed for leather, many a so-called "black diamond" in South Africa, a growing list of ultra-rich and high net worth individuals (HNWI) found ensconced across Africa, rises recorded in income levels above the poverty line to create more middle-income status households (measured in domestic terms: thereby, no middle class *per se*). Many business gurus regard this emerging bottom of the pyramid market as the basis for tomorrow's new consumer goods nirvana, with companies establishing shops to serve their needs, and around 100 million bottles of Coca-Cola and 40 million of Pepsi-Cola drunk every day in hot and thirsty Africa.

China's merchants are entrenched across an unfamiliar continent and trading throughout (with 1 million Chinese currently estimated as living in Africa today – a rate and level of inflow that dwarfs Europe's entry during the original scramble for Africa). There is fast-expanding trade with Asia and an improving business environment in many places. More hotels flourish based on rising tourist numbers. Millions of Africans have commercial ties with foreign parts (China especially), Africa's own companies have gone regional and even in cases global, with some economic giants among them, corporate listings are on the up, capital is flowing in, the private-equity world has "discovered Africa" and the corporate deal flow has been augmented. Cell-phone expansion has been spectacular, closing down the tyranny of uncon-nected distance, and informal markets have grown and spread, while a plethora of product choice confronts Africa's discretionary consumer income classes at all levels.

As Tunisia alone has thousands of retail outlets, you can imagine that in Africa there could be millions, from the *spaza* shop to Walmart, an economic form that will undoubtedly grow. Mahajan too wants to "fix" Africa but in special ways: to see the informal go formal, that too part of the evolutionary process. From infrastructure to commercial networks in all industries, there is growth and technical change afoot as Africa's step forward has come at a time where technologies can be inserted without having to ascend the traditional curves of high-cost research, technology development and domestic-driven innovation.

Yet none of this discounts the bottom half in Africa that make it on $1 a day or the next 20% with $2 or under. Their economic rationale is one of subsistence and survival in a competitive struggle to secure the wherewithal required to join the modern world. The question is whether economic growth, at rates as yet unknown for Africa, might lift them too into another income or consumer class so that they no longer remain the objects of the many "poverty safaris" that often seek their indirect attention.

✳

It is not argued here that Africa could not surmount past performance in future. Yet many postulate that Africa's growth rate can be "forecast" or "projected" or "might" reach, say, 6–7% annually going forward on an unstoppable path through to the mid-21st century. It is heady stuff – whether this calculus is arrived at off the top of the head, by hope, by extrapolation within artificial economic models, or from a good old thumb suck. On this mathematical basis several pundits have reached conclusions that "all will be well", even if just for sub-Saharan Africa, and that Africa's economy will in time then reach the proximate size of America's today. The cardinal difference will be that by then Africa will have 2 billion people, while these growth rates for such an extended period will mean an upside swing way beyond any previously known economic path or experience witnessed for Africa as a whole in the last century or millennium. While such high growth rates have been recorded for China and for India for lengthy periods, both lack the extreme heterogeneity of governance and incapacity to simulate central economic direction that defines Africa's predicament.

For now these projection-driven "economics" images appear to be built on somewhat heroic assumptions, unfounded in contemporary economic history, as measures "beyond trend" experience, without reference to potential upcoming commodity or world economic cyclicity, and excluding any repeat of past reversals or downsides, or even untoward implosions in key economies (as recently witnessed in Libya, Côte d'Ivoire, Zimbabwe and even elsewhere). Achievement of continental growth at 7% annualised for an uninterrupted 40 years would be an unrealistic ask for Africa. Yet the idea may well serve as manna from heaven for politicians who believe that they might be embedded inside such an economic trajectory in which what they have done so far – often highly perverse – has somehow led to the "inevitability" of this presumptive outcome.

Many gremlins still lie within Africa's economic woodwork that could place this image in jeopardy. Some economic pathways and practices have long outlived their utility, such as when planning was à la mode, and *dirigiste* economics the fashion of choice for many. Much of this Neanderthal economics remains as a residual species in Africa, including as preached by those orchestrating policies for elusive "development states", with others advocating liberal doses of elite-driven economic engineering. Many leaders and politicians in Africa still love nothing more than to "direct" the economic traffic, often at fatal cost to the future.

There has been no secret "growth rule" that has guided Africa from past to present. Higgledy-piggledy economic strategy marks the general record and even in some cases much of the present juncture. Economic evolution has been accomplished largely despite flawed political economy architecture, so maybe that strength would apply going forward as well. The causal influences on economic growth have probably been many, with domestic mode survival and competitive expansion among them. Capital accumulation and technical progress with productivity growth have been evident too, and will be germane to future progress. Interactions with the world economy now count for more than in the past.

Given Africa's rich resource endowment, the economic growth might best be built significantly on improved accumulation and expanded capital stock, higher rates of investment and domestic savings, if the continental economic model is not to follow recidivist directions. The large and undeveloped natural capital base across Africa in minerals, hydrocarbons, land and natural resources, even human capital, could provide the essential wherewithal for this improved growth. Yet many in Africa would encourage enhanced resource nationalism as a panacea, with nationalisation, tough regulatory regimes for limiting and controlling the inflows of foreign direct investment (FDI), state measures for industry selection and control, with realigned economic playing fields to disadvantage non-autochthonous corporate entities, and the like. I think all this will cut future growth-rate potential and disadvantage the poorest first.

The arena for economic discourse has widened inside Africa, even while it receives buckets of wisdom in unsolicited advice from outside, including from the UN with its plethora of prescriptions based on many an ideology-driven economic paradigm, and from an army of consultants and hangers-on in the form of the great and the good – including former politicians with at best a few weeks' or months' vintage "in Africa" (Gordon Brown one, Tony Blair another), economic fashionistas, Irish rock stars, British lords, American politicians, many an arriviste, Hollywood starlets, A-list celebrities who have "discovered" Africa, and others self-nominated in a continuing almost endless list of personal and corporate saviours for what *The Economist* in its wisdom in 2003 once called the "hopeless continent". Some offer old or recycled recipes for economic progress. It should be no surprise that this posturing and derivative confusion often befuddles the economic debate.

What is needed is to have no illusions or delusions about Africa's past or its constrained economic future. The numeric realities provide the soundest starting point for avoiding such myopia. There have been many economic fallacies and myths peddled in and about Africa's economies and much future promise promulgated by economists, writers, analysts, media pundits and populists. Few command the relevant numbers and understanding of the boundaries that have imprisoned Africa's economic drama. An absence of historiography has been the hallmark of many airbrushed models of pseudo-economics that have been applied. Economic theorists have built many models conceived outside and out of Africa, even outside its significant literature on development economics. With greater frequency, most have taken to writing for economic fashion and the contemporary take: almost all with a top-down theory ungrounded in historical experience and ignorant of Africa's evolving medieval-cum-modern economic structures. These diverse economic models nonetheless serve as our modern doors of perception. Yet distorted perception is not good enough, and the search for the elixir or "missing dummy variable" in Africa's economies has continued, as the apparent mystery endures. So while many have tried to "explain" Africa, most seem to have failed. What have they missed?

Part 2

Ancient Africa

6

Natural Africa

Natural conditions constrained the continent's evolutionary economic modes and continued to define many subsistence and pre-capitalist forms amid the implanted modernities that developed around them. The power of nature, awesome still, was even more daunting to primitive economies during ancient times.

Nature and ecology shaped the continent's multiple means of economic survival but so too did the dynamics and uncertainties embedded in socioeconomic conditions as they applied in antiquity. The struggle against nature had to be conducted simultaneously with that against many threats to economic existence. Some communities never graduated beyond the economic constraints of antiquity.

Antiquity onwards

Prehistoric forms of subsistence varied across Africa in antiquity and ancient times, even during pre-imperial moments. Ancient Stone Age economies littered Africa from the earliest times. The Khoisan survival mode was just one of them, offering an austere reality that continues to persist in a more limited and degraded form today. These hunter-gatherers had ranged across tropical Africa and had been in earliest times in the Sahara during the era when it was wet: Saharan rock art is testimony to their legacy.

Fragmented throwbacks from ancient economic forms are still

evident in Africa today, prevalent in arenas marked by austere levels of subsistence and much tougher conditions for survival. It may continue this way for many decades.

Many parts of the continent have not progressed much further in the material stakes than in days long gone. Subsistence economies across Africa before colonisation were mainly based on lineage and extended family systems. Backwardness and associated underdevelopment in many zones still portray these ancient imprints. In time Africa broke free from the shackles of the past. The modern era began at the end of the 19th century and accelerated during the 1900s. This was a period of major disruption to earlier ways of economic life.

To gather impressions of Africa's 19th-century dynamics, read the masterful synopsis in Eric Halladay's *Emergent Continent*.[1] This era was one of cataclysmic change, bewildering complexity and considerable violence among cross-continental societies before the colonial world established its Pax Africana. Here we find the roots of Africa's medievalism, today reflected in the juxtaposition of ancient and modern. Some societies disintegrated before colonial intrusion. Others were eventually made captive by more recent African polities, leaving ancient socioeconomies isolated in their wake. Often decimated if nonetheless surviving in reduced form, their populations scattered across the rural reaches. Later, under the aegis of colonisation and emergent post-colony Africa, the mass of people found different refuges – in traditional rural economies, wage labour, migrancy, towns and impoverished shanty-towns, which exploded within the continent's habitat. Over a short span of time, merely 100 years, post-colony Africa was a *fait accompli*, a widely different mode of subsistence, survival and existence compared with the days of the San.

※

Some of Africa's ancient legends and myths of origin indicate how societies adapted their material cultures and social systems to the needs of the diverse ecologies they exploited for survival.[2] The many languages found in Africa reflect distinctive ways of life, often moulded around nature. These myths or traditions of genesis typically set down the benchmarks for culture – the rules for survival and guidelines for relationships with nature and social groups. They have endured into the 21st century to contribute to African identities today.

Old stories they may be, reshaped in the telling, but in them are found the economic foundations of Africa and the rules governing land, animals, property rights, communal obligations, matrimony, kinship, social status and "asset" ownership. Their depth and diversity are striking. These narratives mark the natural and social landscapes, defining kingdoms, families of language and affinity, distinctive chiefdoms, stateless peoples and, in other instances, central authority and incipient state formation. They demarcate the parameters for non-literate economies in ways that did not simply disappear in entirety with the passage of time.

It should be no surprise then that we can find no single or even typical proto-economy in Africa and none that correlates exactly to economic models common to those in the West. This alone should provide a salutary warning to those seeking to transfer the modernist model onto Africa's economic template.

Geoeconomics

Africa is conditioned by long history and its natural conditions, geography and morphologies. Its place in the world has been one that the tides of world economic growth left behind. The immovable hands of geology, geotrends, geography and geopolitics have moulded what appeared to be the unchangeable in Africa: the landlocked, riverine, coastal, desert-like, mountainous, contiguous, isolated and challenged nation-states with their linguistic splits, creating a Tower of Babel and diversity in which the dominant languages for modern communication and commerce became foreign: English, French, Arabic, Portuguese, Swahili and a few others.

Climate had a hand in this drama with alternating wet and dry spells that forged human economic evolution. From 10,000BCE to 5,000BCE it was a humid continent. Then a fierce arid period followed in the long cycles that went from one to the other, and shaped nature in Africa and its ecologies, as well as its economic locus. Modern portents on climate change promise new difficulties for some, perhaps opportunities for others, even if these are not inflicted by the human hand.

Modern Africa stands on ancient foundations spread across its 30 million sq km (excluding islands and huge offshore domains). The ecosystems on this vast continent are more fractured, complex and diverse than any other.[3] This perhaps partly explains why it might have been last to make it through the gates of modernity. Even today nature plays a forbidding role in the economic pathways open to Africa, and shapes the economic forms found within it. The geoeconomic in Africa stands as one key to understanding the continent's history and future.

Africa contains hundreds of distinctive ecologies. South Africa alone has eight eco-zones (Karoo, savannah, fynbos, grasslands, forests, Nama-Karoo, marine/coastal, wetlands). In Zimbabwe there are the eastern highlands, varied areas of lowveld in the north and around the Sabi River, the central plateau, middleveld, major rivers and tributaries in the Zambezi and Limpopo, and western woodlands. In a continent of many states of vast and varied space, the number of discrete ecologies may never have been accurately assessed. Ecologies in Africa include rainforests, jungles, equatorial zones, swamps, deserts, large salt pans, savannah grasslands, lowveld valleys, highveld plateau, mountain ranges, rift valley systems, coastal reaches with numerous marine ecologies, inland deltas and wetlands, the enormous Sudd in southern Sudan, inland deltas, large and small islands, ultra-hot depressions, gargantuan river systems (Niger, Nile, Congo, Zambezi, Orange, Limpopo, Benue, Shire) and many hundreds of huge tributaries. Their influence on Africa's past and present economic structures, socioeconomic survival, subsistence shape and future potential has often been underestimated.

So too has the influence of geography.[4] There are today 16 landlocked states, South Sudan the most recent. Several others have narrow coastlines with large disconnected interiors (the Democratic Republic of the Congo or DRC is one) that to all intents and purposes remain largely "landlocked by geo-history" and vast infrastructural deficiencies. This leaves 39 states with coastal reaches or as islands, holding 75% of Africa's population. A dozen states confront large deserts, with almost an equivalent number configured as micro-states, and there are many isolated or distant islands. Madagascar is almost a world on its own. Population and habitable space are unevenly distributed. When flying over Africa what is striking is its empty quarters, where there appears to be an absence of people, water, vegetative cover, infrastructure and wildlife. The topography is in many zones (in Niger, Mali and Botswana, for example) one of unremitting flatness.

The Sahara or Great Desert, second in spatial dimension only to Antarctica and nearly the size of Europe, is the world's largest ice-free desert at 3.5 million square miles; inhabited by Berber and nomadic Tuareg. The enormous width of the Sahel separates north from south across the continent's upper reaches. In these deserts complex topography and ecologies rule the day and the economic lives of inhabitants. Africa's rainforest below the Sahel is second in size only to that of the Amazon. Hundreds of rivers traverse vast savannah spaces, with several untamed tropical jungles and many enormous deserts like the Kalahari and Namib. Survival in these environs is forbidding, in places impossible – as in the Dankil Depression at over 50°C where salt is excavated by camel in short safaris to collect this treasured prize.

In the Congo the old colonial roads are no longer roadways at all, more like ancient trails for animals as found around the Great Lakes. Pygmy hunter cultures interface with local economies created from the infusions of farmers, loggers, miners, poachers, settlers and militias bonded around quasi-feudal practices of barter and exchange. The older Ituri forest communities have been subjected to terrorism from marauding gangs and armed dissidents from adjacent lands. This eruption of social disorder has been aggravated over the past decade along the vast Rift Valley that splits the continent from north-east to south-west. Around the Albertine Rift on the eastern Great Lakes and the DRC's borders, francophone and anglophone Africa confront each other across a divide in resources and habitat density (over 1,000 per sq mile in Rwanda and Burundi; fewer than 10 per sq mile in the DRC).

Africa's Rivers and Tributaries

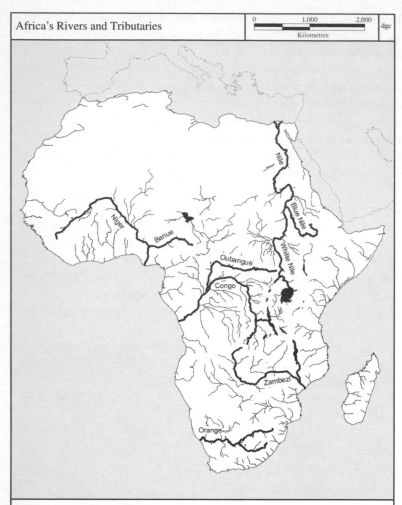

Africa has huge and forbidding rivers, its main arteries connected to numerous tributaries across the vast landscape that drain its main river basins. These have been and remain the focus for many riverine and fishing communities as well as rural subsistence economies. On and around them, many survivalist societies continue to live and exist at material levels that have advanced little over the decades. Some have succumbed to commercial ventures; others have gravitated into relationships with new mechanisms of modernised existence such as tourism.

This is one of Africa's largest internal frontiers of instability. It has left the DRC, today Africa's largest state, with an unscripted future and a latent propensity to shatter into smaller statelets and warring communities. Here ecological stress, unmet basic needs (minimally provided for during Mobutu's *pax corrupta* and since) and unresolved tensions underpin conflicts of huge complexity.

Nature's bounty and its long-term erosion by demographic and environmental pressures has become fatally intertwined with strategic security concerns and struggles over ethnic rights, agrarian resources, water rights, land access, minerals and fauna, leaving many cultures on a collision course. The literal burning of Africa takes place each dry season as grass and forest fires cloud the atmosphere. These conditions are not unique in Africa, but they are found here perhaps at their most dramatic. Even so, Africa has delineated many national parks (of which there are in the region of 250). Put together they would cover land space about the size of the DRC, providing huge reserves for flora and fauna. This excludes marine protected zones along the coasts and inland deserts that probably act as de facto nature reserves merely by their forbidding conditions.

Some foresee that climate change may aggravate Africa's socioeconomic situation. Predictions from the UN's Intergovernmental Panel on Climate Change (IPCC) speak of grave consequences awaiting Africa, with potential for rising mortality as dry lands bordering the deserts get drier and the wetlands around the rainforests get wetter, so possibly compromising domestic food supplies. Sea-level changes around deltas and estuaries might affect coastal infrastructure. Africa's coasts are home to many teeming cities, as well as low-lying coastal plains and vulnerable islands.

Riverine Africa

The huge rivers of Africa were associated with many kingdoms in the past. Riverside and delta dwellers still remain dependent on ancient cultures of subsistence.[5] These huge systems have shaped the economic fabric, both integrating and dividing vast basinal areas spanning many countries, while insulating and maintaining ancient economies along their banks. I have been on each of Africa's five great rivers at one time or another. Their awesome scale, power over local conditions for survival and make-or-break significance cannot be overestimated in any appreciation of how existing river and water systems (including numerous huge lakes), with older inland lacustrine deltas, define economic survival, and even Africa's economic opportunities. It is not much different on so-called minor rivers and tributaries: the Shire, Sabi, Shashi, Okavango, Rovuma, Benue, Vaal, Limpopo and many more. Many proved huge obstacles to early explorers: the travails of David Livingstone seeking to navigate the Lower Zambezi, eventually the Shire, is a classic instance, likewise Henry Morton Stanley on the Congo River.

Along its 2,720-mile length, the Congo River drains six states in a basin of 1.6 million sq miles. Alone it represents 5% of Africa's space. It contains around 4,000 islands, some at least 10 miles long, each a micro-world and natural economy of its own. Massive tributaries push the tumultuous water to the Atlantic to deposit offshore sediments out of which the deepwater oil game has emerged. But inland it defines the economies and modes of survival feasible for its millions of inhabitants. The Congo's navigability (with marginal connectivity along its path) in practice fragments one side of Africa from the other. Many communities remain isolated on its banks while its separate interiors are mostly disconnected. Riverine economies here function much as they did in the distant past. At the time of the Kongo kingdom there was an empire that lasted nearly 1,000 years until the arrival of the Portuguese in 1483, when contests for power brought it to its knees and weakened it irretrievably. By 1665 it had broken into warring factions. The country looks much the same today.

At least 20 major ethnolinguistic groups and local economies rely on the 2,500-mile Niger River for survival. Its course through the lower Sahara confounded early explorers. The river's bend, before it flows south to the Niger Delta, has witnessed many old civilisations (Mali, Gao and Songhay, among others). It forms a focal point for cross-cultural economies and for Sahelian trading from north, south, west and east. A great deal of this economic history finds continuity from ancient empires past to the present era.

A similar tale of cultural imprints and economic dependencies marks the Zambezi's 1,653-mile tropical course from north-west Zambia and Angola to the Indian Ocean, draining on the way several states through the Lozi floodplains and Kafue (Zambia), Shire (Malawi and Moçambique), and the many rivers flowing off the Zimbabwe highveld.[6] Conditions vary along its path, as they do for the economic options feasible and conducted along its course.

This too is the case with the Orange River that rises in Lesotho to cross Namibia and South Africa to the Atlantic, draining 400,000 sq miles of mixed ecologies and economies from its source in the Basotho highlands, near the Indian Ocean, before flowing through the huge Kalahari and Namib deserts to the Atlantic. Many peasant societies continue to live in and around this river system in material conditions not so far removed from those of a century or more before. Others have reached a modernity of sorts, sometimes one of fragility as in Lesotho and even in the north-west of South Africa.

The Nile has around 180 million people living along its main routes in a zone that occupies across its basin about 15% of Africa's space. Its trunk and arteries define the livelihoods and survival of millions and have done so for thousands of years from Pharaonic times, across Nubia and Ethiopia and around the Great Lakes. Some communities are among the poorest in Africa. In South Sudan the Sudd provides hope for an agrarian future that might be different from the present: maybe. The Blue and White Niles travel 4,184 miles from Uganda and Ethiopia, collecting multiple tributaries on their way. The rivers flow through 11 countries into a vast delta system 120 miles wide in the Mediterranean where the old civilisation of Alexandria was born. Here, Lower Egypt and Cairo apart, many communities still tread an ancient path of older-styled economic existence. Only in 2004 did anyone navigate the entire length of the Blue and White Niles.

Rivers are only one of the natural elements that have shaped ancient modes of existence and coalesced with modern Africa's economies.

The continent's many deserts, forests and deltaic or coastal zones have also had an enduring impact, each giving rise to their own survivalist communities. It is no wonder that Africa proved harder to "explore" than other regions of the world.[7] Rugged interiors, parched deserts, malarial swamps, impenetrable forests, disease-prone lowlands, deep rivers not readily navigable, the absence of any Silk Road cutting across the continent, fragmented and fractious polities, and impeded access to the Sahara and to Sudanic Africa – all provided serious obstacles. Many constraints still frustrate communities there today, investors seeking to tap resources, and governments wanting to open up and develop new lands.

✳

While nature remains a powerful force in Africa, there are related socio-cultural cosmologies, combined with geoeconomics, which have shaped its complex patterns.[8] The continent is underpopulated in spatial terms: it accounts for 20% of the world's crust and 14% (at 1,005 million) of global population. This demography will rise to 2.1 billion by 2050, according to the UN. About two-thirds of Africans still rely on various types of agrarian-cum-peasant modes of existence for their livelihood. The 50% of Africans living on $1.25 a day or less make up over half of those at this level in the world. At the sum of $2 a day, another 20% of Africa would be included. Theirs is not the modern world. Fewer than 20% of Africans have direct access to electricity; fewer than 10% have a regular supply. Around 75% of all electricity is consumed in fewer than half a dozen states. The majority of Africans live in mud and thatch huts, impermanent homesteads and rural villages, fragile and pseudo-modern slums, or squatter and refugee camps without any power. At night Africa is truly a dark continent. Energy deprivation rules the day.

With over 2,000 languages spoken on the continent, the local languages of many ethnic groups and the numerous sub-clans within them are foreign to the rest of world and indeed to most other Africans. Many linguistic groups have fewer than 1 million adherents. Most languages cross state boundaries. Few have large cross-country applicability, apart from Swahili on the east coast. Foreign tongues have superseded the vernacular over time, yet most Africans do not command literacy in these cosmopolitan languages. Africa's literacy is nowhere near universal (only 60% for those aged over 15 years). Many still rely for their own histories on contemporary oral traditions.

In the inevitable interfaces between nature and socioeconomic practice, Africans built their subsistence economies and bred their own means of economic survival. Many adapted interstices make Africa a continent apart, deeply rooted in and dependent on the forces of landscape, geoeconomics, ecology and nature's vicissitudes. It explains in part why Africa remains pre-modern in large degree and conditioned by the process of incomplete economic evolution. As the continent where mankind was born, Africa is the one most evidently scarred by its many backward economies, which conventional, modern, simple and deterministic economic models fail to encapsulate.

7

Stone Age triumph and beyond

If nature left mega-impediments to economic evolution in Africa, mankind's innovations proved equal to the task. Stone Age Africa was a world apart from the continent it is now. Roland Oliver depicted it as the mythic Garden of Eden, only then to show it was not really so – or in any literal sense an easy world to master. In *The African Experience*, Oliver has documented this epic tale: some of its relevant salient forms and economic conditions are sketched here.[1]

The cradleland of early mankind swept down from the eastern side of Africa to the southern tip, with pockets found elsewhere, from Hadar in Ethiopia to Olduvai and south to Swartkrans and the southern coast at the Klassies River mouth. The hominoids, before *Homo erectus* emerged, were in the order of tens of thousands. Africa's Eden was eventually outgrown and *Homo erectus* spread over the continent in several sweeps of colonisation during the Middle Stone Age. The hunter-gatherers commanded this landscape and their technologies for hunting and foraging evolved. By the late Stone Age exploitation of the environment had been transformed. It was more varied and intensive. Fixed bases were more frequently established, if you like as Africa's "first towns". Demography and competition pushed these small bands of survivors further and further into the interior as *Homo sapiens* made an appearance around 40,000 years ago. Aridity forced cultural and economic change in hunting, fishing and gathering, eventually leading to pastoralism and settled farming.

Around 9,500–6,500 years ago Lake Chad had become a vast inland sea the size of the Caspian. Technologies had evolved to make a way of life founded around rivers and shorelines with permanent riparian settlements, so encouraging specialisation, notably in Egypt's Nile Valley. Domesticated cereals and exploitation of the fruits of the earth here brought about the first food-producing economy in Africa about 6,000 years ago. In Sudanic Africa animals had come in probably from Asia to change the rural economic base, with cattle, sheep and goats the sources of subsistence as large herds were gradually built up. The pastoralists were also hunters, their endeavours reflected in rock art that depicts them preying on a range of beasts with bows and arrows. With changes in climate the cattle herds were moved south. The movements of peoples and changes in economies continued, giving rise to a wide mix of ethnolinguistic and socioeconomic groups. In the southern belts of Africa the hunter-gather mode ceded ground to the food-producing and pastoralist ways of newcomers. Bantu farmers of varied sorts absorbed or outplayed many of the Khoisan cultures.

Between around 700BCE and 700CE emerged the early Iron Age, with North Africa integrated inside the evolving Mediterranean economies. Iron, copper and bronze made a material difference for tools, hunting, artisans and weapons (for the military elites), as well as in the agrarian modes and for daily household survival. Iron working spread from the Sahara to the Sahel, then elsewhere to the south. The Iron Age brought about the foundations for the long-distance exchange of foodstuffs, commodities and artefacts. The peoples of West Africa and along the Niger came to build larger settlements, the bases for empires to come, and a wide range of economic modes underpinned their subsistence and means of survival.

Even in the later Iron Age the settlements across eastern and southern Africa were more dispersed owing to the economic significance of animal husbandry, yet most tools were fashioned not from iron but from volcanic glass or obsidian. By 1000CE cattle and animals were widespread in these areas as the core of economic life. In time pastoralism and agrarian ways became increasingly intermingled. The new pastures on the grasslands of Africa gave rise to the foundations for early kingdoms and states, even empires, in the lands of the Oromo, and among the Niolitics, Luba, Mutapa and Shona. Different strategies of survival followed these patterns of evolution across diverse habitats, social structures and viable means of economic activity.

To help envisage how the earlier Iron Age pre-colonial societies looked (exhibiting minimal evolution from 200 to 1840) in terms of material culture and homesteads, you can still see the correlates of the past in mud and wood huts, settlement design, structures and stone, artefacts and tools, grain bins and rural interfaces with nature. This is shown vividly in Thomas N. Huffman's monumental work on archaeology in Africa.[2] It has been recorded in a similar fashion for more contemporary economic cultures in Central Africa by Henrik Ellert.[3] The relevance of this ancient social design, economic forms and physical architecture is found in abundance throughout sub-Saharan Africa today. Indeed, William Easterly has claimed: "Seventy-five percent of Africa's current income lag relative to Europe can be statistically explained by the technology lag in 1500."[4] This was a full half-millennium ago, the catch-up gap of significance in which parts of the world, including parts of Africa, moved ahead at a dizzying speed while elsewhere in most of Africa subsistence economies reflected the distant past.

The economic modes of subsistence today, except for the capitalist, were born in Africa and came to fruition in these times. They include the riverine communities, coastal fishing villages, trading and crafts, early mining, agrarian and pastoral economies. Out of them arose the kingdoms and empires that have long gone but whose peoples form the societies of nation-states today. From the Mwanamutapa to the Rozwi in Central Africa can be traced the economic and social lineages of the Shona in Zimbabwe and Moçambique, and from the northern sweep of people down the eastern flanks emerged the societies that later formed the powerful Zulu state.

Slavery and rupture

Hunter-gathers had no essential need for slaves, but could well have taken captives, mainly women and children, to join their bands. With the formation of food-producing economies, labour became more critical and raiding parties acquired booty in captives and cattle. Pharaonic Egypt in its early era had a slave culture, from which arose wider trading in slaves, the practice carried on in Roman Africa. Much later, camel caravans carried the unfortunate to new destinations, especially following the arrival of Islam and Arabs in the north. The trans-Sahara slave traffic grew apace and captives were taken from Sudanic Africa in increasing numbers. An enlarging slave market inside and outside Africa grew even to the extent that among the Tuareg in the 19th century it was estimated that possibly over 70% of the population were slaves. In the tropical forest belts this share might have been 10–20%. The practice found its way into Eastern and Southern Africa, and along the west coast in due course, for instance in the Kongo kingdom. Europe's embrace of Africa opened wider slave demand from markets further afield in the Americas, so that Africa earned the unenviable reputation as the primary source of slaves for the world market.

Slavery practices inside and around the Nile Valley had roots stretching back thousands of years before the international market in slaves found Africa as a ready supply source. It is not just that one begot the other, although the domestic mode of slavery in Africa was well-established when the later-to-be colonisers came to the party. It may have made the modern form of slavery practised easier, when grafted onto the more ancient and already established mode.

The fact and scale of slavery inside Africa bears comment. It was an initial mechanism for Africa's entry into forms of globalisation that basically built on pre-existent domestic practice. Arab caravans crossed the Sahara with slaves for hundreds of years. The East Africa slave markets were widely frequented in and around the Great Lakes, with Zanzibar becoming the hub for this international commerce. Simultaneously, markets for slaves from Africa emerged in Brazil, the Caribbean and the Americas so making slavery in and from Africa a global trade. While the Atlantic slave trade became an intercontinental affair, the east coast was encumbered here too, as slaves went from East Africa to Arabia, some to the Americas, and slavery made its debut in the Cape. Only towards the turn of the 20th century did slavery begin to diminish and eventually end.[5]

The history of the economies of the trans-Saharan world and the slavery that emerged in large measure dominated its commercial practices. This story has been told in a magnificent work by Ralph Austen.[6] The Sahara, the Great Desert barrier to Africa's north/south integration, became a global highway under Arab mastery, founded on the camel and horse, while the caravan tied together many of Africa's northern economies, stopping only at the southern shores of the Sahel. In the Sahara's 3.5 million sq miles only 25% is covered by sand, the remainder of the terrain dry, and gravel, rocky and with plateaus. It is a vast space, forbidding and desolate even today, an awesome vision you can capture on a day flight from London to Johannesburg. Bounded on three sides by fertile Africa, its caravan interconnections eventually married one to the other. Until ocean navigation down the west coast of Africa in the 15th century, the lands to the south of the Sahara had no regular contact with the outside world except via the Sahara and the Arab caravanners. The Atlantic slave trade extended the grip of foreign powers and rich merchants over wider, once-neglected areas of the mainland.

Many economic modes of early survival littered Saharan history during the great periods of wet and dry that engulfed the desert, shrinking it and then expanding it over long periods from 9,500BCE. Hunting, gathering, fishing, herding and farming were all part of its economic landscape at some time in the past. Civilisations had been established on its outer fringes and even inside, for instance in the renowned case of Timbuktu on the northern bend of the Niger River. They all had economic demands of one sort or another and their intertwining was based and built on the construct of Saharan slavery. While inhabitants of the Nile Valley had sourced slaves mostly from Nubia and north-eastern Africa, the practice was not a major feature of the Sahara before the Arab caravans arrived, so it appears, and the period immediately before this was a time of immense disorder in North Africa as Vandals traded blows with Romans. Muslim traders built extensive commercial networks across the Sahara and Sahel for around seven hundred years.

By the 1400s the Sahara had become one of the world's major trading routes, but from 1500–1900 its role declined as naval technologies allowed seafarers to round Africa, the Cape and reach the east coast. The realities of this globalisation in shipping and intercontinental commerce put paid to the once dominant forms of trading in gold and slaves that had been the cornerstone business of trans-Sahara's economies. These duelling competitive pathways changed the course of economic history, for both Africa and the world.

Nonetheless, a vast network of caravan and slave routes had been established through which the Saharan and Sudanic slave traffic supplied around 8 million people to markets in the Mediterranean and Islamic world, a practice that continued up to 1900. This compares with an estimated 13 million slaves that were taken from Africa to the New World.[7] While slaves went one way, goods from elsewhere filled the caravans on the return journeys. Caravan commerce was eventually eclipsed by ships, rail, automobiles and of course aircraft. Complex caravan operations moulded around slave markets were employed, with merchants, coalitions of vested interests, camel masters, Bedouin and various ethnicities involved in one way or another. For buyers there were sellers, for trade there were product markets. At times wars generated slaves; at other times Africa's kingdoms provided these chattels of commerce. The Saharan slave supply was predominantly made up of women and children, while the Atlantic traffic was mainly one of men, each having different impacts on the economies of Africa from which they were drawn.

Despite its cruel consequences, the slave trade facilitated the entry of more varied products, crops, commodities and technologies into Africa, in a brutal exchange as historians have noted, while the kingdoms of West Africa and the Sahel made use of these exchanges to acquire weapons and power. In the last 1,000 years of this trans-Sahara trade many different empires, states and dynasties rose and fell in a shifting collage. Many small and warring states, caliphates and clerical-controlled entities were found scattered in the Maghreb, while the nomadic Berber commanded restricted areas, and a mix of Sahelian and Sudanic powers vied for supremacy, survival and continuity – the ancient kingdoms and empires of Ghana, Mali, Sokoto and Songhay were just some. Horses and firearms often decided who would rule.

Armies were essential for political survival, the military mode being the primary source of strength and capability for the recruitment of slave soldiers, and the means to exact tribute and booty. The dominance of these ancient practices was only later crushed and remoulded by the colonial intrusions from the late 19th century onwards.

It was a dissimilar story but one of equal consequence elsewhere, since domestic slavery had been evident in Africa before the great oceanic slave trade across the Atlantic came to the fore. Slavery had early and great longevity in the Great Lakes of Eastern Africa, well before the Arab slavers entered this market, and it came to supply slaves to Arabia and even the Western hemisphere. The saga has been extensively reviewed by historians, notably in a detailed work on *Slavery in the Great Lakes Region of East Africa*.[8] Many types of slave institution were integrated into the old economies of the Great Lakes not just among the Buganda, Rwanda and Bunyoro but as far afield as Madagascar. There were slaves taken as captives, social entities tied and tithed by kinship, vassal states or communities targeted for plunder, some slaves traded for ivory and goods, and a mix of quasi-commercial arrangements found in this forced enslavement and feudal commerce. These markets formed the backdrop to the later rise of oceanic slaving and played a key role in the ivory trade. The inner African slave trade may have dated back to antiquity while ties of kinship or clientship, along with warfare, were regularly used to enslave Africa's people. Most of Africa's polities had slaves, corvée labour and exploitable subjects to underpin the economic base. Few if any were undifferentiated economic entities. Hausa officials and horsemen counterposed commoners. Clientage, nobility, status and identity shaped social and economic stratification. Historians tell too of how the end of slavery gave rise to the migrant labour system as transformation of the mode of slaving took place under the duress of political edict, colonisation and the demand for cheap labour and changed commercial interests.

＊

Africa's post-slave era led to many profound changes in the economic fabric and in subsistence economies.[9] Before the 19th century most inhabitants lived at low levels of material survival. Romantic notions of pre-colonial economic bliss can be put aside. It was a tough world. The devastation of the Mfecane in the south and *jihad* in the north took place in the first quarter of that century and wreaked social and economic mayhem.[10]

Civilisations then existing across Africa were not stable and unchanging. The residual San were surviving within the limits of the ecologies in which they lived. Settled communities were adapting, in East Africa to an aquatic age on the lakes in the Great Rift Valley and the Indian Ocean shores. On the savannah, "slash and burn" agrarian practices were low-yielding and enabled by miniscule densities of population, a strategy of economic survival put to the sword by 20th century demographics. Most cattle cultures in sub-Saharan Africa were extensive rather than intensive.

Iron working, new technologies and imported crops allowed for Malthusian limits to be breached. Inequalities developed within lineage groups, and not just on the basis of military means. Elders, those closest to the ancestors, controlled production, distribution and most consumption. This inevitably became a mechanism for fragmentation, leading to more village households as juniors broke away to establish new kraals. Control over women and polygamy were common and continue today. Reciprocity and mutual obligation held together the many smallish communities in the absence of formal states. But in time proto-states emerged.

With these conditions prevalent states arose here and there, like the Monomotapa and their successors. The Mfecane established the Ndebele north of the Limpopo in due course. In Ethiopia a state, one of the first, was formed around Axum. More states arose in West Africa and in Congo with the Kongo and Luba, and the Lozi in Barotseland, and in Buganda. Many of these ancient fissures, throwbacks to pre-colonial states, can be found in modern-day irredentism and claims for special treatment from governments. Many cleavages inscribed from the past have remained in Africa's political economy, putting at risk many a nation-state's stability and paving the road to ruin.

❋

Slavery was not, of course, the only prominent mode in ancient economies found in Africa. Many mechanisms of subsistence emerged and evolved in these structurally diverse societies. Here I will take some instances from Zimbabwe, drawing on texts ranging from R.N. Hall's *Pre-Historic Rhodesia*, published in 1909, to another Zimbabwean historian's study of the same areas over similar and later time frames, Stan Mudenge's *A Political History of Munhumutapa c.1400–1902*.[11] The subsistence mechanisms evoked here have been found replicated widely elsewhere in sub-Saharan Africa.

Hall tells us of the ancient gold mines of Central Africa, predating 915CE, and the many unexplored ruins found across the area south of the Zambezi. Here came to live the Mocaranga, inhabitants of the old empire of Monomotapa. Theirs was an economy and tribute system built on agriculture, gold, ivory and trade with the Portuguese around Sofala, with forced labour as tribute from the serfs to the quasi-feudal lords. Slavery was a form found extensively in these environs. Conflicts over the state and power reigned over the period from the onset of the 1500s to 1760 at least. Inland trading stations were established by Arabs, Swahili merchants and the Portuguese up the Zambezi valley and along other routes. A key commodity they sought was gold, but the ancient mines, with origins in antiquity, says Hall, had been established before the empire itself. Africa's potentates had inherited and exploited an even more ancient mining mode. The arrival of the Mocaranga changed the power structure in the area and they became its overlords.

Mudenge recounts in detail the rise and fall of Monomotapa regents and their encounters with their primary and secondary trading inter-locutors, the Moors and Portuguese. It is an account of competitive trading between Arabs and medieval Europe in early commerce with Africa from the 1400s onwards. While the empire, originating as a conquest state, survived a long time, it succumbed to internal disputes over chiefdoms and succession, and suffered from wars, rebellions and decay. It ended in the rise of the Rozwi state over the period 1684–1760. The empire had an economic base with many subsistence and survivalist modes: primitive agrarian cultivation, pastoralism, elephant hunting (4,000–5,000 per year killed during the 16th century), gold mining, small-scale crafts, long-distance trade, bazaars frequented by Muslims and *feiras* with the Portuguese, tribute levied (in cattle or labour, sometimes gold), basic taxation, and with servitude and forced labour in various forms (provided via kinship, loyalty, fealty, vassals, even necessity) as well as periodic slaving.

There was no egalitarian world here. The dynasty and chiefs were wealthy and powerful figures, "Big Men" in modern parlance. The empire was expansionist and held in its tutelage several vassal states or social entities to the south on the Zimbabwe plateau. Portuguese interests alongside Arabs established in this area operated in direct competition, their *feiras* and bazaars functioning as the first retail outfits of long ago. The empire ultimately fragmented as power was challenged among local ethnicities and after wars with the Portuguese. The Monomotapa decline and subsequent Rozwi ascendancy, says Mudenge, was the basis for the later Shona economies on the highveld, subsequently taken over and controlled by the Ndebele invaders from the south around 1838. Then Cecil Rhodes's Pioneer Column with white settlers formed the Rhodesian state (1890–1980) as one of the longest-established modern economies and states ever created in sub-Saharan Africa. (The Union of South Africa was established in 1910, its later republic becoming South Africa in 1994.)

A substantial literature exists on what happened next in Central Africa.[12] Capitalist economies were created which operated alongside and in increased monetary interactions with traditional modes of subsistence, drawing upon migrant labour and the newly established peasantry to meet the exigencies of capital accumulation. Foreign investment poured in and domestic investment added to economic growth. While the older modes faced competitive displacement, the process never reached the ultimate limit. Still today, rural subsistence is substantial, as are urban survivalist forms. Modernity is evident but stands next door to the old. Monetisation of ancient means of exchange took place (in *lobola* or bride-wealth payments, for instance) but not entirely. The original medieval economic mode remains. Now, under the Mugabe regime, limited demodernisation has been achieved, by a reversal in growth and shrinkage of the productive capital stock accumulated from long before.

Zimbabwe is a classic case of deconstruction and self-inflicted economic failure. It is a story of the shift from underdevelopment to modernity over one century, then to self-created extreme backwardness, accomplished within one decade. About 75% of Zimbabweans today live in extreme poverty, in conditions never before recorded. Unemployment is at around 60% or more according to many, and at levels never before seen in the country's entire pre-modern or modern history. Erosion in the means of old-age and rural subsistence, which decayed under capitalism, has become a generalised dilemma for all. The relative glitz and buzz of Harare does not depict the economic saga that is played out in the townships and rural hinterlands, and in the rise of countrywide impoverishment and pauperisation. It will be a long road to recover the past per-head income levels inherited at independence over 30 years ago. This unfinished episode portrays the drama germane to many parts of Africa, the ancient mutating to the new, and the pre-modern to the modern, with many subsistence mechanisms of survival intact and continuing over time, one alongside another, following colonial occupation and the development of early capitalist Africa – with decline to follow.

Discovery and globalisation

Natural conditions, geography and morphology made Africa the latecomer to world exploration. External knowledge of Africa's littoral and hinterlands took centuries to establish with accuracy.[13]

The Maghreb world had opened from Roman times and, much later, explorers traversed the Sahara to Ghana. Legends and gold drew those seeking fortune. It was much later that Europe's maritime powers engaged with Africa, and then mainly on the west coast. For the first colonisers from Europe, Africa was largely terra incognita. Its inner topography, first imagined by cartographers, was learnt only gradually as the result of successive decades of arduous exploration, later modified by colonial experience. Even today, not all of Africa is wholly mapped with precision and in all detail. The European history of Africa that was crafted from the early 19th century was imposed upon far older social landscapes. In Europe there was the perception that Africa had no history.

The sheer scale and natural impediments of Africa made the rate of foreign penetration glacial. The epic discovery of Africa engaged Arab cultures from the 7th century in North Africa and the Sahel, with Europe's venture coming far later. Early foreign knowledge was confined to a few coasts and desert zones in the north. Africa was invented by its "discovery" through outsiders, as a refracted image of the "other", often seen by Arabs and those from Europe as primitive. Yet the first images of the "other" found initial expression not in Europe but in Pharaonic Egypt, in Africa itself. Few, if any, inhabitants inside the continent before the 20th century thought of themselves as "Africans". Ryszard Kapuściński, a Polish writer and traveller, once trenchantly observed: "The continent is too large to describe. It is a veritable ocean, a separate planet, a varied, immensely rich cosmos. Only with the greatest simplification, for the sake of convenience, can we say 'Africa'. In reality, except as a geographical appellation, Africa does not exist".[14]

Though west-coast trading stations were established in the 15th century, this did not lead immediately to travels into the interior where the large, centralised African kingdoms reigned. At this time missionaries ventured only around the edges of Angola and Congo. European circumnavigation to the east coast in the 16th century found Arab traders in command of mercantile outposts. Competition with Arab and Zanzibari slavers over inland routes from the east coast was fierce. From the 16th to the 19th centuries Africans were forced to journey to the Americas in the commerce of trans-Atlantic slavery. Earlier millions had been sent as slaves to Arabia. These events over long spans of time weakened older African polities, without displacing their residual economic modes.

Merchant capitalism from Europe changed the nature of the economic base and the mix of social relationships. Chartered companies and commercial entities penetrated Africa's coasts and hinterlands. Portugal led the charge, soon followed by more of Europe's medieval states. Trading networks underwent major revision. Technologies and capital were introduced from abroad to modify the foundations of accumulation and investment, threatening local sovereignties, and set Africa on a new course. Africa entered the global world economy while the ruling groups in traditional societies came to dominate the trading nexus. Slavery began its long and slow exit from the landscape, and the legitimated commerce installed by the foreigners became the norm.

There was also several of what Bill Freund has called "informal empires". Coastal outposts were set up, missionaries trekked the interiors, explorers sought to raise their flags, treaties were struck, compradors were recruited and trade was expanded, while in the south white settlers and trekboers pushed inland to establish their own land-locked states.[15] Where foreign settlement had been established, as in South Africa, older economic modes were significantly displaced – whether in the Eastern Cape, on the Highveld or in the serial extermin-ation of the San peoples, which had proceeded over the centuries and in which many hands were drenched in blood.[16] The Cape became an outpost of "the West" (a disputatious set of states in Europe) in 1652. Explorers from the Old World later trekked inland from the north, west and east of the continent to carve out niches in the interior, inducing new economic modes in the wake of their travels.

The explorers' journeys included those of Richard Burton, Henry Morton Stanley, John Hanning Speke, Pierre Savorgan de Brazza, Jean-Baptiste Marchand, Samuel Baker and Mungo Park. The formation of the African Association by Joseph Banks in London in 1788 and the Société Géographique de Paris spurred wider interest and a flurry of expeditions. In the 1830s the Geographical Society (later Royal Geographical Society) encouraged this penetration of interior Africa. From 1836 incursions northwards from the Cape redoubt were made, initially by Afrikaaner trekboers, Africa's white tribe. Today's explora-tion for resources and markets by South African companies continues this tradition of intrusion into Africa's spaces from the outside but now from an insider economy, one which has today lost its monopoly on Africa's investment game as Nigerian, East African and Maghrebian companies turn inwards towards Africa in search of corporate spoils.

These arduous expeditions, together with the eventual abolition of slavery, later closing down the slave business of both Tippu Tip (Africa's most powerful merchant and slaver, active into the 1880s) and the Sultan of Zanzibar, changed the economic future of interior central Africa irrevocably.[17] Arab slavers around the east coast had been among the earliest explorers. Later Belgium's King Leopold's Congo Free State imposed its damaging consequences, these lasting long into the 20th century, to disrupt Congo's traditional economies. Contacts and commerce arrived with the missionaries, following the endeavours of Robert Moffat, David Livingstone and subsequent priestly bands (Jesuits and Carmelites among them). Another economic thrust came from early forays by hunters like Frederick Courtenay Selous (perhaps the progenitor of the modern safari hunter) from the 1870s onwards. By now many a global merchant had an interest in Africa.

Even as late as 1790, however, the European presence across Africa had totalled no more than 25,000 people (21,000 then at the Cape of Good Hope). Further colonisation was likewise achieved with few foreigners. The imperial world's rough and ready capture of Africa from the late 19th century onwards brought new and lasting forms of economic focus and social control centred on international trading, settler economies north of the Limpopo, wider-spread plantations, commercial farms, extractive mining enclaves, and a range of modern or ancillary industries. These economic modes included households of masters and servants, a phenomenon now spread across the continent.

Be they loved or loathed, Africa would have been the poorer in its economic base without these long-term evolutionary developments, most of 20th century origin. Simultaneously, the seeds of urban complexes grew, some emerging to become mega-cities. Many commercial, industrial and mining centres based on contract and migrant labour developed alongside a plethora of distant and segmented rural peasant economies (some with a degree of monetisation). As time passed, vast informal mechanisms of urban survival developed in the shanty towns and *bidonvilles* that materialised as Africans left the bush in droves.

All the while, Africa's ancient and peasant economies remained at the edge of survival. Many succumbed to these winds of change, while others adjusted to the onslaught in varying degrees, remaining to dominate the rural environs. Modernisation in rudimentary form did little to eradicate this overall socioeconomic ecology. Commercial ventures did not immediately displace the vast majority of traditional modes of subsistence in Africa, or for the most part directly appropriate all ethnic domains, or carve out the entire hinterland for their own exclusive ends.

In the conquest of Africa the larger powers in Europe took the lion's share, others were left with marginal interests, and the Danish exited. No European power fought another in this quest for a slice of Africa, which owes its economic origins of modern existence to the white conquistadors from over the sea and only later fully defined itself in opposition to the imperial status quo. Colonial economies were built with investment capital and commercial penetration, to develop administration, mines, plantations and towns, with infrastructure. The pre-capitalist world nonetheless survived as a necessary part of this economic architecture. While settlers came to these colonies, the number of whites in tropical Africa outside South Africa was under 200,000 in 1936. They barely topped 6 million at the apogee of white presence in Africa around the early 1980s. Today the number probably sits at or below 5 million in a continent of 1 billion.[18]

Varied forms of subsistence and survival entities emerged: Africa's former aristocrats became functionaries, peasants tilled the lands, wage-labourers filled the towns, while migrant and contract workers were ferried up and down the continent to keep the economic system at optimal rates of capital accumulation. Subsistence wages for most became the basis of payments made, the rural households offsetting the unpaid costs of social survival. All this led to further cleavages, differentiation and specialisation inside the faster-growth capitalist economies.

Colonialism marked out historic watersheds for Africa, at its inception and at its closure. The colonial states mediated the varying claims of its competitive industries, not all with the same interests. Traditional power in chiefdoms and through indirect rule was often maintained. It had not been the aim of colonial powers to take on all liabilities. The so-called "white man's burden" was one shared with many indigenous peoples, as the economic landscapes were changed in fundamental ways, even while the prerogatives of lineage and traditional land rights were left largely to ancient devices.

Decolonisation came in due course following the ravages of the Second World War, partly fought on Africa's soil – in Abyssinia, Libya and the western desert. The "winds of change" were presaged by labour strikes, the surge of nationalism, rising pressures in world politics, and decisions by the colonial and imperial powers to exit their earlier command in Africa. Independence dates were set. There followed a sort of European scramble out of Africa, reversing the interregnums of the previous 60–70 years. Recalcitrant settler economies resisted in Algeria, Central Africa and South Africa, seen as a special case. The exodus of imperial diktat over Africa was sudden, in some cases precipitous, complex and not without crisis, as in Congo. Power vacuums were created and Africa's elites struggled to inherit the mantles of control. Europe executed a rapid but calculated retreat, leaving settler colonial economies to fend for their own interests. Several wars and conflicts accompanied this imperial exodus, with added vengeance created by the disputatious imperatives of the Cold War powers and their proxies fighting hot wars for control and survival in many an African state: Angola, Moçambique, Rhodesia, Namibia and in Southern Africa as a whole.

Africa's post-colonial states were generally ill-prepared and poorly equipped for this sudden transition, and managed to pile mistakes upon their inherited legacies, leading to a weakening of the capitalist project in large swathes of the continent. Political and economic crises multiplied, and development was thwarted following the honeymoon period, as another scramble for Africa began: one led by Africa's political classes seeking power and control. While the era of "strangers at the economic gates of Africa" in the form of colonial states was an interlude of modest time in an era blown away by the winds of change, the new nation-states often resurfaced on the bases of older ways and traditions of governance allied to the traditional ways of exercising power. There had been past pomp and ceremony in the upper echelons of "states" that the colonialists took over. Kings, princes and royal courts, chiefs and headmen were ubiquitous. Their progenitors assumed the mantles of control left behind, with modern economic artifices and organised bureaucracies, which somehow had to be kept running.

It should be no surprise that in Africa's reclamation of its birthright, tradition trumped the modern as institutions took on new shapes, old mores and traditional ways of governance. Several emergent states folded like a pack of cards, their cohesion and durability subject to pressures that could not be easily accommodated. The reinsertion of the old mechanisms of political and social management implied destabilisation when applied to the modern economies. Partial reversion to type thereby took place. Many post-colonial economies encountered decay. Africa had been conquered and reclaimed. Now it sought to reconquer itself.

Part 3

Medieval modernity

8

"Modern" Africa

Africa originated from a primordial past that long pre-dated its contact with differentiated outer worlds. Initial intrusions from outside moulded only some parts of this continental fabric. African societies emerged in their own manner and adapted to the strangers from abroad. To understand Africa today, we must give weight to this "ancient and medieval Africa" in its cohabitation with the modern. Some of the older modes have disappeared or transmuted: what remains is a complex and dynamic mix of at sometimes complementary, on occasions competing, economic modes. As a result, medieval and modern forms of socio-economic structure coexist. Our notion of "medievalism" here is not meant to imply any direct contemporary analogue to medieval Europe, where the landscape exhibited feudal dimensions over several centuries following the collapse of the Roman Empire and through the Dark Ages. The medieval in Africa is a distinctive notion, useful to capture the pre-market and subsistence modes of living, many of which have survived into the contemporary era.

Many houses of strangers – Romans, Greeks, Phoenicians, Ptolemies, Arabs and Omanis, Europe's feudal and mercantilist cultures – brought their economic skills and technologies into Africa to change its destiny irrevocably. More recently, foreigners implanted nascent capitalism, along with slavery, enclave economies and diverse nodes of exploitation which, when their utility diminished, were overtaken by quasi-feudal and, later, capitalist relationships. Today, North Americans, Chinese, Indians, South-east Asians, Middle Easterners, Australasians,

Latins, east Europeans and Russians have contributed to this globalised mercantile intrusion. Africa's own companies have joined this rush for position across the continent.

Capitalist Africa came to be shaped by foreign-implanted mines, plantations and master/servant economies adding to Africa's autochthonous economic mix. The medieval nature of subsistence remained, embedded in econo-cultural matrices. In a kind of Darwinian economic evolution, one model outperformed others to command the citadels of the states that formed in the 19th and 20th centuries. This competitive evolutionary process marked Africa's *longue durée* from antiquity to its modern world. There was no "Big Bang" revolutionary transformation of ancient economies, only their integrated sublimation as appended and changing subsistence communities within fragile, newly formed modernities. Transition from medievalism has been incomplete: the majority in Africa maintain strong ties to the fundamentally pre-modern. In this model can be found, I believe, explanations for the complexity and difficulties in Africa today.

It is essential to ground understanding of Africa's economic experience in this endogenous dimension and not rely solely on interfaces with exogenous worlds. Africa's socioeconomic shape has not been determined by some foreign *deus ex machina*. Even visible modernities (including resource industries) installed through colonialism and post-colonial worlds have failed to transplant wholly the institutional forms typically associated with them elsewhere – in the shape of undiluted property rights, universal modern legalism and individualism, or in economic practices taken as the norm in the West.

The forces of climate, ecology and geography have had distinctive power in shaping African societies, cultures and economies from the earliest times. Eco-cultural dimensions inside Africa created long-standing divisions, a feature observed today. This older saga has echoed in modern Africa as the colonial world has given way to new states, power struggles have become endemic and earlier social orders have reasserted precedent origins. The notions of Africa's medievalism, in which ancient and modern modes coexist, highlight this underside. The paradigm still pervades subsistence Africa. Western thinkers have been slack in appreciating the existence of these older modes of African socioeconomics – and I suspect that the Chinese and many non-Western 21st-century corporations in Africa have little conception of this past or its continuity into the present. The same equally applies to many Western firms and their transplanted expatriate executives.

The conventional wisdom of singular Africa macroeconomies, moulded around a nation-state, does not correspond to prevailing socio-economic reality. Macroeconomic structures in Africa are riddled with proverbial black holes in which either fortune or disaster can occur with unpredictable frequency, creating instability and unforeseen events, and confounding interpretation by outsiders with little knowledge of this vortex.

The "uniformity paradigm" that has been erroneously applied to Africa is a diagnosis predetermined by an economic policy prescription. To use the words of one of the greatest thinkers on economics, Joseph Schumpeter from another context (Schumpeter's review of John Maynard Keynes's *General Theory*): "The ghost of that policy looks over the shoulder of the analyst, frames his assumptions ... and ... guides his pen."[1] There are lessons in the observation about the arduous historical task of modernising Africa. Long-term, multi-decade dynamic processes will be required before achievement, without any quick-fix strategy.

The clash of visions and societies found within Africa today is fundamentally that of conflict between its incipient modernity and the medieval or pre-capitalist modes that dominate many societies within the continent. It was the long saga of western Europe's evolution; it is also Africa's. It may be that modernity in Africa will diverge funda-mentally from what emerged in Europe. That is yet to be known. The quest for modernity is a hard task of history, necessitating patience. By most definitions, much in Africa is pre-modern, and the presump-tion of a single macroeconomy a false one. For Africa this latter idea is largely illusion and at the nation-state level it is equally flawed. Yet ideas presuming overall modernity regularly pervade analysis, media coverage and policy formation concerning Africa.

Africa's vast swathes of pre-modern subsistence or medieval-style survivalist economies have typically been aggregated, submerged, or, at best, inadequately specified within contemporary interpretative works, global economic databanks and institutional assessments (as conducted by the World Bank and the Economic Commission for Africa or ECA). Rarely do these diagnoses reflect the periodic changes, shocks or consequences affecting the bedrock traditional economies, on top of which the modern economies are built.

Some countries do attempt an "accounting" of sorts, as in South Africa where the rubric used is a measure for "non-modern households". Elsewhere estimates for the "rural household sector" have been commonly deployed, then only as a residual based on highly imperfect assumptions. Perhaps any measure is to be welcomed. In some countries there has been a breakdown in the provision of macro-statistics. In 2010 Zimbabwe reported that the country had 110,600 domestic household servants: this was precisely the same number as when last measured in 1985. The reality is that much of Africa has traversed the last century untrammelled at its core, even as it has been changed in superficial ways as a result of being forcibly opened up, dominated or controlled, and now managed at arm's length by an assortment of rival outside powers allied to local power brokers. That this Africa is not "seen" or revealed by the mass of official data says nothing about its pervasive existence.

That the global aid business is now widely considered to have failed in Africa is in part because of its poor reckoning with these continental histories and complex realities. It is another instance of how Africa has been long misunderstood from the outside. Many an aid project lasted only in the short term; some financed only the capital costs of projects, without meeting continuing current liabilities. Many were ill-conceived from the start, ended in corruption, failed to meet aims or even produced negative outcomes, provoked further division over the monetary spoils, and encouraged the culture of dependency. Some states have used aid to avoid or renege on needed reforms. At root has been the delusional macro-view that Africa just needs a financial aid fix, as a sort of substitute for endogenous economic growth.

The problem has extended beyond official aid where strategies to "fix" Africa have been mainly uniform in design and simplistic in nature (more funding, poverty alleviation, and the like) as most have been out of step with Africa's myriad complexities. Likewise, many companies have implemented flawed initiatives to combat African poverty through corporate social "investment" programmes, with defensive public relations images central to such programmes. Many yield no investment outcome at all. It should be no surprise that this record has been a patently weak one: it is as if these companies have never heard of the history of aid failures, or learnt lessons from past decades even while they presume to act as if they know better today than the many who for nearly 50 years ploughed the aid path fruitlessly with little benefit to Africa's economic growth. *Plus ça change.*

Initiatives have often been implemented at the macro level without appreciation of how the economic game works inside many of Africa's economies. This is typically a world that operates around old structures of patrimonialism connected to long-established traditions coming from the distant past. Abundant literature on African societies informs us of the "Big Man" complex, the power of the past, the role of kingmakers (seen in the context of many contemporary politicians and leaders) with their entourages connected to family, ethnic analogues, patrimony and the favoured few.[2]

In many central African states there has long existed the phenomenon of *chefs* and *povo*, the chiefs (presidents, as more than first among equals) and the poor, as latter-day serfs sublimated by what in effect has been the exercise of quasi-feudal power. What might be called the *shamwari* culture – an "old-boy" network, looking after close friends and social or ethnic allies – is almost ubiquitous in tropical Africa.[3] Social bonds provide a powerful force for both those at the top and those at the bottom of the societal totem pole. Pre-existent cultural imprints have a lot to do with how Africa does or does not work. This ancient ethos has shaped decisions on politics and economic policy made within the sanctums of Africa's power elites, including the local distribution of patronage and economic privilege. It is not that time has stood still: it just has not swept away the durable historic and cultural legacies. It probably will not for many decades.

Old traditions in Africa shape a range of economic conditions, rendering the conventional disciplines and economic prisms for analysis weak in their understanding of the wider picture. In most modern diagnoses of Africa, economic models exhibit imperfect and illusory macroeconomic bases, the market hegemony associated with them too easily assumed. Neoclassical economics dominates this paradigm; institutional or evolutionary economic thinking is little used. Politicians and multilateral agencies prefer to deal with numeric composites to provide the indicators and benchmarks of modernity (even for poverty, which is often reduced to mere income relativities). Such measures fail to capture the rough and raw disaggregated worlds of pure subsistence and survival that mark Africa's economic terrain. The peasant household's world, like the shanty milieu, is not just a number: it is a mode of existence, subsistence and survival.

Visions in the mind's eye

Writers have long portrayed Africa's socioeconomic complexity. They offer insights worth reflecting upon, in fiction and non-fiction. Some are literary gurus. Their literature provides perceptive views on Africa's condition as reflected in the mind's eye. Many writers recall their experience, the past and the present, a blend of mixed emotions in some cases, and wrap their stories in a combination of actualities and even myth. Some capture with finesse the drama of underdevelopment; others reflect upon Africa's rush for the trappings of modernity, several on the ambitions and panaceas of venal politicians and emergent capitalist classes.

Nobel Prize winner V.S. Naipaul has written much on Africa's travails, about which he has been quite pessimistic, in particular taking a dismissive view of Africa's history and culture – one that, in my view, is patently contrary to anthropological evidence. African history is an exceedingly rich one. When asked by Elizabeth Hardwick, an author, in 1979 about the future of Africa, the laureate answered: "Africa has no future."[4] This echoed a comment in Naipaul's own novel *Bend in the River* (about Stanleyville, renamed Kisangani) on the Congo's fraught condition, and that it was a place where the future had both come and gone.[5] These were sweeping condemnations, either prophetic (for the fate of Congo was to deteriorate) or extremely naive.

The extrapolation to Africa from only one circumstance is a fatal error. Of interest is that Naipaul's early travels in the Congo were in the mid-1960s, when Africans seen by the author were likened to ancient Britons camping in the abandoned villas of Romans around the 5th century. To me it is neither realistic nor plausible to maintain a nihilistic view of Africa where so much is a matter of passion and on which historiography, literature and modern writings have been profound. If one truly "reads Africa", it is possible to be overwhelmed or perhaps confused – but not nihilistic or without judgement.

In response to Naipaul, Paul Theroux, an American writer, commented: "If Africa has no future, neither do we."[6] A quarter of a century later Theroux revisited Africa in a journey from Cairo to the Cape, only to find it greatly changed and significantly regressed. Africa's past is wholly relevant to its condition, even though its future may remain uncertain. A travel writer's eye can be highly perceptive, as Theroux shows in *Dark Star Safari*.[7] Now a world-acclaimed author, Theroux spent earlier days as a Peace Corps volunteer in Malawi teaching in the *bundu* (the bush) during the 1960s. During his recent journey he finds an Africa more decrepit than previously. Africans that Theroux encountered along the route were, he thought, hungrier and poorer, more lied to, more pessimistic and more corrupt than in decades past. As for the leaders, says Theroux, you cannot tell the politicians from the witch doctors. This is an interesting observation. The *nganga* (in Central Africa) or *sangoma* (in Southern Africa), to which the reference is made, perform honourable tasks in their societies as healers and intermediaries to the ancestors, ultimately to *Mwari* (the god), although there are the usual charlatans, to which Theroux is really making comparison. That the politicians often usurp traditional spiritual roles, as ultimate power or as intermediaries to higher authority, is recognition of their manipulation of older social rituals.

One senses a deep ambivalence in Theroux's nostalgic story, a mixture of regret over an Africa long past, anger at its current manifestation and angst about the problematic future for poorer Africans at large, those left aside by the few who have steered the gravy trains that course across the continent. Maybe therein lurks one problem. In their search for measures of where Africa might stand today, observers from both within Africa and outside can become focused (even fixated) on reference points from Africa's past which have been eradicated by the passage of time. These old beacons may be no guide to the future even if they light up current deficiencies. Here many invest a modicum of hope over experience. In Africa it is sometimes the only way forward.

There is deep insight and reflection found in literary works on Africa by a host of knowledgeable and talented African novelists, biographers, polemicists, thinkers and scribes. They include Chinua Achebe, Ngugi wa Thiong'o, Wole Soyinka, Ali Mazrui, Dambudzo Marachera and J.M. Coetzee, among hundreds of others. One of the godfathers of Nigerian writing, Chinua Achebe evokes serious themes in the widely translated *Things Fall Apart* (10 million copies sold in 45 languages).[8] It tells of the corrupting values of the West that infused African traditional cultures in the colonial era. Achebe proclaims cultural nationalism, a view gaining ground as the continent's Western-controlled roots slip their moorings. The book opens up to all some of the long-lasting customs of Africa, the clash with presumed superior Western values, and how the locals were at odds with the powers of the white man vested in the authority of the colonial state. At the end of Achebe's classic, when the district commissioner orders the principal character, Okonkwo, to be cut down from a tree where he has hanged himself, revulsion ensues and social disobedience follows from this clash with custom: it would bring shame, dishonour among clansmen, and would be an offence against the Earth. The district commissioner gets his way and leaves the scene, choosing the title of the book he will write on the years spent bringing civilisation to Africa: *The Pacification of the Primitive Tribes of the Lower Niger*. Like much that was found in Africa before its long night of colonial history, the old ways have not entirely gone.

Many astute African writers chafe at their dire predicament, knowing it will not pass easily. Some want all-embracing modernity now. Several have paid the price of their impudence in speaking the truth to power.[9] Few have transcended literature and converted their knowledge into political action. There is no Václav Havel found amid contemporary African presidents and none appears on the horizon.[10] African writers have, however, taken up the literary cudgels to write critiques of their leaders or regimes. Ngugi wa Thiong'o, a Kenyan and author of many works, sought to ridicule African dictators and warlords in satire and indictments of Big Men and their entourages. Many Africans empathise with these stories.

Wole Soyinka's memoirs reflect decades of personal adversity and struggle against military dictatorships in Nigeria. Among African writers, Soyinka is the one who has probably been the most informed and active in politics. It is instructive that even in 1996 he should write about hope (soon thwarted) that Sani Abacha might be the last despot in Nigerian history. Soyinka saw Nigerian society clearly, I believe, one with minority beneficiaries organised in a carefully nurtured feudal oligarchy, with sequential transitions custom-built for failure. Even with not inconsiderable support in Nigeria, he was never able to surmount the political barricades.

Others have written about Africa in their own fields of social concern: on the Biafran war, the tragedies in Somalia, the shadows cast by Idi Dada Amin in Uganda, revolution against Portuguese colonialism and serial *chimurenga* (the "people's" war for independence, followed in due course by the war against the people) in Mugabe's Zimbabwe. The majority of texts have focused on political or social questions, few on economic growth.

While few literary works have captured the essence of the oil state in Africa, one author who confronted this dilemma, penning it with thinly veiled satire, is Patrick Wilmot (*Seeing Double*), a novelist and sociologist from Jamaica, who casts a critical eye on Nigeria (depicted as Niagra) where he lived, taught at Ahmadu Bello University, and was kidnapped by security forces in 1988 and deported. We met in London in 2007 briefly and shared drinks and insights into these stories. Wilmot castigates the Nigerian military, the presidential scene, the hangers-on, the state kleptocracy and their allies in globalisation, especially wicked oil companies. It is a tale about the greed surrounding the political system.

Glitterati and celebrities

We also have the fashionable "economic" wisdom of the artistic great
and the good, with Bono and Bob Geldof (among a growing collection of celebrities and glitterati) pushing Africa's aid barrow, the latter
casting a wider canvas in *Geldof in Africa*.[11] Geldof has more recently
raised millions in private equity to invest in Africa to make money – not
music. I must confess to having loved Geldof's BBC documentary on
Africa, with its photo-vignettes and reflections on a vast and luminous
continent and some trenchant off-the-cuff remarks. It is replete with
outspoken anger at the state of affairs suffered by most Africans – and
poetic and impassioned as well.

Nor would I begrudge any credit to Live Aid in July 1985 for having
raised funds for the Ethiopian famine, though some consider that this
gratuity might have merely buttressed the cruelties of the Mengistu
regime at the time. The Live 8 follow-up extravaganza 20 years later
with another concert, global media engagement, rock-star presence at
the Gleneagles G8 annual meeting in 2006 (Geldof placed by Tony Blair
on the Commission for Africa that year) and commitments made by
Western politicians to double African aid to $50 billion over several
years, along with debt cancellation commitments, made Geldof weep.
"We should never need another event like it," wrote the rock-star scribe
in 2006. It was not long before disappointment set in. The capacity to
absorb and "invest" aid in Africa is limited; it takes time to disburse,
monies are fungible, and commitments often mean rolling past into
present projections. There is the cost of delivering aid on the ground,
administrative slippage, even corruption along the chain of donations,
while "investing" more in the Africa aid game, as knowledgeable practitioners like Robert Calderisi caution, could even make things worse.

This one-off rock-shock did not make poverty history. The idea was
manifestly naive. The task is far larger and more daunting, as Africa's
history should tell. Then there is the myopia. To most of us $50 billion
is a gold mine. To Africa's 950 million at that time it was $55 each,
spread over time (say five years), making it below $1 per month or
around 8 cents per day – that is, if it actually all arrived in hand; most of

it would not. Now I know of many in Africa who would like to benefit from this largesse, but to believe that it could "fix Africa" is simplistic in the extreme. The goodwill generated in Western worlds with Africa as a *cause célèbre*, and a natural instinct to support the disadvantaged, has become a fulcrum for rock stars (Irish U2 music star Bono leading the charge). Theroux for one took umbrage in 2011 at this grandiose image in one caustic comment: "There are probably more annoying things than being hectored about African development by a wealthy Irish rock star in a cowboy hat, but I can't think of them at the moment."[12]

Fashion for Africa has induced Hollywood celebrities and the global glitterati to jump on the bandwagon, as demonstrated by a July 2007 *Vanity Fair* special edition devoted to the continent. There you can read how Oprah Winfrey invested in a girls' school in Johannesburg, George Clooney went to Chad to film a documentary (*A Journey to Darfur*) in 2007, Madonna followed Angelina Jolie on the African child adoption trail and Brad Pitt helped launch the "Make Poverty History" campaign. Benefits were run for the victims of Darfur, a spate of Africa-themed movies hit the cinemas (*Blood Diamond*, *Hotel Rwanda*), American philanthropists (Warren Buffett with Bill and Melinda Gates) pledged and delivered gobs of money to charitable foundations and projects, and many sought out South African political icon Nelson Mandela for self-aggrandising photo opportunities and implicit endorsement. Thandie Newton took on the task of fixing Mali's water supplies, Tom Hanks hosted an e-Bay auction to provide free radios to Africa's remotest villages, and Elton John arranged the delivery of 120 motorcycles to doctors in Lesotho. Africa had arrived, at least in Hollywood.

Much of this may be considered harmless or beneficial for some, and perhaps great public relations. The solutions attached to most endeavours remind us of the failed development game of decades past: social-oriented and mega-aid, dubious debt write-offs, tapping into Western guilt complexes, high-profile instant fixes, even a sort of big-bang approach. One enduring mystery is why Western politicians seek or need the advice of rock stars or even Hollywood on these grand strategy questions, especially when they do not on foreign policy, EU security or economic strategy. It leaves me wondering about the durability of these populist fashion statements and their minimal impacts, maybe even distortions about what is really best.

Among the serious diagnoses of those who "worked" Africa from the analytical outside and experiential inside, I read few that today unreservedly recommend any of these panaceas. If only life inside the continent and instant remedies for Africa were that easy and simple.

✳

Anyone who wishes to gain an insight into the huge volume of texts on Africa and its past and present should try visiting specialised Africana bookshops of substance. One in Johannesburg's ragged downtown that I visit often has a collection of 50,000 items covering antiquarian history through to modern themes. Another in Vancouver, Canada, has an equally magnificent collection. London is likewise a treasure trove of Africana, and a few other cities in the world hold Africana archives of great interest. They speak to the enduring fascination that the world has had with this continent over the centuries. What seems to be found too rarely in contemporary economic writings is sufficient understanding and knowledge of this rich historiography and literature, the essence of which describes a world contrary to what today many believe, without due consideration, to be somehow fundamentally modern and capitalist in its nature.

Clearly it is a gargantuan task to encapsulate the essence of this continental history, let alone intuit its economic future. Here I merely seek to capture the skeletal bare bones of this metadrama, so that the complex evolutionary tale can be perceived. The pre-capitalist order ceded control to nascent capitalist-based colonialism. Between colonial and post-colonial states, fusing and evolving, were installed hitherto unknown economic nodes: trading posts, plantations, farms, mines, power plants and electricity networks, dams and administrative centres, tourist entities on coasts and inland game farms. These transformed the economic landscape, creating modernist economic habitats within the colonial and post-colony make-up of *Africanus economicus*. History played its inevitable part in the distortion of old Africa's economic

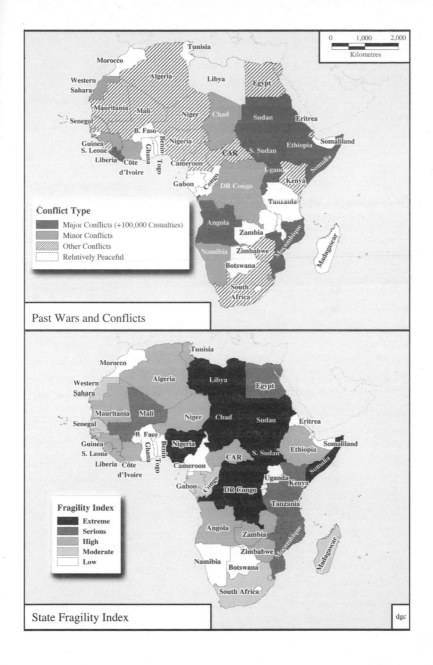

Past Wars and Conflicts

Conflict Type
- Major Conflicts (+100,000 Casualties)
- Minor Conflicts
- Other Conflicts
- Relatively Peaceful

State Fragility Index

Fragility Index
- Extreme
- Serious
- High
- Moderate
- Low

formations. During the 20th century internal conflicts, interstate wars, foreign onslaughts, local rebellions, intrastate wars, guerrilla conflicts, secession, famine, disease and genocide carved out and reshaped political and economic spheres. Complex economic and ethnic struggles, boundary disputes, rival ideologies, religion and contested state power were all at stake. There was no smooth upward path along the evolutionary curve.

Today we find an Africa containing, as pieces of the contemporary economic puzzle, zones of criminality, illicit diamond and gold mining, illegal networks for smuggling, militia and mafia-like activities in drugs and arms, money-laundering, growing piracy, illegal fishing and big-game poaching. Part of these myriad unofficial activities has an oil face – illegal bunkering and crude-oil theft in Nigeria, for instance, as well as piracy targeted at oil-shipping lanes off Somalia. Much of the "illegitimate" in Africa's many shadow economies has become a home-grown business even though outsiders (from Moldova, Russia, Ukraine, Asia and elsewhere, even from inside Africa) have often kick-started and orchestrated many flourishing illegal ventures, taking advantage of weak states and co-opting local allies, even ministers.

This economic history of Africa had profound consequences in shaping the continent. Africa's modern world is only one fragment of this vast historiography, which needs to be kept in perspective even if it comes to loom larger in the future.

9

Post-colony aftermath

The thinkers on development economics in the period when Africa cut the umbilical cords with its imperial masters, and afterwards – among them Albert Hirschman, Walt Whitman Rostow, Harvey Liebenstein, Arthur Lewis, Gunnar Myrdal, Richard Nelson, Paul Rosenstein-Rodan and Ragnar Nurkse – had many theories as to how things should work, but rather less understanding (regarding Africa) of how they did. Some saw development in mechanistic, almost Newtonian terms.

In 1957 Myrdal emphasised the virtues of "circular and cumulative causation" in underdeveloped countries as a sort of economics of the roundabout. The theory could not explain how to get the machine of underdevelopment working and to move forward. Albert Hirschman (1958) articulated counter-theories and strategies for development based on forward and backward linkages. Rosenstein-Rodan recommended industrialisation in a "big push" and cluster strategy, which is a favourite today among business schools postulating the benefits of core competencies and competitive advantage. Nelson (1956) dwelt upon breaking out of the low-equilibrium trap to sever the chains of underdevelopment. For Lewis, the key was progressive absorption of labour within the dual-economy model of capitalist primacy. Rostow (1916–2003) postulated that economic development occurred as economies moved through a series of sequential stages: from traditional society, through the preconditions for take-off, take-off, the drive to maturity, to high mass consumption.

In Africa thesis and counter-thesis were debated, tried and subjected to the tests of empiricism in the search for the Holy Grail: which fix would make Africa's economies take off? Meanwhile, the bloom was fast coming off the rose in post-colony Africa – some economies had crashed on the runway, and the continent entered a period of acute stress before and after the 1980s. It took until the late 1990s for the corner to be turned for many.

Africa had encountered an emerging paradox of "evolution with retardation", as the blight of backwardness remained and underdevelopment was ubiquitous. The post-colonial economic honeymoon had lasted but a short while before many states began eating the inherited productive capital stock under the aegis of planning, experimentation, state controls, militarism, socialism and humanism, and a variety of half-baked economic analogues. The dead hand of bureaucracies and ideology – some drawn from the Cold War and some minted in experimental indigenous varieties – did not help.

Even while subsistence remained of primary concern, amid widespread conflict, the underlying economic fabric and competitive modes remained. Most survived the onslaught of the economic downside and the heavy hand imposed by the all-knowing state machines. This was the era of "state economic engineering" par excellence in Africa. It failed dismally. The motors of the accumulation and investment process slowed and stalled. Aid dependency sought to plug the gap, and then ran out of steam. The debt-financing route became exhausted and trade faltered. What next? The traditional core engines of growth and development – investment and trade – proved insufficient to the task: they had been throttled by state policies and ideologies, taxation and nationalisation. Africa's share of world trade fell, and the inflows of FDI were minimal. This threatened Africa's economic survival, with the continent becoming a net loser in a fast-advancing global game in which investment funds steadily moved to Asia.

Within Africa there emerged parallel and at times conflicting economic worlds. Several stalled economies broke down. Shadow economies and clandestine circuits of informalised merchants and non-state power brokers found havens for survival outside the formal.

Ethnolinguistic Africa

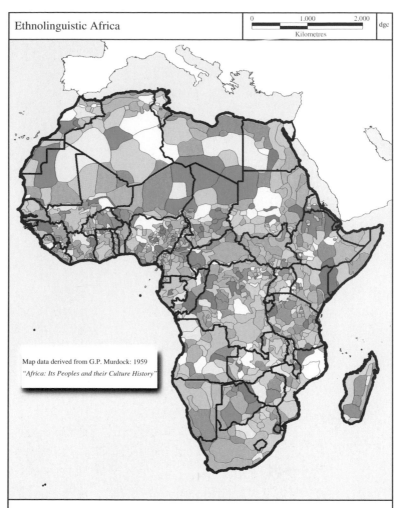

Map data derived from G.P. Murdock: 1959
"Africa: Its Peoples and their Culture History"

0 1.000 2.000
Kilometres

dgc

There are more ethnicities and distinct languages in Africa than elsewhere worldwide. Over two thousand local languages add to the current widespread use of English, French, Arabic and Kiswahili, making for complexities within the nation states that have been overlaid upon deeply embedded and ancient cultural entities. Few countries reflect ethnic or clan homogeneity. Several states have over one hundred ethnicities, multiple languages, and even many official languages. Fragmentation has been one consequence.

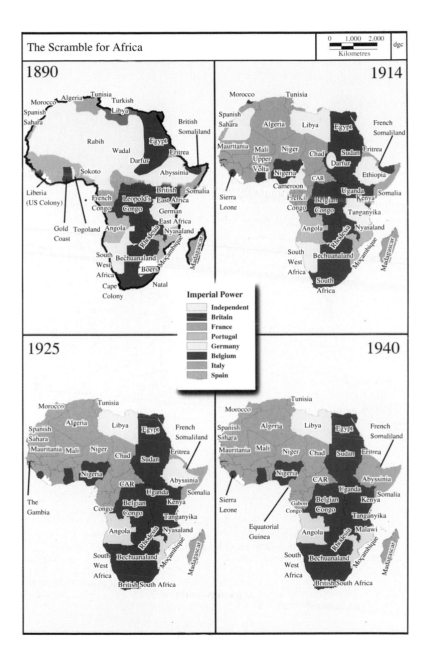

The Scramble for Africa

0   1,000   2,000   dgc
Kilometres

1890

Morocco
Algeria
Tunisia
Turkish
Spanish Sahara
Libya
British Somaliland
Egypt
Rabih
Wadai
Eritrea
Darfur
Abyssinia
Sokoto
Liberia (US Colony)
French Congo
Leopold's Congo
British East Africa
Somalia
German East Africa
Gold Coast
Togoland
Angola
Rhodesia
Nyasaland
Moçambique
Madagascar
South West Africa
Bechuanaland
Boers
Cape Colony
Natal

1914

Morocco
Tunisia
Spanish Sahara
Algeria
Libya
Egypt
French Somaliland
Mauritania
Mali
Niger
Chad
Sudan
Eritrea
Upper Volta
Darfur
Nigeria
Ethiopia
Cameroon
CAR
Sierra Leone
French Congo
Belgian Congo
Uganda
Kenya
Somalia
Tanganyika
Angola
Rhodesia
Nyasaland
Moçambique
Madagascar
South West Africa
Bechuanaland
South Africa

Imperial Power

	Independent
	Britain
	France
	Portugal
	Germany
	Belgium
	Italy
	Spain

1925

Morocco
Tunisia
Algeria
Libya
Egypt
French Somaliland
Spanish Sahara
Mauritania
Mali
Niger
Chad
Sudan
Eritrea
Nigeria
Abyssinia
CAR
Uganda
Somalia
The Gambia
Congo
Belgian Congo
Kenya
Tanganyika
Angola
Rhodesia
Nyasaland
Moçambique
Madagascar
South West Africa
Bechuanaland
British South Africa

1940

Tunisia
Morocco
Algeria
Libya
Egypt
French Somaliland
Spanish Sahara
Mauritania
Mali
Niger
Chad
Sudan
Eritrea
Nigeria
Abyssinia
CAR
Uganda
Somalia
Sierra Leone
Gabon
Belgian Congo
Kenya
Congo
Tanganyika
Equatorial Guinea
Angola
Rhodesia
Malawi
Moçambique
Madagascar
South West Africa
Bechuanaland
British South Africa

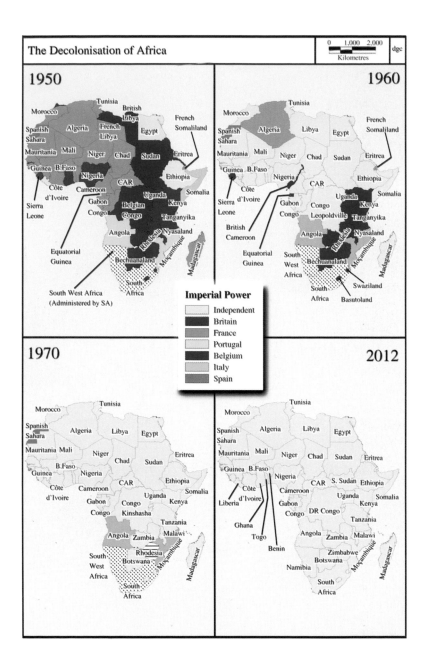

The Decolonisation of Africa

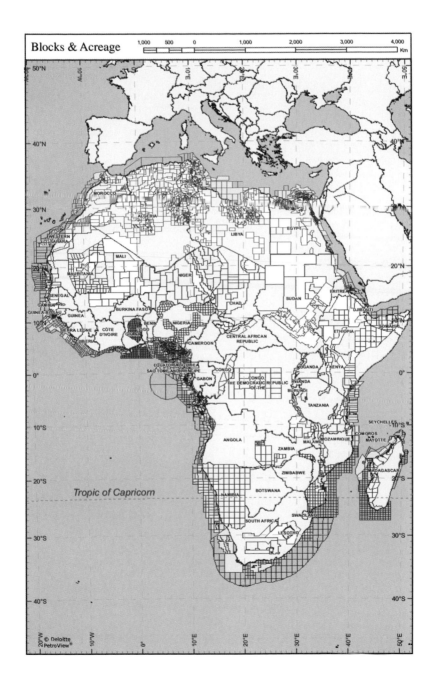

Blocks & Acreage

© Deloitte PetroView®

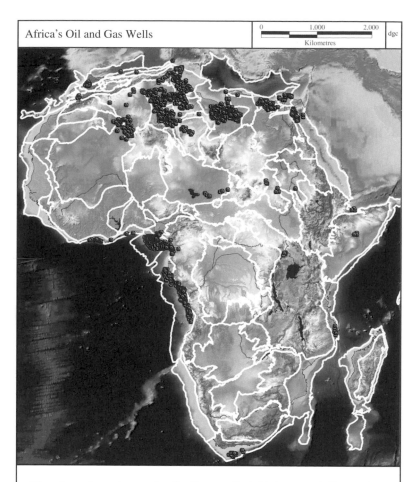

Africa's Oil and Gas Wells

| 0 | 1,000 | 2,000 |

Kilometres

dgc

There have been thousands of oil/gas wells drilled across Africa onshore and offshore. More wells will follow each year over the coming decades. Multiple basins have been opened, and many hydrocarbon basins remain as frontiers, while others are yet to test the drillbit. Drilling has been relatively concentrated in the Maghreb, Gulf of Guinea and selected interior rifts, but exploration well densities remain relatively low in most petroliferous basins. Huge offshore prospective zones will require decades of drilling and large investments in deepwater wells for maturation. Africa is one of the world's great oil/gas frontiers for the future.

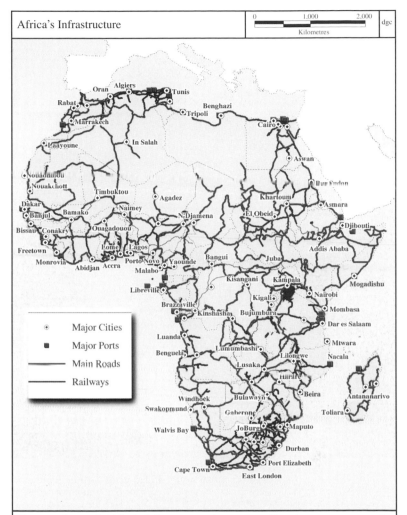

Africa's Infrastructure

0	1,000 2,000

Kilometres

dgc

Legend:
- ⊙ Major Cities
- ■ Major Ports
- —— Main Roads
- —— Railways

Cities and locations shown on map:
Oran, Algiers, Tunis, Rabat, Benghazi, Tripoli, Marrakech, Cairo, Laayoune, In Salah, Aswan, Nouadhibou, Nouakchott, Timbuktou, Agadez, Khartoum, Asmara, Dakar, Banjul, Bamako, Naimey, N'Djamena, El Obeid, Djibouti, Bissau, Conakry, Ouagadouou, Port Sudan, Freetown, Lome, Lagos, Bangui, Juba, Addis Ababa, Monrovia, Abidjan, Accra, Porto Novo, Yaounde, Malabo, Kisangani, Kampala, Mogadishu, Libreville, Kigali, Nairobi, Brazzaville, Kinshasha, Bujumbura, Mombasa, Luanda, Dar es Salaam, Benguela, Lumumbashi, Lilongwe, Mtwara, Lusaka, Nacala, Harare, Windhoek, Bulawayo, Beira, Antananarivo, Swakopmund, Gaberone, Toliara, Walvis Bay, JoBurg, Maputo, Durban, Cape Town, Port Elizabeth, East London

The templates of Africa's infrastructure in roads, rail and ports were mostly laid in the 20th century. More investment has since added to the integration of this hard-wired infrastructure. Yet significant deficiencies exist, operating and usage costs remain high, maintenance has often been lacking, and investment replacement costs to meet demand for new infrastructure exceed over one hundred billion dollars annually. Economic growth has been greatly impacted, especially by problems in energy infrastructure and power supply.

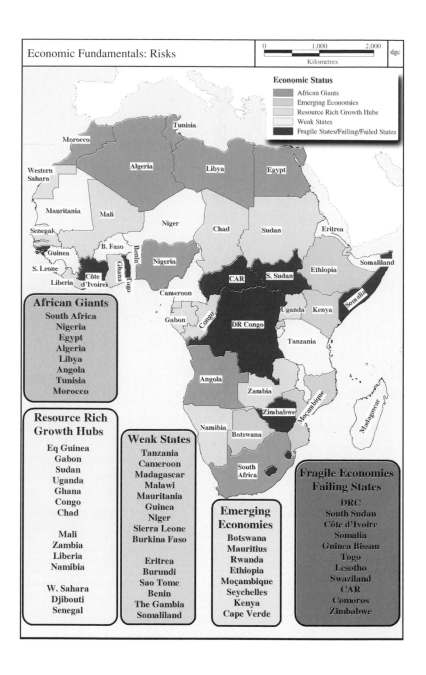

Economic Fundamentals: Risks

0   1,000   2,000   dgc
Kilometres

Economic Status
- African Giants
- Emerging Economies
- Resource Rich Growth Hubs
- Weak States
- Fragile States/Failing/Failed States

African Giants
South Africa
Nigeria
Egypt
Algeria
Libya
Angola
Tunisia
Morocco

Resource Rich Growth Hubs
Eq Guinea
Gabon
Sudan
Uganda
Ghana
Congo
Chad

Mali
Zambia
Liberia
Namibia

W. Sahara
Djibouti
Senegal

Weak States
Tanzania
Cameroon
Madagascar
Malawi
Mauritania
Guinea
Niger
Sierra Leone
Burkina Faso

Eritrea
Burundi
Sao Tome
Benin
The Gambia
Somaliland

Emerging Economies
Botswana
Mauritius
Rwanda
Ethiopia
Moçambique
Seychelles
Kenya
Cape Verde

Fragile Economies Failing States
DRC
South Sudan
Côte d'Ivoire
Somalia
Guinea Bissau
Togo
Lesotho
Swaziland
CAR
Comoros
Zimbabwe

Both Congos – Kinshasa and Brazzaville – witnessed these parallel economic universes. They still do. Many claim that Angola today basically portrays this duality. The absence of efficient bureaucratic states in these cases possibly helped forestall formalist political rivalry (capture of the state thereby not necessarily leading to the full transfer of power). None of these countries is unique or exceptional in this regard: monies and transactions outside "legitimated commerce" are considered important in almost all sub-Saharan countries. Divergence across societies and rising inequalities were accentuated, and the inherited physical infrastructure decayed as the costs of maintenance went unmet and capital replacement programmes wilted. The economics of backwardness spread.

Subsistence and survival

Millions of Africans shifted their existential locus through rural–urban migration to become dependent on massive informalisation concealed within Africa's presumptive post-modern derivatives: its sprawling cities, huge slums and *bidonvilles* found and expanding everywhere. For many, at best, this was an exchange of one form of subsistence for another. For others, it was a move from subsistence certitude to uncertain survival. Africa's "great social transition" in the locus of subsistence simultaneously revealed and concealed the urban medieval economies found inside the image of modernity. Some of the gurus of consumerism saw the transition as a good thing on the basis that economic growth would inexorably follow.

The scale of African mega-slums should not be minimised – and they are growing fast.[1] Precarious urban slum conditions are rife, creating non-traditional networks and hierarchies of survival in their wake. In the Gulf of Guinea it is expected that by 2020 there will be 70 million inhabitants along one narrow 600 km strip of coastline, with Lagos the supernova of this conglomeration. There might be 150 million by 2050. This sprawl of incipient modernism allied to material poverty is matched elsewhere in most of Africa's capitals.

Across rural Africa poverty collides with urban survival options in a world that, while mimicking the slums of old Europe, typically present even worse conditions. Traditional social obligations fractured under the weight of capitalist development and rural decline and so slum dwellers became wholly responsible for their means of survival, however achieved (through street trading, criminality, casual labouring, or begging). No operational minimum income was built into this adopted lifestyle, pushing many to the margins of existence.

The paradox is that these mega-slums grow even as some economies expand. Incomes per head for most drift or fall in real terms. All the while traditional safety nets, mostly in rural Africa, disappear as the neglected rural labour surpluses relocate to the *bidonvilles*. More of the growth in Africa's population has found its way into these fetid and densely packed slums, some among the poorest on the planet. Inhabitants dwell in a patchwork of shelters, often derelict and providing worse conditions than those once faced by the displaced peasants who now live there, most typically retaining residual links of kinship and economic dependencies tied to ethnicity, often to rural homelands.

From time to time this leads to explosive cocktails of combustible poverty and intra-slum or ethnic urban warfare. Periodic state evictions and assaults on this image of misery to "clean out" deprivation have added to rural and urban woes in many cities (as in Harare during 2005 with Operation Murambatsvina, with the forced eviction of nearly 1 million poor, to "drive out the trash"). Wars and social conflicts have added extra burdens to these urban subsistence or survivalist worlds (Luanda is one case), which for many have become infested with gangs, crime and squalid physical conditions where unnatural hazards are extreme.

Survival revolves around fragile squatter modes of tenure, landlordism, inner hierarchies of power and informalism, with fast-expanding zones in depressed peripheries that contain more people "lost" between city and the countryside, in effect uprooted by history. Residents often live literally amid *kak* (shit). Decline and stress within Africa's modern economies has aggravated this Dante-esque situation. Many of these semi-urban informal peasants lead lives of existential subsistence in conditions that informal market modes have been unable to modify. Many are reliant on rural transfers of resources and the "eating" of natural or social capital. Many millions of people living in shanties (perhaps 15% of all Africans) often have only partial connection with the capitalist centres of formal economic power and national authority. The traditional welfarism of old rural worlds can also be found here, with money flowing back and forth to agrarian economic appendages, just as for Africa as a whole around $40 billion flows in annually in remittances that sustain its economies and social structures in a vast and expanding network of structural global dependency. In normal conditions these constituents would be the long-term beneficiaries of surplus capital derived from modernity. Typically, this has not been the case.

Malthusian features envelop swathes of the continent, especially sub-Saharan communities, with technology growth having moved the natural economy little beyond the slow-shifting poverty datum line for subsistence for most, even if not all remain on the brink of marginality, with undernourishment and sometimes periodic starvation. Technology in these agrarian economies remains of ancient vintage. Most of agrarian Africa is decidedly pre-industrial and many peasant communities encounter the daily vicissitudes of life on the edge. Improvements in living standards have often been transitory and not always converted to a culture of permanent growth.

Gregory Clark has shown, taking Malawi as one case (with wider application elsewhere), how many Africans (the rural peasant societies most of all) have a purchasing power parity or standard of living of only about 40% of that found in England in 1800.[2] Nor is Malawi unique on these measures. Today it is far worse in several countries. Comparing per head income for 2005 in dollars adjusted for equivalence, Clark reports 17 countries in Africa at relative incomes then below the pre-1800 English level. Tanzania stood at 20%, Ethiopia 29%, Nigeria at 34% and Kenya at 54%.[3] Amid all the discourse and spin articulated about the economic upside of modernising Africa, these raw realities still stand out.

Thomas Hobbes once described life for many as "nasty, brutish, and short". Hobbesian conditions for many, in some countries the majority, have not been wholly excised from Africa's economies. The disruptive transition from the old subsistence realities may even have left many formerly traditional economies in a worse plight, with greater strategic vulnerability than before. The dynamics of change have likewise led to variances in subsistence income: what is required for survival in some parts of Africa does not always equate to the minimum needed elsewhere. In some places land abundance per rural household, whittled down over time, has now become one of relative scarcity. Many have become in effect landless with little or no claim on traditional rural assets, output or obligatory means of support. Indeed, the removal of many typical Malthusian checks on natural demography – through medicine or external support in times of agrarian failure – have paradoxically magnified pressures on material standards of living in several rural economies. Their "carrying capacities" have not always kept up with the economic demands placed upon them. As a result, lower-level Malthusian equilibrium incomes have not been unusual.

Many scourges widespread across Africa (drought-induced desertification and socially generated famine, with the ravages of disease) have not only induced wider economic fragility but also enforced low living levels that approximately equate to western Europe's rural impoverishment of hundreds of years ago, while real income levels remain about the same as those achieved in ancient Babylonia, Assyria and the classical world before Roman times. Indeed, several countries in Africa still have life expectancies at birth at or below those found in pre-1800 England (approximately 37 years). There is a long way to go to catch up. Under these circumstances, it is fatuous to believe that the economic growth recorded has had a universal or even beneficial impact. The recorded averages in income per head, implying improvement, often do not account for these residues and remnants of the hard-core medieval. In Africa, survival has often meant the survival of the richer or richest – a model now in full swing. This is likely to be Africa's leitmotif for the future.

The critical characteristic in Africa's slow transformation remains the high dependence on rudimentary agrarian pursuits and heavy reliance on one key asset: land resources (in Tanzania, 80% of the population).

Undervalued in market terms, land is the primary resource in most of Africa's arenas. Little is held under private property ownership as found in capitalist Africa or the West, with tradable qualities, transaction potential and instruments for monetising wealth. Lineage ownership and collective usage rights typically follow the dictates of kinship, hereditary chiefs and headmen. This world is quasi-feudal or pre-market in nature and pre-capitalist in structure, despite variable commercial links to wider markets. It will probably take the rest of the century, maybe longer, for fully fledged land markets to develop across Africa.

Socioeconomic pathologies

The easy manner in which many African political leaders have used the social mechanisms and long-established structures surrounding tradition and chiefdom (whether dressed in old or modern garb) to exert authority and control polities over long periods of time highlights how the antiquarian has merged into what appears to be the new. Ancient Africa is never far from the surface. Many leaders have invoked feudal mechanisms of control and power: Jean-Bédel Bokassa was a classic case of aggrandisement, Mobutu Sese Seko another, with megalomaniac pathology. Haile Selassie ushered an ancient dynasty with an imperial court into the modern age. Other politicians have sought dynastic continuity through the promotion of family members (in Equatorial Guinea, Egypt, Senegal, Gabon and Togo) – a contemporary case being Laurent and Joseph Kabila.

The pervasive evidence of presidential longevity and often lifetime authority in power in Africa has deep traditional roots. The average presidential age is high on world standards, while the young dominate the age pyramid. Gerontocratic political order is widespread, found in Angola, Zimbabwe, Senegal, Mali, Libya (till recently) and elsewhere. Africa's politicians are reluctant to step aside for a new generation of leaders. Many have manipulated constitutions to ensure power, seeking third terms even after earlier constitutions allowed for only two terms in office, like the president of Senegal. The 2011 "Arab spring" and changing of the guard in Egypt, Tunisia and Libya, if that is what it was, has been the first substantive threat to this long-established pattern. It could herald uncertainty in these economies as well as elsewhere when the time for leadership change comes, as it will if only by death (though this did not upset the dynastic apple cart in Gabon when President Omar Bongo was succeeded by President Ali Ben Bongo).

Old Africa's social orders juxtapose modernised variants in other ways too, beyond the formality of the state. Many countries exhibit the same apparent disorder in political dispensations, based on the local rules of power and control that prevailed in the past, though without carrying the implicit obligations to subjects typical of classic quasi-feudal structures: warlords, militia, privatised armies, rebel groups of many types, shantytown gangs and armed messianic cults (like the Lord's Resistance Army in Uganda), along with rebels controlling various mini-societies across Africa. Many "social states" (communities ruled locally) inhabit inaccessible parts of the continent under the aegis of local power elites, as in the Niger Delta, Puntland, the DRC, Darfur, the Ogaden and Somalia.

The numbers of dissidents, armed insurgents and rebel groups in Africa are still formidable, documented in *Les nouveaux mondes rebelles*, with their size, capacities and impacts shifting with the political landscapes.[4] Think today of those in the Niger Delta and Somalia, Uganda's dissident militia, more than 20 groupings in the DRC, Salafists in Algeria, militia in northern Côte d'Ivoire, Casamance, among the Tuareg, in South Sudan even after independence, eastern Chad and Darfur, the Polisario, in Cabinda, in the Ogaden, around Liberia and Guinea, and elsewhere, including in Abeyi and South Kordofan where the Nubia mountains have been the scene of bitter armed struggle. Al-Qaeda in the Islamic Maghreb (AQIM) is today a threat to many Sahel states, including southern Algeria and parts of Mauritania, as well as mines and tourism in Mali. Led by Abdelhamid Abou Zeid, AQIM is infamous for serial hostage taking and assassinations. Its nomadic operatives come replete with Kalashnikovs, rocket-propelled grenades and modern Land Cruisers, easily outgunning the ragtag armies sent in their pursuit. All this is not a recipe for guaranteed long-term stability.

Africa is no settled environment of liberalised economies or level political and economic playing fields. In the mix are vast spaces that remain the domains of local power brokers, as in the long-existing nomadic societies and their floating economic modes spanning the Sahara (the Tuareg across five border zones in the Sahara and Sahel). To the inexpert eyes of outsiders these vast domains appear to be owned by no one, but the many outcrops, wadis and oases are objects of ancient proprietary claims fiercely held by clans, nomads, wandering ethnicities and social groups. No-go zones, old demarcations and historic lines are invisible in the desert sand and to the outsider's eye. Here nation-state boundaries exert temporary, even fictitious control. The Sahel's wide latitudes and shifting boundaries, moulded by time and rainfall, broadly divide Africa's Muslims and Christians, contemporary nomads and agrarian societies, encapsulating around 50–60 million of Africa's peoples in ancient or old ways of existence. It was the tsetse fly that halted the horse- and camel-driven Muslim incursions south of the Sahara in older times, creating a semi-religious border across Africa in the process. Today insurgents can cross all these barriers in jeeps and with relative impunity.

In many of these ancient and modern variants of medieval-style Africa the state is nominal at best, its writ over their actions weak and to be kept at length. This arises in part from split allegiances within nation-states, with some groups unwilling to adhere to central authority. This helps to account for the success achieved in the creation of statelets like Somaliland and Puntland (Western Sahara may one day follow this path). These de facto states operate with varying degrees of legitimated personality and partial international recognition. More may emerge on Africa's stage in future. With the existence of the imperfect nation-state, economic fragmentation and future balkanisation could be on the cards in unexpected ways. It is not difficult to imagine another dozen states, statelets or semi-autonomous areas in Africa during the next half-century. An alternative might be realignment in national boundaries, though none of Africa's formal states appears predisposed to any grand pact along these lines. The seeds of Africa's widespread irredentism were planted long ago. Contested claims to autonomy are abundant. Many invoke obscure or eternal socioeconomic grievances to justify separatism: antecedent origins, old empires, kingdoms, language, land claims, water access, animal pasture rights, and even oil or mineral patrimony. In many conflicted zones, like the Sahel, Kalashnikovs have become the weapon of choice. As Paul Salopek puts it: "The Sahel represents the oldest killing field in human history. In the Sahel, Cain is still trading blows with Abel."[5]

In the half-millennium before the scramble for Africa in the late 19th century, most of Africa exhibited this mix of disparate claims and economic modes: small and large village economies, ethnic kingdoms, nomads in the Sahel, caravan traders across the Sahara, bands of hunter-gatherers, oasis-linked communities, forest-based peoples, Central African Pygmy economies of hunter-gatherers (as in the vast Ituri forest in modern Congo, the so-called "forest of death"), Khoi, San and Hottentots in Southern Africa, lake-fishing communities along the Rift Valley and around the deep arteries of Africa's vast rivers, and in many fragmented pre-capitalist peasant systems. Almost all want to stake some independent claim to modern Africa. In some instances this reflects the enduring desire for survival by mode of subsistence, rather than fealty to the modern centralised state. Although much has happened to change Africa in intervening years, significant parts of the continent retain active remnants of times past.

If you read the many reports on Africa's economies from the World Bank, the UN Economic Commission for Africa in Addis Ababa, or the African Union, you will find little recognition of these modes of subsistence and survival. These post-war modernist institutions treat Africa as one macro-entity, as if it existed as such, with disaggregation offered at best at the level of the nation-state, region or industry (energy, banking, tourism, services, and so on). The interpretations inevitably brush away Africa's raw on-the-ground realities. They express modernity alone, unconsciously displaying a marked unwillingness to come to grips with the fundamental conditions found in pre-market and even modern subsistence where raw conditions for social survival prevail. Although all these institutions do specific economic work on poverty and related development, little of substance finds its way into their main "state of Africa" styled proclamations.

Medieval and modern marriage

Modern Africa is not really "modern" at all. Rather, its old economic modes enjoy mutation within, alongside, or under the driving force of the installed capitalist economies. That does not make them modern *per se*. Despite rising dependence on monetisation, this too is no criterion of sufficiency in this regard: it is the level and nature of devolved practice and connections to subsistence mechanisms or survival levels that defines the non-modern on display.

If you look across Africa today even, there is plenty of evidence for this pre-modern situation. Chiefs play important roles in both the traditional and the modern political economy, especially in linkages to the state, straddling the economic worlds of both. As with modern states, myths of origin and legitimacy are used to sustain power and contemporary order. Though the same is true of Africa, the mythologies are different. In South Africa, the most modern state, this has been taken further to legitimate many traditional chiefs with the largesse of the state, funded by taxpayers, as with King Goodwill in Kwa-Zulu. President Jacob Zuma exudes traditionalism, partly through polygamy, while simultaneously acting as a modern head of state. This is a form of the contemporary production of tradition built on the actualisation or modification of ancient ways. Several societies exude endorsements of "nativism". Many older traditions have been maintained through membership societies, cults and religious practice and in totems, oathing and state ceremonies. Even Nelson Mandela felt obliged to make a *lobola* (bride price) payment (in this case in cattle) in respect of Graca Machel when they married. Much *lobola* nowadays has been monetised, modernised if you like, the old form remaining, the new different in substance.

Almost untouched traditions remain widespread in some parts of Africa, as found by Tim Butcher when in recent journeys tracing the paths of Graham Greene across Sierra Leone and Liberia he encountered the "devils" or masked figures guarding the spiritual secrets of the jungle communities, with some relying on ritual cannibalism as a source of power over man and the spirit world.[6] This is probably an extreme circumstance, yet it conveys to many the power of the old. The contemporary marriage of medievalism and modernity is a theme in V.S. Naipaul's latest work, *The Masque of Africa*, in which on visiting several African countries it is found that "magic", *sangoma* or *nganga* (traditional healers and spirit mediums), with reliance on and use of *muti* (medicine), ritual practice, animal slaughter and traditional religious ancestral worship, held considerable sway.[7] At the same time, oral histories provide myths and equally the means to modify or modernise them to suit new circumstances, especially in economic adversity.

Significant local power is still in the hands of Africa's chiefs, notably over economic practices and rights, making them like quasi-independent "vassal states". It is as if there were a multitude of micro-statelets within the conventional nation-state, the mix found in varying degrees across Africa following independence. In Africa's clan-controlled states this power typically devolves to elders. It is not uncommon in authoritarian regimes (Zimbabwe, for example) for the chiefs and their communities to be punished if there is rebellious nonconformity with the powers of the land – namely the chief, *chef*, Big Man, boss, president.

Not all assets have always been under communal or a chief's command. There existed in ancient Africa some limited de facto private property dimensions in terms of a few demarcated means of production, though this was cast inside wider networks of social obligation. In land rights, usufruct typically applied in the form of lineage ownership, and little has changed in this respect over hundreds of years. Yet land fragmentation or partial economic transformation can be found. In some countries land has been sold, rented or leased by traditional authorities on negotiated terms, which typically include payments for chiefs and headmen (effectively pay-offs), and even in some cases without central state permission.

Across the continent, core ethnic affiliations allied to old economic interests often lie beneath conflicts, with economic growth miracles doing little to reshape primordial social identities. Western implanted modernities have had only around one century to flower on African soil. Most primary affiliations are far older than any of the looser identities forged around Africa's nation-states, their resilience affirmed by social fissuring experienced this decade in Côte d'Ivoire, Kenya, Sudan, Libya and elsewhere. Residual composites of old kingdoms, courts, dynasties, sultanates and even princes (many in Nigeria) remain present in large parts of the continent. A few are throwbacks to the time of older caliphates. Many of these medieval institutions perpetuate the semi-feudal relationships in the modern era, typically with state orchestration, some translated into the economic realm and politics, their influence not negligible. Millions of African villages (or kraals) are still primarily controlled by chiefs and headmen, clans or cohorts.

The Dark Continent's formal nation-states enclose not only the traditional authorities from centuries past but also many de facto statelets, combined with multiple zones of often shifting irredentism. This could lead to greater balkanisation. Yet against this tide are found pressures seeking to hold Africa together. There is a tug of war afoot. Africa may not achieve classical equilibrium in its nation-state structures for many decades, even in this century. If this is so, there may be continuing instability – and an unstable future.

I O

State complexities

Human societies have created political structures or states since time immemorial. Even in Olduvai there would have been some type of implied consensus or writ, about which the record is absent. Typically political forms have reflected societies' own image, and the origins of Africa's states have been etched in time with lineage, Big Men and authoritarianism as prominent features. Some states have explicitly limited property rights. Others have enhanced them, thereby setting down boundaries and economic limits, trapping their future in history – a view well articulated by Francis Fukuyama in *The Origins of Political Order*.[1]

State evolution has never been linear. It is more chaotically sequential than many would like to assume. In Africa this allows us to understand the coexistence of the medieval with the modern, not just in economic shape but also in the political economy. In a simplistic account it might be inferred that many societies in Africa went from small bands to larger "tribes" to post-colonial nation-states, and partially back again, in an *etatism* based on reversion to type in state evolution. Centralisation of authority and control over the means of coercion helped define this process. It has been one in which Africa's states have become more hierarchical, elite-based, stratified and unequal. Modern nation-states were brought into Africa, not born in Africa, in a form of cohabitation or mixture with tradition.

Often as products of occupation and imperial coercion, most of Africa's states bear the marks of this mixed marriage of imposed, and at times self-determined, malformation. Lineages of founding ethnicities have often translated into monarchic or secular dynasties of sorts. The sheer geographies of Africa have complicated this evolutionary consequence. Once colonialism dissolved, the return to patrimonial control and governance with political decay was almost inevitable. This time it has emerged within conventional, if mostly artificial, nation-state boundaries.

Political economy of control

The specifics of the state have captured attention in writings on Africa. States provide the overarching architecture governing economic conditions. Some perceptive thought here comes from French schools of political economy and anthropology. It was Jean-François Bayart who coined the term *la politique du ventre* (the politics of the belly) to describe Africa's paradigm in *The State in Africa*.[2] The work sets out a non-dependency approach, with Africa positioned not as a victim but as the creator of its own circumstances, long involved and implicated in its own extraversion or engagement with the outside world. Africa's authoritarian regimes exploited *la politique du ventre* in their own interests. Dominant classes operated to forge commercial advantage, the state becoming the mode for execution of these strategies. Accordingly, democracy from the early 1990s onwards has largely been a fairy story.

Africa's political spheres have been almost invisible to outsiders. Western chancelleries deal with formal institutions, while Africa has made its economic decisions behind closed doors. The post-colony is a sort of Potemkin village in action, with symbolic gestures of reform and compliance made to donors and foreign institutions. These practices have a long history, all the way back to slavery when it was key to Africa's enrichment for the political classes and compradors of the time. They account for many a coastal elite's command over the hinterlands, as in Angola, Guinea-Bissau, Tanzania and elsewhere. Successive waves of globalisation have permitted these cleavages to be enhanced and differentiation to emerge. Contrary to images of comprehensive colonial command, vast areas in Africa were left to their own devices:

in Chad, Angola, Sudan, Congo and elsewhere. The vacuum provided space for local power players. Once the colonists exited, these political forces re-emerged into the sunlight. The public and private, argues Bayart, have never been wholly separated in Africa, allowing for later flawed privatisation of the state. Meanwhile, many African wars have been instruments of in-group regulation and accumulation, rather than measures to forge nation-states along the post-Westphalian lines found in Europe. The state salariat also indulged in this primitive accumulation. Hybrid states, many led by presidents accumulating fortunes, emerged in consequence. The looting of the state was often spectacular. Measures to mislead the foreign master became normal conduct, actions by day reversed at night, invisible to the outsider.

Africa's constitutions have long been subject to negotiation, convertibility and malleability with state apparatchiks in the role of mediating gatekeepers. Following independence, the extraversion of commercial relationships with the outside world converted to the quest for local hegemonies, with Africa's elites seeking commercial benefit and control. These initiatives opened new pathways and means of existence, many under the guise of the state. The global pathology on Africa as dependent and subservient has served as a useful alibi for many functionaries. Foreign scholars entrenched this view, seeing the domestic economic formations only as bricks in the construction of capitalism in Africa, and not as continuing entities with fundamental aims of subsistence, survival and more.

Ancient societies and economies have never been monolithic in Africa, as often depicted in the Western historical narrative. Many an escape route from one economic locus for survival to another has been evident. Where economic backwardness has existed it has often been a consequence of many constraints and often deliberate choices, led by the benefits accruing to some of competitive failure, and not as an eternal condition. Western models have not recognised that many of Africa's states moved closer over time to the ways and functionalities of ancient antecedents. Informalisation in Africa has grown rapidly, and this feature of state structures has often been turned into an economic turnpike for informal income and wealth accumulation. Contracts and special deals have proliferated inside and outside the state apparatus and its enlarged economic nexus. Often officials openly operate business directly with state machines, a common malaise in contemporary South Africa, from ministers to bureaucrats.

There is little separation of the corporate and the state milieu in many parts of Africa. This has led to kleptocracy and grand larceny, as was common in Zaire under Mobutu Sese Seko. It reflects the notion that the struggle for power and the state is essentially one for wealth and accumulation. "Our turn to eat" is the metaphor for this practice. One consequence has been the decline in productivity in the state systems around the continent. It places the state in the role of the merchant house for acquisition. For many, the state reflects an opportunity to secure commercial involvement with central governments and municipalities; these corrosive economic impacts are rarely addressed in economic reforms. In many cases commercial factions, networks, clans or mafia align in temporary or permanent syndicates to carry out this plunder. Usually the president must be more enriched than others, as a sign of power. This is well known and certainly reaches *radio trottoir* (pavement radio) and the "little men" of the street, who understand better than the outsider the cultural underside of economic machinations.

Whether one argues that similar actions occur elsewhere or not, there is more than meets the eye to the meaning and nature of the modern state apparatus found in Africa. These proto-modern entities rest on still-existing autochthonous social foundations. Nation-states in Africa have endured a short lifespan.

The argument presented here contrasts with that of those who see the partition of Africa and the outcome of the 1884–85 Berlin Conference to divide Africa into spheres as the primary (or almost sole) source of contemporary difficulties, as the "curse of Berlin", a harbinger to change that somehow "retarded socioeconomic development" in Africa.[3] They claim that colonial powers like the French had a *chasse gardée* with established dominions firmly established on the map, and a century of pestilence followed, with Eurocentrism at the helm even after decolonisation. In this is seen, implausibly, the reason for the absence of Pax Africana.

From this have emerged myopic calls for rectifying boundary

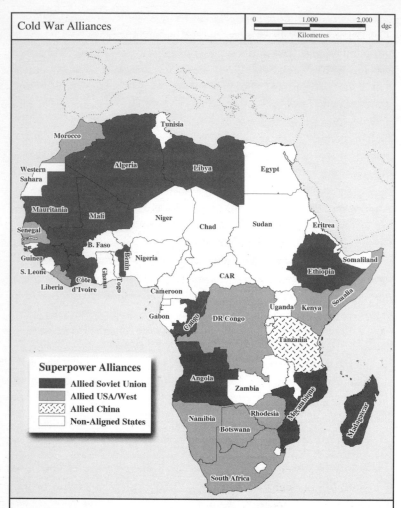

Cold War Alliances

0   1,000   2,000
Kilometres

dgc

Superpower Alliances
- Allied Soviet Union
- Allied USA/West
- Allied China
- Non-Aligned States

Cold War client states littered Africa. USSR/Western and Sino-Soviet conflicts, in ideology and periodic hot wars, created a heavy toll on Africa's economies. Many post-Soviet appendages took years to recover from faulted economic pathways. Western powers largely retained commercial interests after the fall of the Berlin Wall. Russia waited for over a decade to return to Africa, focused on business. China shredded its ideologies and began large-scale mercantilist lunges into Africa in the 21st century.

distortions with a continental *indaba* to realign "bedevilled Africa". This is a most unlikely expectation. The hand of history will play a more profound role. In these romantic and nostalgic images, Africa's paradise was lost as Bismarck, with Europe, committed the geopolitical equivalent of the "original sin": the chancellor united the Germans, but divided Africa. Such views stand against the tide of history, which cannot be undone, and outside an appreciation of realpolitik.

This "curse" thesis represents the displacement of economics to the benefit of the political: it sees Africa as victim only, in an argument that goes against the evidence of economic empiricism worldwide, and raises the question of what brought Africa its malformed modernity. A more radical version of the thesis claims that colonialism actually pre-empted and even reversed modernity in Africa, in an inversion of well-established and widely shared conclusions about that epoch of world economic expansion.[4] The argument is that modernity might have happened anyway and the colonial project retarded the inevitable progressive tide. These ideas express extreme hope beyond reasonable expectation: they stand contrary to the economic record on growth and capital investment in Africa (on which almost all economists agree). These are not the only revisionist ideas to be found on Africa over which the intellectual conflict has matched others.

Kaleidoscope

Many insights on Africa's states may be gleaned from analysts of its political world. John Reader's *Africa: A Biography of the Continent* is a work of grandeur that examines Africa on a macro-historic scale, reminding us of its epochs in the making and its truly vast dimensions.[5] The text is dominated by a detailed panoramic overview of mankind's early footsteps in Africa, ancestral economies and evolution in civilisations across the landmass, with interfaces built through trading, slavery and colonialism. It clearly elucidates how the past influenced the present, the ancient roots of Africa's societies, and the problematic and continuing lurch towards modernity.

Our modern era is merely a footnote to this panoramic setting, one in which Africa's initial dreams of modernity turned to nightmares as 70 coups in 32 states marked the 37-year period from 1960 to the overthrow of President Mobutu in 1997. More coups and instability with serious conflicts have followed. By 2010 sub-Saharan Africa had experienced 81 military coups and at least 125 further failed attempts. Most recent have been more military coups and the nightmares of Côte d'Ivoire, North Africa's spring, continuing havoc in the DRC, and the split of the Siamese twins of Sudan and South Sudan. Electoral coups might be added to this list.

Today Africa's states have large official armies, military reserves, paramilitaries, presidential guards, security forces and militia of informal sorts. Algeria has 484,200 people in these categories, Eritrea 321,700, Ethiopia 138,000 and Nigeria 162,000. Africa-wide there are around 2 million or more people under arms inside this military complex. We must add to this total rebel entities and dissidents of all sorts. One lesson is that we should not necessarily expect a stable Africa to be the norm.

Many reasons why the state of the continent reached an impasse over the last half-century are detailed in other chronologies.[6] One depicts how hope in the 1960s changed to realism in the 1970s, decay in the next decade, with new directions sought in the 1990s. Strongmen, wars, corruption, poverty and manipulations by Great Powers brought Africa to its knees, a supplicant for aid and charity, the continent distinguished only as the world's poorest. Is this the harbinger of more to come in the 21st century? Imperialism was seen to have cast a long shadow, external pressures combining with internal failures in leadership to cripple its hopes. For one observer, "Africa has little influence and less power, a fact that attracts major powers like vultures to a carcase to be exploited."[7] Hope was once placed in an African Renaissance, but caution is required here: it needs to be funded by the West. Paradoxically, the fanfare on this grand scheme, led by Thabo Mbeki with presidents Obasanjo and Wade, has largely dissipated. The message was that Africa must control its own game. Would control be enough? Not really: to survive and prosper, Africa must be competitive in a globalised world.

Writers and political analysts have long sought to diagnose the causes of the crisis and dissect the dramas plaguing black Africa over 50 years of independence.[8] This was a time of the "second scramble" for Africa, a struggle for power, from the mid-20th century onwards – more tumultuous than the original scramble of the late 19th century. Within a generation around 10,000 African polities were sublimated or amalgamated into around 40 colonies and protectorates, the so-called early-modern states of Africa. At the end of the Second World War only Egypt (a corrupt monarchy under British tutelage), Ethiopia (a feudal empire), Liberia (a decaying republic founded by freed American slaves and run as an outpost of the plantation system) and South Africa (under minority white control, soon to embark on apartheid) were not under direct imperial rule, exercised by a mere handful of foreign powers. Within a decade, blown by the winds of change, most colonies were swept towards statehood while the Cold War intensified across Africa. Independence proved a cruel gift, for some a poisoned chalice.

By the early 21st century Africa's prospects seemed bleaker than before. It suffered at the hands of Big Men and ruling elites whose aims to hold power (using patrimonial systems) primarily led to self-enrichment. Acquired wealth was liberally squandered on economic folly, luxury and excess, with the culture of corruption pervading all levels of society, costing an estimated $148 billion annually (25% of Africa's GDP, according to an African Union report). The new elite-controlled players entering the political firmament rapidly adopted the habits of their predecessors, leading some to wonder if this was some form of internal "sub-imperialism".

For many states the narrative was one of predatory politics for personal gain and the hollowing out of public institutions. Apparatchiks were enriched, the masses forgotten. In examining wealth and income inequalities across Africa, empirical evidence for this reality is not hard to find. Several authors have commented on the unequal outcomes found in states with "black gold" – Angola's war and the venality of the ruling *nomenklatura* is an oft-cited instance. There have been huge costs in ruptured lives and resource mismanagement, an issue that has attracted considerable contemporary critique, in an analytical context often much misunderstood.[9] Its manifestations were replicated in other places. Many foreign writers lament such conditions and Africa's plentiful deficiencies. Yet we must remember that over more than a century the shift from multiple pre-colonial societies to a few narrowly controlled regimes has been one of the most dramatic intertemporal shifts in history.

In today's medievalism abundant forms of traditionalism (ethnicity, patronage, with patrimonial practices) have been applied as mechanisms to capture the "liberated" nation-state, almost always contested among Africa's power elites. It is not always the case that Africa's residual institutions (chiefdoms, lineage, ancient agrarian economies and old cosmologies) were completely at the service of incumbent elites and predisposed only to agendas moulded around predation in its citadels of power. The power of the old ways remains, even if dressed in modern garb. This nexus stands between the past and the future sought by more sophisticated and techno-competent middle classes. We should take care not to neglect the complex internal economic shapes that make up the Africa matrix. It could take many generations for this debilitating form of hybrid political economy to erode. In the interim the associated patronage, patrimonialism, nepotism and corruption may continue to distort economic growth and modernisation.

Many political intricacies have shaped shifts in power within the states across the continent.[10] In almost all countries, patronage has been in the hands of Africa's political gatekeepers, as modern temporal powers linked to the external world as one form of continuity in world historical experience. Challenges to such control became the norm. The commandeering of the post-colonial state led from 1960s optimism to later pessimism as this political artefact gave way to retribalised cultures of authoritarianism within the enfeebled state machines.

The complexities of Africa's politics are difficult to diagnose and straitjacket, so that no single model can be found. Africa's inheritance at decolonisation may have presented a poisoned chalice in one locale and a cup of plenty elsewhere. Pan-African ideals (another still pervasive myth among political elites) rapidly wilted as irredentism surfaced along with secessionism. The continent splintered into competing factions. New elites asserted primacy and control by contesting the institutions of state power. In most cases it is remarkable how Africa's contestation then was not only about economic issues *per se*: in almost all states politics has been heavily underpinned by struggles over identity, in-group primacy and ethnicity, which are deployed widely as vehicles to capture the state and retain power. The crushing of formal traditional powers (chiefs, monarchs and ethnic minorities) was sometimes part of this agenda, allied to the toxic mix of militarism, Marxism (with brands of African socialism) and a few pliant client enclaves founded from 1960 onwards during the Cold War.

Khaki fatigue eventually set in as military and liberation movements entered the ministries of Africa to harvest the bitter fruits of social struggle, resulting in many economic failures. During the 1980s and early 1990s, structural adjustment administered by the Bretton Woods institutions was proffered as the cure, causing retrenchment and taken as a curse by leaderships that became adept at stalled reforms and pseudo-democracy in the 1990s. As the medicine proved indigestible, many crises worsened.

Finally, the continent became a prime target for the benevolence of numerous NGOs (Africa's fifth estate), often seen as new imperialists by some Africans. In the local milieu and spaces vacated by imperfect states, a wide range of organisations (traditional entities, churches, voluntary associations, social groups, issue-oriented claimants) emerged to fill the void. Popular protests, elite mobilisation and multipartyism became the order of the day in many arenas. This sweep towards democracy was still-born. Many a political dinosaur, patriarch and father figure left the political stage in the 1990s (some returning later), often through hastily convened national conferences, as in francophone Africa, yet the democratic space soon closed again.

Despite its nominal unitary state architecture (in principle intended to consolidate authority), Africa was more varied at the turn of the new millennium than at any point since the initial scramble – the result of internal fiefdoms, warlords and warring factions within failing states. These conflicts were mostly shaped around identity, ethnicity and inherent state legitimacy. The political context set the framework around which economic modernity arose. If nothing else, this tells us that the inherent dynamism of the past 50 years of political whirlwinds will probably remain as the *longue durée* continues. This time many states have the largesse that resources could (but will not necessarily) offer in the quest for greater stability. It would be a grave misjudgement to assume that any "end of history" has been reached in Africa. "Flat Africa" has never existed – and it is most unlikely to in future.

Africa has a bewildering variety of states in a constant process of adaptation. Some almost constitute mega-states (for example, Angola, Sudan, the DRC, Ethiopia, Nigeria and South Africa) – all sizeable, all with modern industries and all with large populations.[11] Evidence to the turn of century revealed that these big states had not performed well, their dysfunctions apparent and their performance contrary to the myth that "bigger is better". Warped conditions and general underperformance were connected to leadership conflict, rebellions and wars, looted commodities (minerals and oil some) and failures in international governance and best practice. Africa's six largest states account for nearly 60% of all Africans, with Nigeria perhaps mattering most in terms of oil and population and South Africa as the continental anchor economy.

Size is but one variable to consider among others. Many small or micro-states have fallen on hard times and endured deep crises in Africa – notably Lesotho, Liberia, Swaziland and Eritrea. In large and imperfect states (Angola, Nigeria and Sudan) there are other optics to consider. Their futures look likely to differ structurally from those of the DRC, Ethiopia and South Africa. In Nigeria today, 67% of the labour force toil in agriculture, little of it modern by any degree, and real incomes for the bottom 60% of households have barely moved over the last 30–40 years. While income per head there was 8% of the US level in 1960, today it is under 2% – one measure of decline and relative backwardness. Each state thus has its own path and economic trajectory: the claims for scalar determinism are weak.

The uneven character of African states is evident from many country studies. The old colonies of metropolitan Portugal – Guinea-Bissau, Cape Verde, São Tomé and Príncipe, Moçambique and Angola – illustrate the different legacies of empire.[12] Lusophone Africa was built on the back of 500 years of Portuguese engagement in Africa. The contrasts between each Lusophone state are substantial, reflecting their varied circumstances and divergent post-colonial histories. Modern trajectories followed abrupt ruptures from Lisbon, the seat of a backward imperial power that rapidly decolonised following the Portuguese coup of April 1974. It is another instance of Europe's dynamics shaping Africa's legacies.

All these Lusophone-led, later revolutionary states acquired their independence built on centralised Marxism. The models withered when confronted with rude economic realities on the ground. While the ideologies fought for may have differed from the outcomes sought by British and French neocolonial collusion elsewhere with elected elites, they became degraded nonetheless. In effect they reverted to type, suggesting that Africa should be viewed as a fragmented world, a complex story. The experience shows us why Africa's states should not be lumped into one basket according to their former colonial powers.

It is instructive to reflect on the external forces that shaped Africa from outside the West, notably the former Soviet Union/Russia (only now elucidated in the literature outside the Russian language).[13] Many of Africa's links with Russia over the centuries were almost invisible. But in several ways, Russia shaped many an African legacy. In Leninist and Stalinist views, Africa featured as largely unknown and exotic, its revolutionary credentials often discredited. Soviet engagements were primarily opportunistic. Soviet presence and involvement connected little with any resource extraction, being more driven by ideology. Many thousands of Soviet technicians and military advisers entered Africa during the Cold War, when Marxist ideology was the core business of many states. Now the ideology of Russian engagement in Africa is business, with minerals and oil high on the 21st-century agenda.

Soviet aims were to shape the political climate and influence local regimes in power. The Soviets supported surrogates in Ghana, Guinea, Mali, Algeria, Egypt, Congo, Ethiopia, Somalia, the People's Republic of Zanzibar and around the critical cockpit of conflicts in Southern Africa (in Zambia, Moçambique, Zimbabwe and Angola). They tended and financed multiple factions within African liberation movements.

The Soviet Union and Cuba acted in tandem, especially in Angola where residues of this intervention can be observed in the military-political and economic complex. Soviet legacies are still evident in the one-party state syndrome that found Africa's minority-oriented elites receptive to authoritarianism.

Africa slipped off the post-Soviet radar screen for some years, with Russia re-emerging in Africa only during the 21st century. In the hiatus, Africanists inside the Russian elite took a back seat to the new orientation of Russia on the world stage. The Africa "experts", or *africanistika*, in Russia have long been clear that the country's interests in Africa are driven by state policy. Scientific socialism never took lasting root on the lines of Soviet models inside Africa (Mengistu in Ethiopia being its most ardent adherent). The Soviets exhibited little practical regard for the vast majorities that composed Africa's medieval world, except as pawns in the global struggle with the West (and in Sino-Soviet fratricide waged in Africa). Today a similar realpolitik drives the interests of Russian companies and Kremlin-style diplomacy.

Russia's acquired knowledge of Africa was designed largely to serve its Kremlin masters, this having been eroded as the axis of the country's engagement with Africa in the past separated in the mists of time. I would predict, however, a more extensive Russian hand in Africa's oil and gas future, shaped by its state companies, especially Gazprom, already in Algeria, Equatorial Guinea and Libya, with Nigeria and Angola as key targets.

Many foreigners, especially Americans, have encountered a duality of hope and tragedy amid complexity in their Africa sagas.[14] Some have seen Africa's embrace by the West as one of betrayal and disaster, aided and abetted by African leaders in exploitative machinations over resources. The West has often been accused of acting as if Africa had no history other than that of Europe in Africa. Observers often generalise on finding hope in the dignity of ordinary Africans, crushed by naked power and extortion exercised from Abuja, Brazzaville, Kinshasa, Monrovia, Kigali and Bamako as well as in the recesses of the interior by warlords and assorted plutocrats. The end result is disappointment about the promise of hope perceived in Africa's future. This, I suggest, is too pessimistic: it reflects the often undiluted expectations of foreigners about Africa, which is very much a work in progress.

Many outsiders are mystified as to why this continent of promise does not perform to another's dream. The dream is replaced by damnation when the dreamer finds that Africa just does not accord with their expectations. It is apposite to the failed state syndrome, a complex one, and almost Africa's leitmotif. Things have fallen apart in many societies, and some attribute this disorder in the late 20th century and even now to the foundations of the state, which has lacked the revenues to administer fractious polities, so making predation more rewarding than stable governance. There are shreds of truth in this optic except for the fact that sufficient revenue generation from Africa has not been always lacking: its retention in Africa and proper usage have more often been amiss. Moreover, the shallow roots of Africa's state are often unappreciated abroad. Mystification at sudden state collapse or catastrophism thus becomes almost inevitable.

What then really drives Africa's political paradigm? According to renowned French thinkers, no conventional order exists.[15] The model in practice is said to be one in which the political elites in Africa maximise their gains (maintenance of power being one of them) directly from the orchestrated state of uncertainty, confusion and chaos that reigns in many polities. According to this explanation, Africa has undeveloped, weak institutional structures, where informal and elite-controlled systems are the dominant characteristics set against a background of economic failure, with corruption the norm amid widespread retraditionalisation. These systems shape the continent's multiple crises of modernity, while African politics appears inimical to development as envisaged by the Western or Cartesian mindset.

This diagnosis has some merits but there is no unmitigated uncertainty always found within all African states. The informal operates alongside significant formalism (bureaucracies riddle the continent); more African companies exist that seek the virtues of productivity and aspire to world-class standards; and corruption is not the only "Africa way". The existence of traditional mores and customs is a deeper issue, one that has long been there but finds new expression inside African polities. The modern manifestations of traditional practice in statecraft and economic strategy in Africa should not be neglected or forgotten. They evoke a mixed paradigm: one modern but simultaneously medieval in nature. It may not reflect a marriage made in heaven, but it is the marriage made in Africa.

Informalism and illicit network-driven challenges to the orthodox state shape historical drama in parts of this continent.[16] There is evidence of the private (sometimes semi-state) interfaces of smuggling and fraud, the plunder of natural resources allied to "privatisation" in state institutions (often without actual privatisation) and the growth of private armies across the continent. Many illicit networks have global linkages, with the use of public office for private gain widespread. Crime has proliferated and is found to be strongly linked to political disorder, while the deformities of economic space have allowed corruption to flourish. Parts of sub-Saharan Africa may be returning to the proverbial heart of darkness through "shadow economies". Locals with foreigners forge felonious state connections in modes of predation, war and extraction. While plenty of cases justify this view (the DRC above all) they do not provide a full account of Africa's economic realities.

Congo collapse

The tale told of the Congo basin in the "modern" Democratic Republic of Congo may offer a lesson for those wishing to "see" inside one part of Africa. Tim Butcher's compelling travelogue *Blood River: A Journey to Africa's Broken Heart* is about a modern-day roughshod journey along the course of Congo River in the footsteps of Henry Morton Stanley (who did this in the 1870s). It amply portrays the present scene in Africa's largest state.[17] The Congo River is over 4,500 km long (excluding its many tributaries) and sits in a basin larger than the whole of India. This gargantuan river "swallows all rivers" and casts an awesome shadow within the heart of Africa, the natural analogue to Joseph Conrad's tale of deprivation. The Congo has rarely been a land at peace. Its enduring history has been one of menace and still is today. Its peoples have weathered slavery from several quarters (Arab and Portuguese, Belgian and African). The contemporary economic structure is one of a failing and fractured state, its past glories long eroded, with new edifices needed to patch together this impoverished quilt of fragmented subsistence entities.

In this forested and disparate set of ecologies there are almost no paved roads to be found any more outside urban centres, colonial roadways having returned to overgrown footpaths at best. Perhaps around 1% of the roads built during the colonial era have remained in the entire country. Memories of slaughter, genocide, atrocity, mercenaries and even cannibalism are fresh. Tutsi/Hutu social divides, Congolese and Banyamulenge power struggles, inter-ethnic wars, Rwandan and Ugandan troop incursions, Mai Mai marauders and continuing conflicts (usually many more than one) have been its modern manifestation amid the usual trappings of prosperity for a few indigene and foreign investors. For all its richness in minerals and resources, this Congo – call it DRC if you like, another figment of the modern imagination, for it is neither democratic nor a classic republic – is still a zone run by combinations of gendarmerie, military, security forces, rebels and police, with UN forces in the east. By no means all power is in the hands of the nominal state that carries its latest name. Little is truly modern about this land, and its presumed status as a functioning state is a charade belied by episodic collapse and internal discord.

UN peacekeeping forces struggle to maintain a semblance of control in and around the Great Lakes, which the Kinshasa government evidently cannot. Local fiefdoms operate for self-preservation. The Congo basin is home to around 200 ethnicities, say contemporary anthropologists – operating in a free-for-all manner, as a sort of anarchic self-help system. Even pre-colonial balances between chiefs and subjects eroded long ago through Mobutu's ruthless rule, a cult of personality that elevated *les grosses légumes* (Mobutu's fat cats) to positions of power, pillage and rapacious influence. As one interlocutor remarked wryly, "Where logic ends, the Congo begins."[18]

Can we really take seriously the proclamations about Congo made in macroeconomics as a reflection of the real world found here? I think not.

The gigantic Congo arena does not correspond to the norms promoted by modern economic theory, the long-lost Washington consensus, OECD visions on Africa, or even edicts emanating from a far-distant African Union. The ethos of the market-driven and rule-based world has retreated inside this uneven economic landscape.

Some find relative safety or security provided by the group, goons or the gun. Others seek their sanctuaries of escape from these tyrannies of modernity inside primeval forests and hidden recesses afforded by the bush. Butcher, traversing the Congo in the 21st century, finds a country in evident structural decline. It is splattered with old, backward communities, fragmented and "undeveloping" demi-mondes hidden in a decaying and disfigured history, much of it warped by anarchy and plunder from militia. Most inhabitants hang onto a grim subsistence at levels almost unchanged from the time of villages and mud huts observed by Stanley in the 19th century.[19] Very little appears to have changed in large parts of this Congo in the long epoch since Africa's greatest explorer walked across this vast terrain. Yet it has done so, as the recent testaments of some formidable authors inform us.

We must not forget that many a Cold War warrior of convenience was born in Africa. The old Congo (modern DRC) had its chaotic condition influenced heavily and disastrously by Mobutu's Zaire.[20] Congo's story has been one of rampant kleptocracy and contradictions at the heart of this pseudo-state, with a populace left in (almost literal) darkness. It is not merely a caricature of one individual responsible for this entire collapse. Zaire's freefall required the complicity of thousands of ethnic and co-opted collaborators inside the country, Africa's elites from elsewhere and meddling foreign powers. It is a history of internal machinations and outside interference that may have left the cowed Congolese acquiescent to rampant state power. Mobutu cultivated myth and omnipotence, traits found elsewhere among some of Africa's politicians today. Many find little right in this maelstrom, and are ultimately confounded by earlier images portraying the country as an ordered colonial society. It seemed as if Africa had to deconstruct before it could be built again, a process alien to the Western mind. Expectation provided no indicator of the shambles that Zaire became or the makings of the failed state that the DRC inherited. Our images of Africa, the lesson suggests, should certainly never remain static. It is another reminder that development in Africa is not guaranteed, even in what should be prosperous states: Zimbabwe's implosion is a signal indicator.

Analysis on the Congo-DRC conflicts, the genocide in Rwanda and the involvement of several African armies in this conflict helped unravel Congo's mixed polities and failed-state syndrome. Anyone who has had trouble making sense of the complicated drama that has endured since 1996 should join the queue.[21] Many forces were at work: the multiple intricacies of ethnic conflicts, warlordism, pillage and interventionist politics that remade the eastern Congo, north and south Kivu, and its Great Lakes region of porous frontiers alongside six African states. There is no guarantee that these volcanic social eruptions could not happen again. Wars and serial atrocities this century (maybe 5 million casualties by some counts) have imprinted a legacy of disorder and deprivation wholly incomprehensible to the outsider. Here the ultimate apocalypse flowed from state collapse as opportunity gave way to the political economy of pillage. It is enough to make some recall the misty and illusive benefits of Mobutism, perhaps one reason why Big Man rule has been associated with relative "stability" in Africa, if scored merely on the years of longevity racked up by so many politicians.

Efforts to establish normalcy in Africa have been manifold, with UN forces, foreign funding, EU election finance and the usual well-intentioned Western initiatives among them. They have not succeeded, and the Congolese will, one day, have to make order out of this chaos. This untamed heart of Africa, a vast terrain drained by the Congo River, could someday be an economic powerhouse. But this cornucopia may be a long time in coming, as in Moçambique, which at least illustrated that adversity can be reversed on a slow, if rocky, road to economic recovery.

Anyone who claims to know the Congo should think again unless they have read Gerard Prunier's detailed portrait in *Africa's Great War*, a modern tale of unremitting conflict, mayhem, multiple militia at work, foreign African armies ensconced in Congo with predatory and punitive intent, rampant economic decline, political and human catastrophe, and grisly consequences.[22] Congo is undergoing a vast transformation with differential modernity edging its way slowly forwards. It is morphing out of earlier clichés into unknown shapes. There is no need to try to "explain" this past decade-and-a-half of the Congo's recidivism, the drama continuing, to those who can read this intimate story of a "country" on the skids. It is a lesson not only about state fragility, failure and decline, but equally about what has gone wrong in the economics and understanding of Africa's largest "nation-state".

The economic costs to Congo and to Central Africa have been huge. Millions have been pushed to the edge of survival and as many others to premature death. This apocalypse has taken place far from the faded modernities of Kinshasa and Lubumbashi and the mines and plantations that remain scattered across the impoverished landscape and lush tropical rainforests. The resource potential of Congo in minerals, potentially oil, and natural bounty is immense, yet standards of living for 90% of the population are among the world's lowest.

Even so, I have seen this Congo paradigm of minimal material change replicated in many parts of Africa, including in so-called modern states. The tragic story is not unique. There are many places and states evoking similar tales with Malthusian status. You need only to travel the hinterlands and byways, off the roads and into the vast spaces of Africa's worlds of origin, its rural heartlands, to witness this predicament. Several countries and areas I visited 40 years ago and since have advanced not an iota in economic terms and remain today just like they had been perhaps a century before. Some have even slipped backwards.

State origins

To understand how Africa's political and state collage and its foreign nexus have formed, it is necessary to return to the distant past. Answers relate to the epicentres of modernity, their geopolitical distribution, the question of who sits atop them, and how they emerged in these domains. Africa's collection of modern states had long gestation patterns. They were moulded inside the global history of exploration and empire-making as part of a larger world canvas. If we delve far enough into Africa's history, there were many incursions by predatory proto-states pre-dating European colonisation: Moroccans crossing the Sahel to conquer the Kingdom of Songay in 1591, the establishment of Islamic theocracies in northern Africa, and a multitude of rivalries and conflicts between Africa's pre-colonial polities, warrior states and kingdoms. They too shaped the modern in socio-political Africa.

The emergence of the continent into the world system was deeply entwined with the ascendance of Europe's empires, which absorbed old regimes and brought forth myriad post-colonial states. It was a confused, heavily contested and chance-ridden passage of history. In Africa today, competition for resources and markets partly reflects these older imperial thrusts. Forays into Africa sprang equally from merchant networks, the wanderings of explorers, scholarly interest and cultural fusions between Africans in power and the rest of world. The dramas of empire creation and dissolution across the Eurasian land mass had little impact on Africa except in the Maghreb under Ottoman rule from Constantinople. By the 1570s Ottoman grip on North Africa matched the scale of Roman conquests in times before. This empire on African soil was eventually eroded only in the early 20th century. An Egyptian domain had been carved out in Sudan and as far south as Equatoria towards modern Uganda over 1821–79. The opening of the maritime commons, however, transformed the geopolitics of empire and laid the foundations of globalisation, which later became of great significance to Africa's modern world.

During the 1830s the British were the first to imagine a global market, inspired by Adam Smith (*The Wealth of Nations*, 1776) and rampant mercantilism. Marx and Lenin also had aspirations, albeit different ones regarding world political order. Militant ideas and armed acolytes also shaped Africa's domains. While the defunct views of 19th-century thinkers might have worn away, their interests have not, as witnessed by the long struggle over Africa's markets and resources. It was the source of slaves from Africa that counted most, pre-Renaissance demand initially driven from Arabia and later with Europe implicated, in a trade forged by Iberian success in opening the New World. Residual traces of Spanish and Creole cultures remain around the continent, notably in Angola, Equatorial Guinea and São Tomé and Príncipe, but also in East Africa. African colonisation came late onto the world stage, the neo-Europe created in the Cape an exception to this delayed foray. Ultimately, the reach of Europe's empires stretched far and wide, sweeping around Africa and inland, edging out Arab-influenced African empires (Islam having broken into Sudanic Africa south of the Sahara from the 11th century). Both moulded Africa's proto-modernity, reinforcing separation from ancient models of existence.

America's engagement with Africa remains modern, with the country primarily entering these domains as Europe's empires faded after the Second World War. As we have seen, Russia's demarche under the Soviet flag was mainly political, ideological and military in nature; it was only in the 21st century that it took on dimensions connected to investment, significantly in minerals, oil and gas. Chinese and Indian intrusions, although somewhat aggressive, are of recent vintage. In this game early advantage went to Europe's state and private companies or national champions. Today there are more challengers on Africa's soil. While Europe modernised, its colonies remained mostly pre-modern and a mix of survival forms prevailed. Many modern companies have adapted to these old circumstances and cultural knowledge about medieval Africa in old Europe has long lapsed. Colonial bureaucracies formed their own world and laid the foundations of post-colonial states. Much knowledge from this era eroded with the departure of the colonialists. Following independence, most African bureaucracies expanded greatly, as governments inflated their roles to dominate the economic architecture. Few abroad have complete intellectual command of this set of structures. Cultural dissonance and economic disconnect were two of the causes and consequences. This limited understanding of Africa is widespread in corporate relationships with Africa's states and their many entities and ethnicities even today.

In part the Western worldview of Africa was formed from old foundation myths made up of purely "tribal" constructs, sometimes crudely. The modern mythology is that Africa is made up of a series of fully fledged nation-states. Neither matches contemporary realities. Some serious historians argue that colonialism "invented" tribal Africa as a means of divide and rule, allowing the collapse of multiple identities into one manageable concept of tribe. They claim that this primitive distinction is false, the model does not always work and these identities were manufactured. There may be instances to justify all these claims. Yet because for the majority of the 20th century ethnic identity was and still remains a fait accompli in most of Africa, I find this idea overacademic and unpersuasive, even if at the outset some domains might have been partially ordered this way. Ethnicities of many sorts were important before, during and after the great scramble for Africa. They remain so. Most regimes across Africa still hold to distinctive ethnic, "tribal", clan or minority ethnographies. It is also the case that ethnic identities have evolved in often complex ways that reflect 20th-century modernity. Revisionist historians and anthropologists have at times sought to displace such notions. Yet even where the colonial lexicon may have been insinuated upon social order, it nonetheless built upon pre-existent ethnolinguistic cleavages and significant cultural differentiation.

Nationalism, strongly evident in decolonisation, did not wholly erode these sociographies in Africa. The struggle for power and control embodies many of the old elements still in the mix. It some states it is the kernel of the issue, whatever the public spin to the contrary. Complex ethnic dimensions in Africa often confound foreigners in their relationships and links with state personages. Most have little real understanding of these facets and social complexities in the make-up of evolving African identities, which play important parts in the economic and commercial world.

※

The idealised image of the nation-state is our dominant contemporary but flawed myth. Cartography shows defined "states" on a typical map, most having less than three generations' vintage. Literature treats them as if they were eternal and unchangeable with power built around them, empires creating them, Africa taking control of them and companies dealing with them. Yet they do not always "behave" as pure nation-states. It is into this fluid overlap of statehood and underlying socioethnic and economic morphology that we must look for Africa's deeper architecture.

The work of historians shows that empires have distinctive limits in reach, capacity and lifespan. Global colonialism in Africa, built on an unprecedented scramble (the term coined by *The Times* in September 1884), reached its cartographic completion within one generation, with shallow and contentious foundations. In Africa it lasted only around 75 years (Rhodesia and South Africa were exceptions), approximately the scope of three generations. Here can be found the seeds of many of Africa's dilemmas. Some point to an incurable "genetic flaw" inside any empire as being one cause of dissolution as the world shrank, while land empires became contentious, often leading to failing states. America and the Soviet Union challenged the handful of European powers that commanded Africa, reshaping the traditional paradigm to break the colonial mould. Conflict in European theatres cut this Gordian knot in the colonial worlds, unleashing African interests in their own power game, to eventually implicate all.

The scramble for control in independent Africa followed as decolonisation unscrambled past regimes forged by empire. During the Cold War, Sino/Soviet rivalry with the West aggravated Africa's difficulties in a bipolar world order. If world stability was achieved, it was not in Africa, as evidenced by armed conflicts in the Maghreb, the Horn of Africa, Angola and Southern Africa. Ideological struggles engaged all. Dramatic consequences played out for capitalist Africa then and since. Instabilities wracked the continent as Africans struggled for succession in rivalry over the title deeds of empires lost. This power struggle was non-consensual. Newly born states mostly sought to replicate received structures, inheriting flaws from the past, since there was no escape from history even though a few attempted this forlorn task. Nor did the end of the Cold War bring Africa the legacy of stability, although it did provide commercial space for Anglo-American companies from the West.

Histories of empires and nation-states in Africa – fractious all – cannot provide any guarantee for future stability or even allow us to predict that existing cartography will remain the same. Historians note that the empire of the West did not come to an end in the bonfire of colonial vanities called decolonisation. Competition on a world scale has long been there, but may just be more visible nowadays than in earlier times. Africa illustrates this uncertainty better than most. The ultimate devolution from empire may be a long one, although changes in Russia had rapid and dramatic impacts in states such as Angola and Ethiopia, among others. Retreats from empires past opened the continent for many new pretenders, most with commercial intentions.

It was in the following 50 years of African independent rule that most modern companies became installed in Africa, and more recently non-Western ones, while imperial footprints remained in state structures. Corporate Africa, apart from the progenitors of chartered and colonial companies, is part of the modernity play. These links with Africa's states are fresh. Space has widened for foreign companies in Africa, but emergent proto-commercial empires (Nigeria, South Africa, Morocco, Angola and Algeria) have come forward as surrogate replacements for the old imperial order, seeking to take their share of Africa's economic pie. Intuition and informed guesswork may be useful guides on the shape of the continent's states and economies in times to come.

Part 4

Search for the Holy Grail

I I

Economic tracks

To understand Africa's economies, we need to consider what the economic thinkers claim as knowledge or truth about the continent. The intellectual journey to understand this perplexing mosaic resembles the search for the Holy Grail: in an endless quest to "work out Africa". This remains a Herculean task. Commentary is of course vast, with countless books, treatises, journals and papers in the discipline of economics alone, not to mention the media. If economists, the diagnosticians and "medicine men" of the modern age, have partly failed to explain Africa's economic story adequately, despite so much effort, what could have been the reasons?

Many writers on Africa's economics entertain macro-fantasies, some attributing to the continent potential well beyond its capacities of the moment. Advocacy economics currently reigns unrestrained, built around single issues or specific solutions that will apparently bring economic nirvana. Many have mooted – some indeed still do – massive aid funding as the panacea to "fix poverty". Others, sometimes with vested interests, are prone to generalise solutions from specific cases or strategies – a fatal flaw given the continent's diversity, histories and massive economic complexities. In Africa, one size fits no one. Today another characteristic, evident outside Africa, can be found in South Africa, where pundits regularly offer thin opinion on Africa, and places they have never been, or on issues with which they are patently unfamiliar. Many non-economists are particularly prone to such pontification.

One weakness of economics in Africa at large has been the very history and scale of the literature, the huge volumes of often diffused data, the myriad experiences and sometimes confusing configurations that make up the multitude of interpretation of Africa's complex economies. Even "pure" economics is not enough here. We need to recognise the magnitude of the task. Valuable sets of insights have flowed from many a pen, and many differences of interpretation contest for space in the African sun.

We can put aside the economics done by the quick-fix artists and parachute economists who come and go as fly-by-nights, with little appreciation of the depth and challenge of the task. Another particular weakness among Africa's economists and thinkers is a tendency to assume that if a word is uttered by someone with an overseas academic label, it deserves acceptance. It often does not. Africa remains part-prisoner to the power of global ideology, even in economics. We can also largely dismiss the many doctrinaire economists seen in the 1970s–80s who came to treat Africa as their private laboratories for activist and neo-Marxian praxis. Some still linger in the intellectual corridors. Several gained access to the echelons of government, economic strategy and policy to provide advocacy that in retrospect can be seen as ill advised. Moçambique, Ghana and Tanzania, among others, were once beneficiaries of this dubious largesse. Other economists were distinctively experimental, ideology-driven and, in the worst cases, non-empirical and ahistorical. Many were not even economists at all, yet preached perverted versions of the dismal science from the parapets of politics.

Economic complexity

The literature on development economics in Africa is extensive. It emerged intellectually without much recourse to intimate knowledge of Africa's modern industries. Much stems from world development theory going back to seminal works on economic growth in the late 1950s. Interpretation from that period onwards rested mainly on "dual economy" models (the dichotomy of capitalist and subsistence) and later multiple variants (like formal and informal sectors). These have been mixed with strains of neo-Marxian thought (including dependency theory imported from Latin America). All had the weakness of confining the residual masses to a chosen category of convenience (subsistence households, the underclass, and the poor, rural, exploited: take your pick).

In contrast, deeper analysis reveals socioeconomic complexity, with multiple mechanisms of survival and transitional interfaces with modernity. A lot of this work appears to have been forgotten. Yet the simplistic dualism of the "modern and residual economy" still litters even mainstream diagnoses of Africa's economic game. Many observers of Africa, inside and outside the continent, have little knowledge of earlier intellectual currents. As a result, many economics writers base their analysis on assumed dichotomies in theory and empiricism between the modern and non-modern reflecting the dual model employed half a century ago – with poor explanatory power then and even less now. Consequently, many conclusions drawn are mistaken.

In particular, it is erroneous to conceive of some single modern economy, still further to regard it as the single cause of all the conditions elsewhere in the economy. The modern economies have never been the *fons et origo* of all economic endeavours in Africa. The implantation and growth of capitalist Africa is recent in the continent's long and convoluted history.

From a diagnostic viewpoint, this state of affairs is highly unsatisfactory. There is, it would seem, no continental scale model to explain how Africa's modernity exists alongside, and in complex relationship with, more ancient economies based on divergent means of subsistence and survival. We are thus left with only partial analysis. As a result of these shortcomings, there has seldom been clear understanding of the continuing role of the original and ancient, reshaped over historical time, in *Africa economica*. Western myopia on this matter is as profound as it is misleading.

Modernity on the continent is in greater evidence than before. Yet modern Africa provides only a part of the more profound picture in which the daily struggle to survive involves hundreds of millions of Africans and their traditional communities, with often little connection or complex relationship to the nation-state machineries. Pre-market economies are entrapped in older worlds at the edge of the modern, inhabiting blank spaces unmapped by economic cartography, hidden from contemporary visions and data on step-by-step orderly economic progress. Medieval parts of the continent's economic sphere can exist alongside ultra-smart urban areas across Africa and amid its most modern first-world trappings and artefacts. The one world is centuries removed – in foundations, structure, significance and connectivity – from the other's economic modernity. In Africa, where much happens, little of this may have really changed.

Economists have tracked many economic themes in the diagnosis of Africa's economies, looking for the elements that might explain economic pathways, benign or blighted. To this set of analyses should be added a wide range of work on Africa's political economy by non-economists that deserves attention.

Emphases of key interest mould around a mix of issues: capital accumulation and investment, the role of non-economic constraints in development, macroeconomic performance and balances, correct economic policy advice, the dilemmas faced by economies with economic traps from which escape is needed, aid and financial assistance to overcome underdevelopment, the failures of economic leadership in the continent, the musings of those seeking to apply preordained global agendas to Africa's economic future, and, in sharp antithesis the critique of capitalist economies and ethos in Africa as causes of economic backwardness.

✳

The accumulation of capital, following its emergence and penetration in the early years of the 20th century, is essential for long-term economic growth. To understand this process there is still no better guide than Sally Herbert Frankel's *Capital Investment in Africa*, a masterpiece on the economics of investment by a South African economist of world renown, published in 1938.[1] That so few economists today consult this deeply empirical, measured analysis is a sign of the lack of depth in the knowledge and writings now passed off as the "economics of Africa".

Frankel was professor of economics and economic history at the University of Witwatersrand and a distinguished economist with a grasp of the entirety of sub-Saharan Africa's economies, situating their then-rapid emergence inside the capitalist evolution of the world economy. His analysis dwelt on the entry of Africa into the world as a continent of outposts with obstacles to colonisation, reflecting the long struggle to develop even the Cape. There followed an economic revolution in gold and diamonds setting the basis for resource-based growth. Many an economy in Africa today sits in this early analogue situation.

Here was the case of natural capital unlocked, and the seeds of funding for shaping modernity. It was a saga of periodic and sustained inflows of capital and investment, invested in resources and industry to create an economic base within Africa, setting the foundations for growth over the following 70 years. In current-price terms, many billions of dollars – in investments in equity and bonds, and in private and public funding – flowed into Africa as the continent at last truly joined the world economy. Without this capital from abroad, Africa would not be what it is today. Over the years, many an African state has in effect been living off this capital inheritance built on foreign funding with subsequent domestic reinvestment, corporate risk and market commitment.

More recently, economists have sought to come to grips with economic failures to be found in Africa. Some have hard lessons to impart. It is no secret that Africa's downward drift inspired Western aid and debt-relief initiatives, remedies that were intended to plug the savings gap, infuse capital, allow for growth and cut extreme poverty. Over the past 30 years or so over $500 billion has been poured into Africa in this manner, yet little appears to have resulted from this Western largesse. Now some advocates seek to magnify this flow of funds, in addition to which corporates provide social-related funding and investment. Aid programmes have been subject to damning criticism, with many economists tagging this as another failed strategy.[2]

Many critics dismiss conventional excuses for contemporary economic failures: the delayed economic impacts of slavery, legacies of settler colonialism, insufficient foreign aid and World Bank structural economic adjustment, negative impacts from globalisation, indebtedness, geographical determinism, harsh environments and biased international economic forces. The Cold War did indeed leave deleterious marks, but thereafter Africa has done too little to rid itself of its residues in flawed economic regimes. None of the excuses adequately explains why the sub-Saharan world went backwards for nearly 30 years to the start of this century.

In recognition of the pre-modern, writers have drawn attention to the role of non-economic factors as the midwife to distortions in several of Africa's economies: the thugs in power, the lack of good governance, cultural factors (in the form of inherited practices, communalism, gerontocracy, acquiescence and passive acceptance of authority), African socialism and experimentation, political pomposity, deluded leadership based on entitlement, identity politics and heavy doses of fatalism. If the finger is placed on the social matrix as a blocking mechanism, then infusions of aid or even investment can hardly offset the problem.

All these elements are said to have made for impoverishment. Into this vortex came corruption, to bind social entities in a project of subjugation, with Western political correctness helping to mould the mix and add the final touches to Africa's backwardness and misery. Aid enabled responsibilities to be shifted onto others. Western guilt and allied compassion have proved easy to manipulate. More aid becomes worse aid. In this diagnosis the social matrix led Africa to defy economics (rather like ignoring gravity), strangle business growth and install high-cost cultures with low productivity. It encouraged low savings rates, induced capital flight and raised barriers to foreign investment. Clearly, aid on its own is unlikely to fix this predicament in future and it is rejected today as a fix by many commentators.

Africa cannot be expected to catch up soon with Europe in any material sense. It remains in a state of suspended hope, with Africa itself required to break the cycles of slow growth, often laced with terror, poverty and mediocrity. Foreign aid has often acted as a band-aid or placebo for underdevelopment. Yet I remain to be convinced that improved growth cannot be achieved: it has happened before and in several places is doing so again – though certain political mores remain

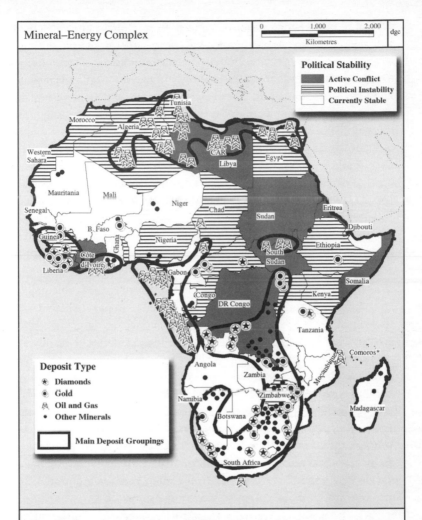

Mineral–Energy Complex

0   1,000   2,000   dgc
Kilometres

Political Stability
- Active Conflict
- Political Instability
- Currently Stable

Deposit Type
- ✳ Diamonds
- ◉ Gold
- ⚒ Oil and Gas
- • Other Minerals

[ ] Main Deposit Groupings

The continental space of over 30,000 sq km is rich in natural resources, minerals, diverse energy fuels (uranium, coal, coalbed methane) and oil/gas potential, including unconventional shales, with vast offshore waters and Exclusive Economic Zones providing rich hydrocarbon provinces. Africa holds large command in world reserves of sensitive minerals. The under-developed mining complex is spread around large areas within the continent. Some resources have been linked with conflicts in the past and present.

inimical to market forces and the serious reconsideration of economic strategies is required to obtain long-term higher growth rates.

The breakdown of many agrarian societies in Africa can be traced to mismanaged central power. The peasantry or majority have often been left to fend for themselves. The social matrix is often the only protection against increasing impoverishment in Africa's rural societies. It is typically the bedrock of survival for many. Yet Africa has grown and will grow further. The issue here, however, is the congenitally flawed history and current record of underachievement that all this implies. If potential expansion in GDP of only 1–2% per annum is lost for some years (equal to less than the growth deficit vis-à-vis competitors), the long-term cumulative effect will be considerable and catch-up will become a very long game indeed, maybe impossible. Crucial here are the opportunities for structural transformation that Africa has forgone but its competitors have grasped. The cumulative damage mounts with time.

Imprimatur

What then should we make of the official economic views on African macroeconomic performance presented by the main multilateral institutions: the African Development Bank and the Economic Commission for Africa, typically in conjunction with the World Bank and the IMF? Each year these bodies issue "state of Africa's economy" styled reports, complete with data and graphics to mark Africa's progress, and valuable sources they may often be, as is other basic research conducted.[3] Yet such analysis of the modern in Africa usually excludes treatment of the majority of older economic modes that are ancillary in shaping and driving the Africa economic locomotive.

These multilateral institutions often reflect best the economics of modernity, while the critics explicitly and often better deal with the economics of underdevelopment. It seems that rarely is there any meeting of minds between the two camps, let alone intellectual and empirical consensus on paradigms, theory, models, method, issues, analysis, or policy. Why? I think it is because both wish to fix Africa in their own way, often along preordained lines. Thus economic schisms reflect divisions between "worldviews" (perhaps even economic traditions too).

Allied to the orthodoxies of the multilaterals are the proposals that have emerged from a series of commissions over the years, from the Brandt Commission to the Blair Commission on Africa, with similar policy-inspired products issued from time to time under the auspices of governments in Europe, the Swedish and Danish among them. Few such efforts or outcomes lasted for more than a few years. The life cycle of the economic wisdom peddled by foreign political dignitaries in Africa is measurably, perhaps happily, short.

Two large volumes edited jointly under the aegis of an adviser to the World Bank, *Political Economy of Economic Growth in Africa, 1960–2000*, present the writings of many economists on Africa.[4] While examining policies generally, there is a special focus on opportunities, anti-growth syndromes, regimes of control, economic geography, shocks and state failures, and retarded growth. Though much can be garnered from this set of studies, there are difficulties with the paradigms used and hence their diagnostic insights. The advent of national statistics allowed for cross-country and intertemporal estimates, and became a treasure trove for econometric bias in much of this analysis as macroeconomic numbers set the frame for the interpretations contained. Point-in-time data, regressions and the "magic box" of econometrics will never fully explain Africa's syndromes and dilemmas. Underlying the theory, models and data used is the idea that "correct policy" might be all that is needed, as if Africa's modes and economic histories could be so manipulated. In this mould Africa, it appears, was just not making the "right choices" – a fair point and yet a naive one. For most authors, Africa's apparent negative destiny could be readily offset by interventions, appropriate investments and sound economic policy choices, several of which involved redistribution. Well, it has all been tried before.

The story behind Africa's deprivation is one of a complex economic slide over the past decades. Long-run economic divergences with East

Asia have become embedded as both had begun the era at much the same economic levels. Nigeria and Indonesia with oil endowments and once comparable economies parted economic ways. In Africa there was only slow accumulation in most countries and poor productivity growth allied with the demise of rural Africa. The future was sacrificed in spending booms, civil conflicts, looting, autocracies and unproductive government consumption, all found high on the list of deficiencies in Africa's growth experience at this time.

Though this economics work advanced a range of theoretical ideas, none would explain exactly why Africa's economic history has been as it has. The elegant equations lacked authenticity and grass-roots veracity, even while the macro evidence contained some gems of truth. The view in many places seemed to be that if only Africa had been governed by others, rather the venal leaderships that arose within it, all would have been well. This set an agenda for reform, no bad idea, except that here economists and their acolytes have long been wailing at the crosswinds of change. In the second volume of this magnum opus in case studies across many countries, specific industries and markets came in for examination, as a useful antidote to the macro-speculations of the first volume, in which metrics trumped economic shape and history. Careful reading of several case studies highlights the competitive modes of economic differentiation and issues around subsistence that help explain Africa's economic evolution. Together these volumes provide one of the few detailed contemporary efforts to define Africa's economic malaise. The conventional macro explanations they advance, however, fail to capture the holistic drama of Africa's flowering seeds of economic evolution, partially exposed in the economics literature before the 1960s, and little tended thereafter.

Many non-official works have also examined the continent's intractable economic past, current problems and ways forward.[5] Often these present non-orthodox optics on economic growth and come with a development-state philosophy. Several nostrums could here be accepted: treating Africa as a vague abstraction in simplified general theories is fraught with error; gradualism in the development process is likely, as no great leap forward can be expected from one stage to another; the intellectual choice of development cannot be represented as some smorgasbord of options, models from elsewhere and paths elected from the experience or bottled wisdom of others; and shifting global economic realities will always retain significance. There is no "African" economic theory applicable only to Africa. I would agree with all these notions.

It seems that no matter how many case studies and macro perspectives are produced, the search for the elusive African dummy, the statistical or theoretical artefact that explains the continent's poor performance, continues. Maybe the eternal quest for this silver bullet will continue unabated. Homogenised scholarship has played a role in this search, based largely on econometrics divorced from reality, and shaped by fashion in economics, especially from World Bank research on Africa. Across the economics field you can find multiple micro insights yet no coherent framework within which to situate them.

In many analyses there is plenty of food for thought. Two key issues bear reflection. First, many argue that the continent has been marginalised inside the world economy, while new directions afoot need to be led only by endogenous-driven accumulation and local growth determinants. Fair enough: but how will Africa's past experience suddenly be transformed? Second, the scale of the informal economies is shown in many research studies to make a mockery of the assumed exactitude of Africa's statistics and economic models based upon them, while illustrating the weakness of modern economies to provide enough employment to absorb the output of the continent's burgeoning demographics. If this predicament is to worsen, as it will, how then will net per-head growth be sustained in the long term?

Gurus and cognoscenti

Few have written more on the diagnosis of Africa's economic condition in a quest to reorient policy than Paul Collier. Some of these writings have been integrated in works related to wider world issues, such as *The Bottom Billion*.[6] Many others have appeared in journals and within compendia collated by and with colleagues. Influenced by early sojourns in Malawi and Ethiopia and their dire poverty, and work on civil wars in Africa, Collier devised a schema of "traps" that supposedly caught Africa in their vices and arrested development. If only it could escape these traps, founded on conflict, natural resources, the dilemma faced by the landlocked, and the travails of governance in small countries – yet this will be easier said than done.

Much of Africa exhibits one or more of Collier's traps of misery. Wars in Africa there have been and plenty continue, their causal roots complex. Some states have resources at issue and have badly managed their bounty: Collier has denounced the "resource curse" which has led to the "survival of the fattest" (actually a condition that pre-dated resource discovery and exploitation and is found even where no resource development exists). Nearly one-third of Africa is ensconced in land-locked states surrounded by bad neighbourhoods, a fact of geohistory and evolution, with large interiors within littoral states effectively land-locked and equally condemned; and bad governance reigns, not just in small countries. To my mind this is not a suitable theory or explanation of how Africa came to emerge and become so eviscerated. Rather it is merely a refashioning of the descriptive, based on partial (if real) conditions found. We should not be blinded by the images of eternal economic traps, just as Mauritius was able to escape the famous Malthusian trap projections of Nobel laureate James Meade, proclaimed in the mid-1960s as a fatal destiny.

In the mould of economic redeemer, Collier propounds a series of policies to remedy Africa's eternal conditions and escape the traps of the past and present. They include many ideas about better-targeted aid, new laws and charters, realigned trade policy, and even selective and fine-tuned military interventions. As with many others it partly reflects the democratic and quasi-evangelical economist at work, with several novel solutions, wanting to fix Africa.

These ideas were further elaborated in Collier's *Wars, Guns and Votes*, which examined the political economy of violence, the political power game and the failure of elections to deliver economic advance. Collier then thought that the world was getting safer, Africa with it. Yet since 2009 the hand of history has given us revolution and civil war in

Libya, continued strife in Somalia, the ongoing imbroglio in the DRC, the debacle in Côte d'Ivoire and the bloody birth of South Sudan, with irredentism and subliminal conflicts entrenched in more states across the map of Africa. Is it just the modern economic traps of history, bad politics and serial conflict that have led to Africa's economic condition and repeated difficulties? I think not.

Economists have also sought to identify some of the factors now moving Africa forwards.[7] The backdrop has been progress over the first decade of the 21st century and optimism for the future. Some wonder whether Africa will be the world's next development miracle following a quarter-century of economic failure. Yet growth is not coming from industrialisation. Poverty remains scattered around Africa like potholes in the road to redemption. The telling observation is that in the early 1970s Africa, India and China had comparable levels of per head income: so what went wrong in Africa? The aid record appears flawed, maybe even counter-productive. Some 70% of states have experienced one or more forms of armed conflict since 1980. Over 30% of states continued to be in conflict in the 1990s. Conflicts continued in the last decade. Old conflicts once settled often reappear in new guises. It raises one problematic question: was war or conflict an economic model of choice?

Another view is that adverse economic conditions, including in some cases austere natural conditions, have bred this strife – with large costs to economic growth. The nation-state building process has been costly in time, resources, treasure and blood, not dissimilar to the Latin American independence era of the 19th century. Perhaps Africa's economic birth pains were of an equivalent nature, just at a different time and place. Hope today remains for a long phase of catch-up. Yet it looks as if Africa is still not over the maturity hump. Some remain sceptical about the stability of Africa's states, viewing recent changes as ones of magnitude not a shift in the character of the politico-economic fabric.[8] Many still perceive Africa as fragile, with demography a remaining challenge (70% of its urban classes live in impoverished slums) and massive informalisation everywhere. Little of the recent economic progress can be attributed to the so-called democratic dividend, itself a disputed reality in the face of pseudo-democracy, hybrid regimes and managed ethnic head counts that marred many modern elections. Institutional foundations remain weak and may make any economic miracle short-lived. Not even the so-called "boom at the bottom" might be enough, especially if Africa has not learnt lessons from past economic failures. Will it?

Some commentators continue to believe that an orchestrated "big bang" in aid is the way forward. Jeffrey Sachs, a former Harvard macroeconomist, known for radical shock therapies applied to post-communist states in the 1990s, advocates mega-funding now (with a global estimate of $250 billion) as the solution to extreme poverty, Africa's most of all. George Soros notes a messianic fervour about him. Sachs never thought that in the 21st century he would witness the type of poverty seen in Africa.[9] It proved to be a wake-up call. Sachs, who first arrived on the continent in 1995, should be modestly informed on its problematic aid history. Yet the solution mooted, portrayed as "a great titanic battle of morality", appears to be the old "1% theory" (this share of the rich world's income to be diverted, mainly to Africa). There is little new in either this idea or the number mooted. What is more recent is our knowledge that it has not worked before. There are a plethora of reasons to think it may not if ever tried again.

Sachs's economic litany – despite claims to apply "the science of economic development" – is more akin to missionary advocacy rather than clinical diagnosis. His perspectives are enhanced by the grand ambitions found in *Common Wealth*, as a call to arms with proposals for mega-aid programmes to "end poverty traps", global solutions to climate change, fixing world water needs, redesigning demographics in a crowded planet and (while we are at it) rethinking American foreign policy: all a tall order for the power of one.[10] More recently, Sachs has advocated a focus on gross national happiness rather than GDP, inspired by such initiatives in Bhutan. It would be impossible in Africa to measure this elusive definition of paradise. At best it is a vague idea of little economic substance, notwithstanding its embrace by a few outliers in the world of the cognoscenti.

As an experimental economist Sachs devised a six-point plan with strict timetables applied to real-world micro-laboratory conditions (dubbed Millennium Villages) set up in Africa. All that is required, apparently, is to scale them up – big time. Yet when this is put to Africa's authorities, there is a sense of underwhelming ennui, if one encounter between Sachs and Uganda's President Yoweri Museveni is anything to go by (as indicated in the Africa edition of *Vanity Fair*, 2007). Listening to Sachs's impetuous urgings, Museveni manages to emit the sounds of silence: a series of "mmms". When Sachs is later asked how the meeting went, he thinks it was "very good". Many can tell you that implied "silences" in Africa are normally a very bad sign indeed. The idea that this sort of grand socioeconomic engineering could be modelled and installed across the continent's vast rural world is faintly ridiculous, devoid of appreciation of how Africa works.

This generic mix of economic evangelism and cognoscenti concern for Africa was well summed up in Paul Theroux's review of Tim Jeal's book on Africa's greatest explorer, Henry Morton Stanley.[11] It is worth quoting in its entirety:

> *Poor Africa, the happy hunting ground of the mytho-maniac, the rock star buffing up his or her image, the missionary with a faith to sell, the child buyer, the retailer of dirty drugs or toxic cigarettes, the editor in search of a scoop, the empire builder, the tycoon wishing to rid himself of his millions, the school builder with a bucket of patronage, the experimenting economist, the diamond merchant, the oil executive, the explorer, the slave trader, the eco-tourist, the adventure traveller, the bird watcher, the travel writer, the escapee, the colonial and his crapulosities, the banker, the busybody, the Mandela-sniffer, the political fantasist, the buccaneer, and your cousin the Peace Corps Volunteer.*

While many modern-day faith healers have come to Africa (and left in due course), there will undoubtedly be many more to make these discoveries of Africa's poverty and safaris to fix all in future.

Davos man

Nothing appears to dampen enthusiasm for the fad of economic talk shows on Africa. Some indeed have become a fixture on the global business calendar. There appears to be a vast policy paraphernalia and world-connected political class with corporate acolytes that work off these five-minute diagnoses, perhaps best summed up in the image of "Davos man". Here the formulaic command the podium space, with droplets of quasi-economics fed to the media and public in a regular diet of Oprah-style discourse, moulded around newly emerging themes selected to capture attention. They add little to our understanding. Whatever their place, it is not to enlighten us on Africa's deeper economic realities.

Brainstorming sessions, thematic statements, workshops and plenaries with networking (known often in Africa as notworking) follow well-worn paths, as if they were continental wedding ceremonies designed to match selected politicians in Africa with the corporate elites. Few involved are willing to challenge government power head-on. Fewer ever get close to the dirty diagnostic that is Africa's economic reality. Corporates in the room usually want to marry Africa. Many sharing these artificial stages, often televised for larger effect, sing on song with similar harmonic tunes and issue statements of opaque conformity. Glad handing and politically correct optimism are typically the fare of the day. Even so, the celestial bodies that move Davos man to annual confabs worldwide and to periodic Africa meetings do issue several documents on a regular basis to measure the continent's status within the everlasting process of competitive economic change. They mix economic waffle and the pragmatic, issuing league tables on who has moved up or down in the stakes for economic glory or repentance, with attention to the constraints on doing business in Africa, a matter of implied importance to the corporate world. As with most cardinal or ordinal ranking, little is actually explained by the numerics. It is not even a decision-making guide to corporate strategy.

We should not leave aside the soft or hard economic left of modern times, with its generic antithesis to the Davos model and its critique of

Africa's states and their economies.[12] The general thesis of this genre is that Africa has been looted from the start, from the era of the Atlantic slave trade onwards. Arab and Omani slavery, let alone Africa's own forms of enslavement, are often neglected in these missives. From Live Aid to Make Poverty History, the G7 and G8 Africa summits and the Blair Commission – all have been depicted as public-relations spin at best. On the left it is typically said that Africa's central problems result from one or more variant of the following potpourri: uneven development, "unequal exchange", rampant income and wealth inequalities, neoliberalism, exploitative debt, financial chicanery by the North (wherever that might be), phantom aid, distorted investments, capital flight (including lost human capital), militarism and looming sub-imperialism, with elite-led African capitalism by and for the ruling *nomenklatura*. The aim of many analyses of this sort is political not economic explanation.

All these faults and sins of commission are naturally resisted by Africa's heroes of the struggle, the comrades and the civil societies across the continent. Some or all of this may even be true: it is a tale of good and evil, with a cast fit for purpose. But rather than explain Africa's growth and transitions from the past to the present, it typically portrays Africa simply as a victim – "poor Africa", moulded and manipulated by the outer world, unable to act on its own (or if it does, then perversely) and paternalised. This raises the question of what might have happened to the continent had it not been "exploited". We might equally wonder why most in Africa appear to want more of this excessive "evil", with increased investment, along with the sublime bourgeois trappings of enhanced economic modernity.

In the search for fashionable explanation, many cite inadequate political leadership as the problem for Africa's economies, arguing that politicians ("crooked and incompetent") and predatory governments lie at the root of African poverty.[13] Though this may be valid when applied in certain cases for limited periods of time, it cannot stand as the sole or a satisfactory explanation for economic backwardness across the entire continent. It may tell us what transpired in some cases, not why this became so. We need to discern the deeper histories and structures that moulded Africa's economic world. There is more complexity in under-development than flawed leadership allied to predation and political deficiencies. Today there is overabundant talk on leadership that passes for analysis, providing a weak diagnostic framework for complex economic realities. It is almost the default position for many "thought leaders" ruminating on the many deficiencies of politics in Africa. Most seem oblivious to the competitive modes and histories that lie behind the economies of Africa's nation-states.

One recent attempt to get to grips with the contemporary political economy argues that Africa's poverty is attributable not so much to inadequate financial means, problematic aid, poor infrastructure, or trade access issues, but rather to the fact that Africa's leadership has in some manner "made this choice".[14] For political scientists this seems a natural conclusion. Yet it tells us little about the economic transitions involved. It echoes comments from many earlier observers going back decades. So it is no new discovery. There is no doubt that in the 20% ascribed in the "80/20 rule" our model suggests, the political nexus can play a critical role in economic growth or decline. The flip side of fixation on leadership is seen in the abundance of meetings prevalent across Africa about "leadership strategies" and "new-generation leaders". The idea appears to embody the notion that if the captains of the ship can be changed, all will be well. It has happened before, with little long-term economic consequence.

The story elaborated is nonetheless with insight on many issues that preoccupy political analysts. Africa's leaders often make bad economic decisions and conflate the state with their party or personality. Many aspirants enter politics to get rich, the converse of what is often found elsewhere. Personal rule trumps democratic transparency and the political class leeches off the impoverished masses. In this endeavour they deploy an armoury of manipulated regulations, edicts and practices to enhance family interests around presidencies, party-managed companies and personal wealth. There are few if any punishments for the bad choices made, and little domestic accountability, while the state kleptocracy thrives on top of bureaucratic machines designed to serve the ends of their political masters. Big Man rule and the mechanisms of neo-patrimonialism hold sway in many countries as partial causes of Africa's failure to "make" modern states. Presidents and their entourages, with allies, manage to become donor darlings, and little is done to shift the economies forward, at least as they could so perform. Hence land tenure remains 80% under traditional title, often as "dead capital" and wasted as an exploitable resource, so penalising potential economic growth. Civil services are stacked with party hacks, ethnic allies, the kinship-connected and the faithful dependent on the imperatives of political continuity. Corruption and predation are rampant. The continental aid game facilitates this inertia with the consequence that development is widely regarded as something that might come from without, as in a cargo cult. In this milieu state degradation and economic underperformance is not uncommon.

Yet the "leadership" question must surely fall short as an adequate explanation of the nature of economic change in Africa even if it is of great concern. It may identify one corrosive lubricant making for steady underperformance and even in some cases catastrophic decline. Longevity in power of political incumbents in Africa typically enables this process of serial downside to be unhappily accomplished. Indeed, it does not take long for this *muti* (medicine) to work its wonders. Numerous instances of political greed, ineptitude, self-interest and larceny are found in Africa, while private industry is in places an elite-linked system of rent-seeking allied to the political power of the day. Yet economies in Africa have grown despite these many leadership faults.

Similarly, political commentators have lately taken umbrage at the wider imperfections and alignments of political elites, fingering them as the reason African capitalism has, it seems, failed.[15] Elite capitalism is sometimes regarded as the problem. Africa is seen as locked inside the stalled stage of mercantile capitalism, lacking any bourgeois revolution, on the road to nowhere. Hence the continent is somehow marching backwards, and yet the evidence of economic growth tells us the opposite. Undoubtedly, independence entrenched elites that often reinforced inequalities inherited from colonialism. Non-producers still control many countries, with capital accumulation and private industry partially compromised. Fossilised pre-industrial or pre-agrarian social formations may limit economic growth as stunted subsistence systems have perpetuated in post-colonial Africa. No one represents peasant interests. Deindustrialisation continues apace. While these observations contain some veracity, they inadvertently mirror early 1970s economic discourses of dualism (classical or neo-Marxian). The underlying view is that the existent modes found are few: mercantilism as private capitalism with peasants, the state elites squatting above both. It is thus a somewhat simplistic model, aggregated in nature, and of old vintage. That Africa might still be seen in this way reflects the continuing hold of past thought. Economic theory, empirical work and even Africa itself have all moved a long way since then. Economic history indicates that Africa (that "big word" again) is far more complex and dynamic than the established academic image of (even modified) dualism.[16]

To do full justice to the copious literature on Africa we need to delve deeply into historiography. Africa has been blessed with many a fine historian. I have cited a few in the text and in the Notes and cannot hope to summate their many and different studies and interpretations, which add to our knowledge. All that can be done is to make this acknowledgement, as applicable to the multiple interpretations of Africa coming from social science and anthropology, which have an equal claim to legitimacy in helping us to understand a continent in long and evolutionary transition.[17]

Panorama

Well, there it is: parts of Africa as seen by many authors writing about Africa, the diagnosticians from economics and the social sciences, the medicine men of the modern age, the scribes of tomes that have presented deep and often contradictory understandings, along with novelists, journalists and analysts, fantasists and mapmakers – all trying to capture the essence of the continent or wanting to "fix Africa", some outraged by its non-conformity to modernity or the seductive liberal charms of the richer world. I like to think there is something in all these writings, even the growing number of scribblings on a mythic future without any problems. But mere quantity is hardly enough: where should we turn to find Africa's economic essence?

Without doubt the continent's story is panoramic and highly complex. For long it has been dramatised in journalism with glib phrases such as the "hopeless continent" or its antithesis, the "Africa century". Shards of truth lie behind these epithets, yet many deeper dramas of greater economic significance need recounting. Many contemporary authors, most from outside Africa's borders, who write on Africa and its imperfect modernity, do so with prescriptive intent or damning indictment. They seek to remedy Africa or at least its flaws, even to "save Africa", typically from Africans, and from the perceived blemishes left on the corporate or African soul.

Some writers are evangelical in their wish to redeem the continent; others emerge as quasi-politicians aiming to engineer and change Africa's world. Moral exhortations are high on these agendas. Many appear to retain an occidental guilt and sensitivity about past injustices wreaked on Africa and its populace, the "wretched of the earth" in Franz Fanon's immortal phrase. I am less convinced that this adds to our understanding. Almost all in today's moral militia (writers, journalists, activists, politicians, even economists) feel that they have found the solution to Africa's ills. Yet few seem aware of the many past economic remedies that have failed: initially delivered by way of independence, then aid or more trade, later poverty alleviation initiatives, finally humanitarian interventions and sometimes armed might.

Now too there is rampant moralising about corporate social investment. Not surprisingly, these palliatives often fail, some dismally. Many are doomed from the start. There is almost a state of mind ingrained in many contemporary utterances about the corporate world's obligations in Africa, with ambitions and claims for finding and sorting out all that is wrong by means of an expanding bag of tricks related to the export of best practice in managing the continent's economies and resources. What luck if this task were that simple.

Like Sisyphus in Greek mythology, many who invoke advocacy will face a perpetual uphill battle, condemned to repeat forever the thankless task of toiling to push their chosen rock of reform up the

African mountain, only to see it roll back once again. Africa will not lightly take its cue from the outside. In his famous essay *Le Mythe de Sisyphe*, Albert Camus concludes: "The struggle itself is enough to fill a man's heart."[18] While this may hold truth, it has not always been enough to fill African bellies and avert the drama around *la politique du ventre*. Whatever the outside world may want, the Dark Continent largely creates its own history and will be the main architect of its future. To discern what that might be, perhaps we should return to the past, find out how Africa arrived at the present impasse – if that is what it is – and examine the seeds from which Africa's future will sprout.

The diversity of opinion – in historiography, political analysis, economics, or contemporary comment – should be instructive for corporate players and state officials seeking to read Africa. My own experience is that few read its past in sufficient depth, much beyond a partial take on headlines: "If it's Angola today, then what is there on that?" seems often to be the approach. Sometimes I wonder if the task of interpreting Africa – itself an invention of sorts: Europe's imagination, Africa's mythology, perhaps the reverse – can ever be accomplished. Many of the writers cited have alluded to the same problem. But I believe it is important to reflect all these studied opinions, scholarship and wide collective experience across the continent, and also the profound journalistic flashes of insight on the part of some writers. Africa is a work in progress; so too is our understanding of its full range of economic complexities.

Pliny the Elder, who got little right in describing Africa, is said to have remarked: *Ex Africa semper aliquid novi* (out of Africa always something new). It may have always been this way. Maybe it will remain so: certainly it was during the classic scramble in a continent for the taking, now a prize with riches to be secured in a race engaging many more. Yet in Africa one might say equally that there is always something old and enduring from the past, a set of societies often spread apart in time and space, a world that has not everywhere been a mimic of the modern. The road to that nirvana will be a long one.

Very little in Africa even today equates to occidental modernity. Yet it is towards this slice of the continent that most have gravitated to find Africa. Perhaps because of its myriad characteristics, so at odds with global norms and structures, many in the West have long sought to interpret Africa in their own image, remould and remake it; in short, fix Africa. The task to remedy Africa occupied past *missions civilisatrices*. It is one that contemporaries ardently, if unconsciously, practise and might even recognise if they properly read Africa's vast and informed economic history.

Yet things are changing. How fast they will move, where and in what circumstances, is not known with any exactitude. In looking at this emerging future, let us consider what appears to be known, and review some of the trajectories mooted in the economic explanation of Africa, to divine what might be interpreted.

12

Future imperfect

Africa's economies are complex in their origins, structures and growth profiles. No one mirrors exactly another. History has shaped them. Present economic configurations constitute a mix of the old and new. There has been economic growth at unseen rates in the last decade that indicate higher potential to be realised. There is new dynamism across many economies in Africa even while the hand of history still weighs heavily. Africa has greater linkages to globalisation than ever before, but remains imperfectly integrated with the fast-changing world economies. The idea that Africa's "true post-colonial age came to an end in the last quarter of the 20th century" may be seductive for academics, some in search of new nomenclature to classify the era afterwards, but the overriding evidence is of continuity from that past to the economic and political paradigms found today.[1]

Africa ascendant

Could Africa be on the cusp of an era of a decades-long boom, unlike the cycles in the past that have wilted under local difficulties and external market pressures? What might this economic future portend?

These questions were on the minds of the hundreds of corporate and state executives at the 5th Africa Economic Forum in Cape Town in 2011. In and around Africa similar optimism is widespread. The storyline has gained traction worldwide: it has become almost conventional wisdom. Countries and companies are seeking to take advantage of the rising tide of economic progress anticipated. Cities within and beyond the mainland, on islands and in the Gulf and Asia, are marketing their virtues as the elected gateways to Africa's emerging riches. Many "economic cheerleaders" prognosticate on this future: politicians, diplomats, banks, analysts, rock stars and academics. Just about all punt the idea of Africa's inevitable and unmitigated economic success going forward.

Officials from the World Bank had forecast growth in Africa of "at least 5%" for the next five years. If realised, this would bring Africa's GDP to a minimum of $2.44 trillion by 2016 (based on Angus Maddison's long-term numerics for Africa). This would be significant in that Africa would have extended the long cycle of growth for nearly 20 years, excepting the blip of the last global recession. As if this was not enough, Justin Lin, the World Bank's chief economist, the first in this post from the developing world, claimed in 2011 that Africa could grow at 7% for the next 30–40 years: "there is no reason why ... this should not happen", he noted.[2] I can think of a few.

Capitalist Africa was being portrayed in an almost revolutionary mode. Barriers to growth had come down, more were expected to fall. Market signals appeared promising. Foreign investment capital was flowing in. Private industry was bullish. Afro-pessimism had witnessed its twilight, according to many. The Africa giant, once sleeping and at times bedevilled by nightmares, was stirring. Equity market capitalisations had risen; more companies were listing; initial public offerings (IPOs) flourished and mergers and acquisitions were at levels rarely seen. Corporate Africa was taking advantage and shifting portfolio into the continent. The bogey of indebtedness had been largely tamed, with highly indebted poor country (HIPC) write-downs and more prudent fiscal management. Markets for middle-income Africa were expanding, Gini coefficients were improving and poverty was decreasing according to the official data. Trade volumes had risen and new emerging partners were linking to Africa's star. Many in the diaspora were "coming home", with skills and funds. Macroeconomic stabilisation was emerging in more economies. There was the evidence of an oil/gas and energy boom, with rapid development in commodities and minerals markets – these locomotives of growth being likely to push forward the unlocking of natural capital to Africa's benefit. The patrimonial relationships of old Africa were believed to be transforming under the exigencies of economic complexity and growth. It would all just be a matter of time.

Davos man had taken notice of Africa. The view was reached and endorsed that the "mindset of Africa" had changed. Leaderships in Africa in government and among the corporate elites had been converted to the economic cause, seeing the light on the proverbial road to Damascus. Government reform was at unprecedented levels. Home-grown companies and "champions" presented new business models. "Middle-class" income growth, rapid urbanisation and the demographic future were taken as foundations for economic dividends to come. McKinsey had endorsed this view.[3] The IMF had forecast that seven of the ten fastest-growing economies in the world over the coming five years would be sub-Saharan. Gold-plated imprimaturs of official endorsements poured forth.

The old stereotypes of Africa appeared to have been overtaken by the new realities. Past predilections and instincts to block economic progress while guarding the economic citadels, with the pillaging of economies, had been converted to the maxim of enlightened self-interest in widening evidence of trade, investment and exchange. "Africa ascendant" was one slogan and pitch for this spin and upbeat certitude. There seemed to have been a quantum shift in Africa's economic landscape. Facts, data and trends were presented as evidence of these positive shifts in Africa's political economic outlook. Had old Africa died, with Olduvai and its derivatives replaced by the unrestrained march to modernity? Were Africa's economies positioned for Walt Whitman Rostow's stage of economic "take-off"?

The cartography of conflict was presented to show fewer states at war or in some conflict. Less state fragility was implied and talked about widely. On one image that I perused while writing, the 1970s map of Africa showed 17 states at conflict then, 18 in the 1980s, 14 in the 1990s and 9 in 2011 for sub-Saharan Africa, while over 90 conflicts had marked the landscapes from 1949 to date. In this 60-year period

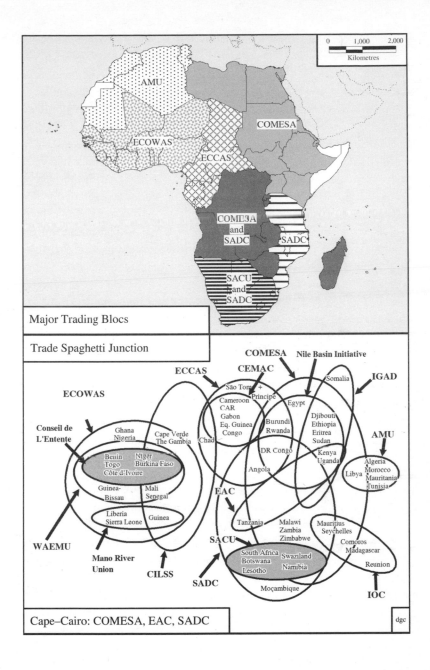

Major Trading Blocs

Trade Spaghetti Junction

Cape–Cairo: COMESA, EAC, SADC

213

there had been over 150 warring parties on Africa's soil. (I think that the full count, including those with arms and awaiting opportunity, could probably yield a good number today.)

On the indicators "measured" there were downward trends reported for political troubles in Africa, an elliptical concept it should be granted. The political scientists, ever eager to go quantitative, claimed that "political hardening" of regimes in Africa had softened on trend. Improvements in governance, transparency and anti-corruption were indexed in ordinal rankings published by a variety of organisations and NGOs. Life expectancies at birth from 1970–75 onwards showed advances, except for several imploded or problematic states (Congo, Zambia, Zimbabwe, Lesotho, Swaziland and even South Africa), as signs of past material uplift. But not all appeared well.[4]

Roadways to ruin

Despite the gloss, portents about the continuing malaise in Africa's political economy remain. The ancient and the old have not gone away. Lineage-based systems were undiluted, often redeployed within the unexpected miracle of economic success. Conflicts anew have occurred with frequency (Côte d'Ivoire is one left unresolved for over a decade). If there were two steps forward, they have often been accompanied by one step back. Has Africa merely grown without grasping what Henry Kissinger, remarking on Chinese economic success, had once called the "long arc of time"?

In poor Africa today – exemplified by Zimbabwe – economic backwardness and political regression have been the marks of distinction. Several conflated economic pathways to ruin have been followed. At the core has been the false idea that wealth is found in mere ownership of the land – which is never the case. Land confiscations magnified the devastating economic consequences of this fallacy. The regime has been on an economic mission to capture all private white-owned land, and lately foreign mines and businesses, not in party or autochthonous hands. Some initiatives were based on confiscation without redress, others on extreme "indigenisation" programmes. These currently require all companies, foreign included, to give 51% equity in their firms to locals, for which read party allies and friends: the anointed *shamwari*. In 2011 over 175 mining applicants were denied options to invest on similar grounds. This economic pathway will have long-term costs in terms of investment and future growth.

Zimbabwe's parastatals, many "parasiticals" in effect, have racked up huge debts and have often, like the state oil company Noczim, been looted. Few state firms, one being the power utility Zesa, command even a modicum of efficiency. Enrichment of military leaders bedazzled the pauperised masses. The kleptocrats have not put their hands back in their pockets. Income per head has fallen off the charts and unemployment has reached seemingly impossible levels of 60% plus, maybe much more. Informalisation has become extreme, one observer describing Mbare, the capital's main township, as nothing but one giant flea market. Real average wages in the primary industries today are probably little better than they were 50 years ago. Millions have fled to economic pastures elsewhere. Industry is a shell of what it was in the past, its capacity utilisation driven down to pathetic levels, in 2009 reaching only 10%. Zimbabwe has been overtaken by Moçambique and Botswana, both once much smaller economies. Agrarian recovery is slow and lags performance from over a decade before. The national cattle herd stands at 5.8 million, below what it was in 1970, with lower-quality beef stock and a lost opportunity.

The government in Harare operates on barebones financing. It owes its own parastatals around $87 million in unpaid debts. Financially, many of them are under water. Around 75,000 "ghost workers" are still on the state payroll, costing $135 million per year. The Reserve Bank is mired in debts it can probably never repay following theft and confiscations on a grand scale. Dollarisation has yielded turnaround at the bottom, with continuing small improvements, but with little change in psyche or economic management among the top echelons holding power and acquired privilege. GDP has shrunk by over half in real terms over the past decade, devastating all. Life expectancy, once over 53 years, has fallen sharply. This has occurred in short order and in the absence of any war. Like empires, Africa's modern economies are complex adaptive systems. The road to ruin can be readily engineered with but few wrong moves.

In faster-growing "emerging economies" such as Uganda the traditional kingdoms persist. The Buganda kingdom (with approximately 6 million of the country's 33 million people) exercises political muscle and exhibits a lack of timidity towards presidential power off the back of a list of long-held grievances, including claims to large traditional lands. The Acholi, Busoga, Ankole and Toro kingdoms press equal claims on ancestral bases. The Bunyoro kingdom was blessed, so it thought, with discoveries of oil beneath their traditional soils around Lake Albert. Elsewhere patronage politics has not disappeared. While there are potential economic limits to patronage (only so much can go around in jobs, positions and resources), it appears to be endemic and allied to strategies weaving its benevolence into more and more nooks and crannies of the economic fabric even as capitalist modernity bears its fruit.

In modern South Africa, where much has been achieved, party and state control, cadre deployments, parastatal indulgence and mechanisms of empowerment mandated in charters and a plethora of laws have forced economic "transformation" on the compliant. The difference from most of the rest of Africa in this case has been the formal legalisation of the patrimonial and its socioeconomic engineering at an extremely high cost. Amid its evident wealth and successes in modernity may be found seeds for the emergence in time of a dysfunctional political economy. Many economics observers speak of a possible economic slide in future. It remains no ordinary country. The government system lacks efficiency. Wastage in public outlays is extensive. Presidential claims on budget allocations have risen sharply; 42% of cabinet ministers have outside corporate interests; over 60% of members of Parliament have significant shareholdings in companies, 45% as directors; 60% of civil servants hold business interests in private companies (some $5 billion annually going from public funding to entities in which they hold assets); and 33–50% of provincial political representatives have similar business engagements including as company directors. Around $30 billion or 20% of the state procurement tender value is estimated to be lost annually from graft and mismanagement while irregular state spending has risen. This stands alongside acute poverty for probably 40% of all households, with around 100,000 self-employed today seeking their living in excavating the discarded rubbish from dustbins on the streets in the hope of providing bread for their dependants.[5]

All three of these economies have lit the economic firmament in the past. More contemporary instances of regression to crisis can be found over the past few years – for example, Lesotho, Swaziland, Madagascar, the DRC, Somalia, Libya and Sudan. In Swaziland over 63% live on less than $2 per day under the tutelage of the monarchy and its various economic entities used to indulge in excess, the king having 13 palaces accommodating in luxury a retinue of 14 wives. Other extreme disparities are found elsewhere, power and accumulation being considered part of the natural rights of rulers. Economic growth cannot disguise the decay and crumbling of central governments in many countries, the economic modes often outlasting the machinations of the political regimes. Authoritarianism and the divides of identity remain notwithstanding growth and the practice of pseudo-democracy, behind which often lies the enrichment of tyranny. The nation-state project in Africa still needs to transcend the ties of ethnicities, clans, party and political identities fused within its make-up and modus operandi.

It is within this cauldron of asserted optimism amid older realities of the political economy that many have come to "project and forecast" the continental economic future as "Africa ascendant". Here the continent's image has been repainted with an airbrush. Some say it is the last frontier for growth, corporate gurus proclaim blue-sky economics will colour the future, and others foresee Africa "rising". The leitmotif *du jour* is Africa's economic "take-off". How are these judgements reached, and what are the economic implications and realities in the future calculus on Africa?

Futurology and numerics

We can assess the critical projections that have been made. Let us focus on the mid-century, by when there will have been a further 38 years of economic change, nearly two generations in Africa's future demographic life cycle. During this time possibly around 1.3 billion people will be born in Africa, somewhat more than all living now, but another 300 million or so will die, leaving 2 billion on Africa's soil by 2050.[6] Compare this with an estimate that around 15 billion people have lived in Africa since around 50,000BCE, in effect from the initial footsteps of *Homo sapiens* onwards. It will not then represent a zenith in Africa's demography, since some expect Africa's population might reach 3 billion by end of the century. Where will there be an economic pinnacle?

Most architects of the projections will probably no longer be around to witness the accuracy or otherwise of their forecasts. It is naturally accepted that to predict that far ahead is impossible. As an attempt at futurology, projection might be taken to hold heuristic benefit, setting out contours for feasible economic expectations. Notwithstanding the usual caveats (and noting that the data used here differ from Angus Maddison's GDP numerics based on 1990 real dollars), an exercise in such quantitative speculation was conducted by the Pardee Center for International Futures in Denver with the Institute for Security Studies in Pretoria in 2011. It set down perhaps the high-water mark in "optimistic" long-term economic projections, in *African Futures 2050*.[7] While the model used for forecasting the future embodied a complexity of variables (inevitably disputable), I am not concerned here with its intricacies, just the economic numerics and outcomes.

The baseline at 2010 indicated income per head for Africa at $900 in constant dollars, compared with $500 in 1960 (with $150 "lost" in the mid-1990s). Naturally, there are enormous variances by country, region, class and segment. From 1960 onwards Africa's economic growth rate had touched over 6% annually on five-year moving averages only once or twice. The futurists argued that Africa's GDP would exceed $13 trillion by 2050, further ahead then than the United States and the EU in 2010 (this projection was based on a GDP compound growth rate of 5.1% for 2010–50). While the baseline GDP for 2010 was not indicated, I have calculated it at $1.8 trillion on these parameters. These projections therefore prognosticate per-head income in constant prices at around $6,500 in 2050, way up from $900 today. If so, Africa would have maybe "arrived" – except for evident regional and related income disparities, and poverty, which would remain.

Many in Africa and beyond would love to see all this happen. Yet is it realistic to expect on the basis of known past long-cycle growth-rate trends? Here the magisterial source data of Maddison are our only real guide to cycles over the *longue durée*. While these data differ in baseline and constant prices, the cycle growth rates derived are valid for comparison, whatever the calculus. Let us recall then these long-cycle growth rates over different epochs.

Maddison's figures for Africa's GDP present us with the following annual real constant-price growth rates: 0.15% for 1500–1870, then 0.7% for 1820–70, moving upwards to 1.3% for 1870–1913 and 2.8% for 1913–60. For 1960–80 economic growth continued at a rapid clip, at around 4.5% – the most promising growth experience then to date. Growth over the next decade was at 2.3% but below net natural demo-graphic expansion. For 1990–2000 Africa's GDP notched annual rates at just below 2.8%, barely offsetting population growth. The golden decade of 2000–10 found Africa's GDP expanding at 4.8% on average, aided by the world commodity boom. On the longest measurable economic cycle from the 1st century to now, annual growth-rate perfor-mance was only 0.05%, with the last 1,000 years at a roughly similar rate, the last 100 years moving at just over 2.2%, and the last 50 years at under 3.8%.

For annual growth of per-head income, Maddison recorded the rate at: 0.05% for 1500–1870, 0.58% for the 50 years 1820–70, then 0.57% for 1870–1913, 0.91% for 1913–50 and 1.8% for the period 1960–80, after which decline set in. For 1980–90 growth rates were negative at –0.6% annually, and GDP per head stagnated with no growth for another ten years, to leave the 1980–2010 growth rate at only 0.7% per year. The best result found was in the 2000–2010 decade at 2.36%. On the latest cycle of 50 years (1960–2010) the rate of 1.1% has been achieved. To go back further in time, for the last 2,000 years growth has been at an annual rate of under 0.07% and for the last 110 years at 1% – no stellar performance. The large and growing gaps with Asia and Latin America reflect Africa as the global laggard.

Such economic contours provide perspective on the future and expectations for any projections. First, the achievement of high, continuing secular growth over the long-term cycle has been hard to secure. Small variances in growth rates, especially in early years, have had a devastating impact on GDP and per-head income in the long term, when measured at future dates. An annual growth rate of 5% or more (let alone 7%) for 40 years has never been achieved in either GDP or income per head. The advent of even one tough decade does serious harm to the growth profile. Ups and downs have been a consistent element in Africa's economic past, with no guarantee that cyclicity could not strike in future. Crisis – whether domestic, or in conflicts, or exogenously driven coming from investment flows and world markets – has been a prominent feature for Africa.

Extrapolations from decade-long golden periods or current high growth rates for parts of Africa mislead: they pose dangers for interpretation and risk leading to fantasy. For instance, the AfDB estimated growth rate for Africa in 2011 was radically scaled back within six months from 5.5% to 3.7% because of developments in North Africa. As a result, one-third of the growth earlier projected had been lost. In September 2011 another downward revision was made, to 3.2%. The growth rate had been cut by over 40% within 12 months. Reliance on the much-loved assumption of *ceteris paribus* (i.e. all things remaining equal) can be heroic. If future economic growth of Africa's GDP based on $1.8 trillion for 2010 (at constant prices) progressed at "only" 4% annually, GDP in 2050 would be not $13 trillion but $8.6 trillion – a huge deviation. If the rate of growth was only 3%, Africa's GDP would be $5.7 trillion. If it expanded at the rate of the last 50 years (ie, at 1.1% annually), in mid-century Africa's GDP would be just $2.8 trillion. One must take care when drinking the Kool-Aid.

With the per-head income base in 2010 at $900, growth rates at (a) 4%, (b) 3%, (c) 2% and (d) the historic growth rate for the last

50-year cycle of 1.1% yield respectively the following per-head income for 2050: (a) $4,321, (b) $2,935, (c) $1,987 and (d) $1,394. All these scenarios stand far behind the $6,500 mooted for the heroic economic growth trajectories for Africa's GDP based on uninterrupted annual growth of 5.1% for the coming 40 years. This illustrates the power of future demographics and the sensitivity of outcomes to small downsides in long-term growth rates to be achieved. *Quo vadis* Africa?

No one truly knows what shape Africa's economies will take in future. Its economies could in principle formalise more of the informal, clandestine and shadow economies to allow capitalist Africa to command more economic space than before, and power the continent forwards along better growth trajectories than in the past. The weight of the pre-modern lingers and has been centuries in transition already, with important if modest consequences. No one can intuit growth paths with precision for four decades. Nor can the constraints and opportunities be defined today with any absolute rigour. If growth trajectories follow old pathways, Africa will slip further behind the rest of the world. It is expected that the world economy will grow, with Asia's expansion drawing greater strength. Many competitors to Africa's plurality of states exist and have their own ambitions. In this competitive struggle for position, Africa has long been the world's weakest link, with many of its modes of economic survival locked in slow-growth evolutionary paths, and even some of its modernist economies trapped in economic dead ends.

Another burden may await Africa down the track: incomplete economic maturation and difficulties in sustaining high growth rates as time passes. It is a fact of economic record that even South Africa, for all its modernity, has over the course of the last 90 years rarely crossed the 3.5% real GDP growth trend line. It continues to find this rate one that it cannot easily escape on the upside, for now at least. The government's dream is that 7% annual GDP growth should be achieved. But it appears as a mirage even while it is accepted to be the minimum to slay the dragons of unemployment and poverty, these aggregated in numbers to yield the crude "misery index" of failure. This has not stopped the futurists waxing forth with unbridled optimism about South Africa's growth to 2050, one projecting this at an annual 5% in real terms – well above any historic trend. All this contrasts with the reality that the country's GDP per head was 24% lower than the world average in 1994, and by 2010 stood at 33% lower. Hubris often becomes infectious. Even Mario Ramos, the chief executive of Absa, one of the country's major banks, wondered recently whether Africa was not the "new Asia ... the power to claim the 21st century is ours".[8] It is most unlikely.

In the debate on economic policy in South Africa, business and government seem to portray the image of an enduring "cold war" conflict: their ideologies standing worlds apart. South Africans like nothing more than to discuss and "unpack" their solutions with never-ending rounds of party or state meetings, *indaba* and *bosberaad*, even over the *braai*. Every few years the government issues conflicted blue-prints for growth, some wildly ambitious and typically unrealised, even unrealisable given the economic configuration: congenitally *etatist*, seeking central-planning-driven nirvana. Political analyst Moeletsi Mbeki boldly forecast the country's "Tunisia Day" by 2020, give or take a couple of years. This may never happen yet the economic slide can be calibrated.

These prognoses raise critical broader questions for Africa. Is South Africa's fundamental economic dilemma some modern limit to capitalist Africa's evolution, as with Algeria's state-capitalist model (and 25% unemployment), as one sort of middle-income trap, or rather an iron ceiling, one perhaps to be encountered for economies in Africa that later attain more advanced levels of maturity? Only the future will tell.

Official visions

Despite recent actual growth rate erosion, today's official growth story is one of almost unrestrained optimism. The World Bank's strategy for Africa in 2010 concluded that Africa was on "the brink of an economic take-off, much like China was 30 years ago, and India 20 years ago".[9] The usual caveats followed: on productive employment, with the need to accommodate 7–10 million youngsters in jobs every year; on food insecurity; the large number of fragile states that may be stuck in the famous "low-level equilibrium trap" (actually a wonderful reverse image, given that in all countries of this sort there is nothing of equilibria about them – instability dominates); infrastructural deficits; power and energy deficiencies, and the like.

The bank's ten-year vision released in 2010 foresaw Africa's per-head income (at $1,440) as 60% higher by 2020. This would mean growth in average individual incomes at about 5% for each year forward without any slippage, once more the projection of the future beyond the historic record. By 2011 this strategy had already been watered down: now it was for at least 20 countries to have income per head 50% higher, implying growth rates at 3–4% annually (actually the real rate would need to be 4% for all or more if others only scored 3%), with another 20 countries enjoying income per-head growth at 1–2%, and nothing said on the rest – the 15 countries that did not make this cut. While the prognosis mooted the idea that five countries would achieve middle-income status in this time frame (for some reason Comoros and Mauritania were cited), the list of the top 20 growth performers included Malawi (already in meltdown), and Steven Radelet's "list of 17" for emerging Africa so-called, which had identified among others Lesotho (an economic quagmire), as part of the would-be renaissance.[10] Here the expectations have been in line with many "visions" articulated elsewhere (Nigeria 2020, Cameroon 2035, Uganda 2025), providing political comfort to the architects' images of the future.

The World Bank (after consulting multiple stakeholders and NGOs) has it seems taken to the fashionable task of socioeconomic engineering like a duck to water. It believes Africa's present can be redesigned or at least tinkered with to shape economic growth, as do many. Strategies for climbing the stairway to heaven are many and wondrous: co-ordination with development partners, capturing synergies, knowledge generation, fostered learning, leveraged finance, cemented client-driven strategy focus, programmatic approaches, increased multisectoriality, high-impact operations, game changers with "quick wins", dynamic multilayered monitoring arrangements, and the like. It is a litany of econo-speak and managerialism that would make George Orwell proud. All would provide the "fix", in an ever-expanding smorgasbord of orchestrated interventions, options and instrumentalities – to somehow preordain and actively shape the willed economic outcome. I recall all this being discussed and tried before, under other guises, in earlier development plans, with different nomenclature, to little avail.

The African Development Bank (AfDB) naturally joined the party, issuing its *African Economic Outlook 2011* to similar enthusiasm. It focused on emerging partners to Africa, meaning the usual suspects: BRICs, Turkey, South Korea and others – whoever is for now on the up. It suggested correctly that Africa's widening trade matrix meant global connectivity was more than just about China. The AfDB reported that, while in the 1990s Africa was struggling, it was today "converging", even if traditional partners were still sourcing the bulk of world FDI inflows, around 72%. Convergence is an elliptical idea in the short term, it must be said: it really requires decades to cement its place. To be safe, the AfDB asserted that the new players and linkages were not setting Africa onto a backward path due to claims about lowered governance standards, re-indebtment, deindustrialisation and more reliance on resource extraction. Yet many cases of this paradigm in Africa, even today, have been suggested by others.

Nonetheless, the AfDB estimated that around 25 countries would not cross the 4% GDP growth mark in 2011–12. The lower-growth performers would probably include South Africa, Algeria, Egypt, Côte d'Ivoire, Cameroon, Sudan and Morocco, to which we should add Libya and even Tunisia, many being hefty players in economic scale and demographics. Only ten countries might make this benchmark on growth in income per head, leaving the rest below, with ten countries at under 2% growth and three with negative growth. Another 40 million people in Africa would enter the 15–24 age cohort by 2020 alone, many more after, and hence the employment task would remain unforgiving, even greater than before. On the growth stakes, the AfDB prognosticated sub-Saharan GDP to grow 6.2% in 2012 and North Africa (with Sudan) to recover off the floor and rack up 5.1%. Already this prognosis has been thwarted.

Then too, AfDB's economists have turned their hand to the

long-range, 50-year projection game, issuing an unofficial prognosis (*Africa in 50 Years' Time*, released in September 2011) built on AfDB's *Vision 2050 Project,* pushing growth estimates and projections for Africa out to 2060.[11] Acknowledging that the future is shrouded in uncertainty, it nonetheless offers a quasi-official heroic view, much influenced, one suspects, by images of current buoyancy and optimism in Africa's economies circa 2010. Here steady growth is foreseen, untrammelled on a linear upward path for half a century, most countries expected to be then at middle income status, the Africa-wide GDP at around $15.7 trillion (with the crucial caveat, however, that this is measured in current market prices, unadjusted for inflation), with income per head put at around $5,600 for the 2.75 billion inhabitants expected in 2060. In this piece of "modelling" of the "high case scenario", real GDP growth per annum rises to a zenith of 6.6% in 2020, thereafter slipping downwards towards 5.4% in 2050, while on the "low case scenario", Africa's GDP reaches $12.25 trillion in 2060, the growth rate peaking at 5.5% in 2020 and ending the day on 4.5% per annum, so leaving income per head then at only $5,617. While citing the usual litany of "drivers", this piece of futurology is wholly speculative. It follows the well-trod macro-path of benign extrapolation, its projections well in excess of realised long-term historic trends, without recourse to any interruptions on the economic stairway to heaven. As an idea there may be nothing amiss in this largely statistical exercise, and yet its numeric aridity, presumptive claims, gloss on the demographic challenges, and implied faith in wholly efficient and reformist states, without any realistic reference to Africa's often torrid political economics, makes one doubt its economic legitimacy and futuristic veracity. I know of no corporate investor that would bet the farm on this impressionistic image.

The World Bank and the AfDB have not been alone in trumpeting contemporary Africa's economic virtues. The chorus has been joined by the private-industry world of companies, accounting firms, consultants, assorted pundits and the media. The investment case for Africa is now touted almost universally as evidently compelling, perhaps irresistible. Now is the moment to invest in Africa. It is Africa's turn to shine.

Rating agencies have joined in. Moody's has claimed that the pace of growth has fundamentally altered. Funds, with funds of funds, lined up capital and commitments. Private equity shifted gear. The continent was at a historic turning point, the corporate giants having "discovered" Africa. It was the next big thing. Mastercard Worldwide sang a similar song.[12] There have been new stirrings since the dawn of the 21st century, it suggested. Among the elected top ten transforming economies for the future was even Zimbabwe. Together these top ten countries controlled 67% of sub-Saharan GDP. Many economic drivers would navigate the route forward, including notably urbanisation, the mythic "demographic dividend", rising consumer income, economic hubs and growing markets. Optimism is infectious. Why not a 10% growth rate for Africa, one economist said; the emulation of China was on the cards, remarked another. The cheerleaders took easy command of the economic stage. Africa had "arrived". There would be no going back.

If there were an award for bullish optimism, it might well go to Renaissance Capital. Its upbeat report, *Africa: The bottom billion becomes the fastest billion*, published in mid-2011, signalled an epic economic shift in motion.[13] It was easier than ever to catch up, it asserted. Others had done so, why not Africa? Nigeria would move to double-digit growth and become a trillion-dollar economy by 2027, overtaking South Africa before then by a good margin. It might well do so, one day. Sub-Sahara outside South Africa would account for $4.5 trillion by 2030, assuming nominal GDP growth at 10% per year, on a path of 6–7% real growth – the heroic growth rate deployed here too. This might even be conservative, it intimated. This was heady stuff.

At the heart of this projection lay our old economics friend, the Rostow model, and the stages of growth syndrome. In this analysis Africa had emerged from traditional society during 1960–80, even though 70% of Africa today still remains in or connected to agrarian modes of subsistence. The preconditions for take-off were set, typically needing modernity to dominate the traditional, which presupposed continental economic flight within 10–50 years. Take-off, however, could be different for Africa, Renaissance argued: it would be services-led, not based on manufacturing as the engine of growth. The mobile phone syndrome was evidenced, Africa recording famous and fabulous growth rates for unit numbers sold and the spread of communications. Could this random correlate, however, be associated with growth causality inside the marked deindustrialisation witnessed in Africa, and how long would it be from take-off to maturity (Rostow allowing 50–100 years for industrial revolution to become rooted and spread)? Could Africa be that unique, that different?

The time required for these sequenced shifts from post-traditional society to maturity could be anywhere from 50 to 150 years. Here, however, fewer qualms were exhibited on this problematic periodisation and stage succession – and none on the inconvenient realities around the lingering and large pre-modern in Africa's economic landscapes Africa, it implied, had somehow mastered the growth paradigm. Future demographics would be the critical driver and present an unchallenged competitive advantage over Asia. The fire of youth would ignite the continental economic machine, not its presidential palaces. The urban influx too would generate huge growth, even if (for reasons unexplained) it had not done so before: this time would be different. High economic growth would, however, need sizeable investment rates, typically at 25% of GDP for the 7% magical benchmark annual growth rate to be reached and to work its charms. Few of course had ever done that before. Why then would Africa differ?

Here the "catch-up theory of economics" was invoked. The critics, we were told, had it all wrong; apparently the ideas of Vladislav Inozemtsev, a Russian economist, concerning countries stalling at the middle-income phase were "irrelevant" to Africa. Nor would the problems of weak Western economies hold Africa back: it had China and others in its firmament. If the Middle Kingdom stalled, so what: many countries did well enough without reliance on the China card. The growth in Africa would, moreover, almost automatically move it away from autocracy towards democracy, another fillip towards growth. Weaknesses in infrastructure and bottlenecks in energy and power would be eliminated in time to raise the trajectory further. What could possibly go wrong? With this constant refrain, and with analysts coming to the same consensual conclusion, using much the same variables in a roughly similar configuration elected for the "drivers" in the pending economic miracle, I could not but wonder about the old Latin dictum: *repetitio est mater studiorum*. Was this confluence of like-minded views knowledge anew, from divergent sources, or the herd effect of the choir of economists and fellow travellers on song?

Inconvenient realities

The optimism portrayed above has in effect become a dogma in official and corporate worlds. What of the deeper economics and structural histories in Africa, the pre-modern and majorities across Africa's subsistence economic fabric? Could they be so rapidly minimised or airbrushed away by the palliatives of faster or never before achieved rates of economic growth?

The Tripartite Free Trade Area sought between the SADC, the EAC and COMESA is now envisaged as a potentially formidable economic giant, with 26 member states having a combined GDP of approximately $740 billion, a large chunk of Africa's economic weight. But it could turn out to be another Africa dream too far. Each bloc has special trade exclusion clauses, sensitive products and competitive positions, and exhibits reluctance to open up. The problem, and the reason these constituent pieces of the trade puzzle have for so long, 30 years in some cases, not managed to integrate their flows of goods and services, remains: intra-Africa flows are still a fraction, around 10–12%, of Africa's external trade with the world. Indeed, many economies remain highly restrictive to outsiders, even competitors from Africa. Africa does not really trust open markets: Nigeria still prohibits an extensive list of imports; Uganda wants local content rules applied even within the EAC states; tariff and non-tariff trade controls are ubiquitous across the frontiers. Moreover, vulnerability to world trade shocks and outside markets will continue. Even internal crises have their damaging consequences, as the headwinds of the North Africa downside in 2011 demonstrated. All this leads to the view that maybe there has emerged a "twin-track" growth trajectory: North Africa barely recording economic growth in the near term, sub-Saharan Africa expected to manage short-term respectable growth.

In the list of least developed countries, the category created by UNCTAD in 1971 to depict the world's poorest (on which I used to undertake economics work in the 1970s), Africa has always featured prominently. At the time 30 countries were so designated. Now 48 countries are listed, and of these 33 are from Africa. Only Botswana, Mauritius and Cape Verde have moved off this list, all small economies and the latter two island states. Angola and Equatorial Guinea should soon exit this category. But many others in Africa will struggle to emerge from this bottom-of-class classification, even within the next decade or so, and some may never.

Progress on cutting debt/GDP ratios in Africa's economies took place over 2000–11. Write-offs from multilateral and foreign creditors made a huge dent in this profile and some fiscal rectitude helped, although it has already been eroded in several cases. Public debt in many of Africa's economies is not yet an economic drama that has disappeared, though progress on past trends has been made. Today the IMF places nine countries in the category of distress, ten at high risk of debt distress, another ten at moderate risk, and ten at low risk. In effect, half of Africa is still regarded to be at significant risk. By 2011 private investment in sub-Saharan Africa stood at 15% of GDP, below the norms in the developing world (18–19%), with Asia at 30% or more in certain countries, and the OECD at 24%. A quarter of Africa's economies currently have a foreign-exchange buffer of less than three months of imports, the mark of relative fragility. Economic security is not evident for all.

Among the greatest constraints on African economic growth has been infrastructure – especially in the areas of energy and power, but also transport, roads, rail, ports and logistics, shipping, airports and air links, water and irrigation, and health and sanitation. Critical has been infrastructural deterioration across and between countries, its dilapidated state, embedded inefficiencies and inhibiting high costs, the growing lag behind competitors elsewhere and the associated problems of greenfield infrastructure funding, with $93 billion per year estimated as being needed for the future.[14] Half of this is required just for maintenance. Costs for Africa's infrastructure replacement have doubled in the last five years. Some fragile states face near-impossible burdens and even the resource-rich nations lag, despite acknowledged but often poorly monetised natural capital wealth. The funding gaps are large, growing, spreading across the continent and critical for the all-important power industry on which modern economic growth is dependent. That much is certain.

Over 30 countries still have regular power shortages, with periodic blackouts, brownouts and systemic deficiencies. Infrastructure could shape up to 50% of Africa's rate of economic growth/decline, in both directions. Some argue that, if improved, infrastructure and, especially, power systems (in the equation of "no power equals minimal or zero growth") could add up to 2–3% to future growth rates in some economies. Yet it has long been this way. Nigeria is a classic case of inadequate power and energy undermining growth and potential, yet it currently seeks long-term 7% annual growth rates amid sharp rich/ poor divides (with 593,000 bottles of champagne imported in 2010). As Africa's economic growth profile lifts, these constraints will become more apparent, potentially placing an embedded ceiling on normal economic expansion and in so doing intensifying competition between industries and firms reliant on power, electricity and energy supply. High-growth-rate optimists often presume that these inherent limits to growth can somehow be easily breached or simply ignored. They are dreaming.

Africa is still vulnerable to local and foreign shocks that could act to undermine high-growth projections. They include international economic events, so-called "idiosyncratic" shocks related to health, famine and disease (costing an estimated $12 billion annually); natural disasters (droughts, cyclones and floods); and the unpredictable bugbear of conflict and political violence. The costs of Africa's conflicts over 1990–2005 amounted to more than all the aid received, at around $284 billion. In some countries conflict had cut real GDP by 30–40%. Zimbabwe did even worse, without any war. The average conflict in Africa has turned the normal country economic clock back by around 10–15 years on the growth cycle. Few take account of this risk, and no one seems to care.

Today we find within many countries a mix of modest affluence

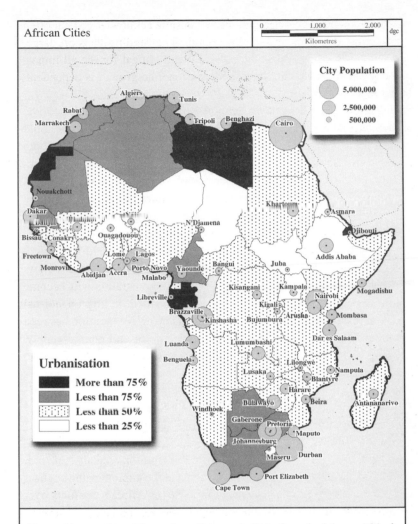

African Cities

City Population
5,000,000
2,500,000
500,000

Urbanisation
More than 75%
Less than 75%
Less than 50%
Less than 25%

From old or ancient cities and small towns built in the colonial era, Africa's cities have grown apace and are home to increasing numbers. Millions have flocked to slums and market centres in an escape from rural economic backwaters. Urban subsistence is no less tough than in the areas left behind. Future demographics will ensure that the majority will be urbanised over the next few decades. More and larger cities are expected.

and miserable conditions for most inhabitants against a background of apparently paradoxical conditions: uneven growth, great natural wealth, social instability and raw underdevelopment. Africa contains many states aligned on this model. GDP and incomes may rise but the numbers, and even the share, of very poor people remains at best stubbornly large, producing for the fortunate countries a sort of middling-income, failing state. Nigeria may be one and even "modern" South Africa too on this poverty-spectrum measure. Then there is the periodic perversity of dynamics ingrained within world markets. Although the 2008–09 world recession hit Africa like others, it left a less negative imprint, the lower-income countries faring better on the growth profile – mainly because of their lesser integration with the commodity world. Today Africa at large is seeking more exposure to world markets.

Overall, we can see that Africa is growing, has grown faster in its recent past, and may even do so more – perhaps for longer. It may have more economic drivers, but it will need to keep on the road to nirvana for longer and not deviate off the best pathways in order to achieve the projected outcomes hoped for by so many. The multiple economic modes found in Africa will realign along these economic roadways going forward, but it will be an uncertain and unpredictable journey. For those positing realisation of the upper boundaries in growth rates for 40 years, I predict tears at or well before the end of the line.

Middle-class "magic"

Perhaps the most seductive tale about Africa's economic journey concerns the rise of Africa's "middle class" – taken as evidence of the emergence of the continent, the foundations for its promise, and the economic driver of choice for most of the pundits. This tale has been told by numerous sources, including the AfDB, the chattering classes and voices from the corporate front.[15]

You can see evidence of the middle-class phenomenon if you travel to Africa's cities, on flights, in five-star hotels and within the suburbs of urban substance. Crucially, I mean here the middle class *per se*, that is as a socioeconomic "class", rather than simply the "middle-income" category measured in local terms. The latter is a wholly different animal, and much larger, as it is measured typically in relative income terms against domestic economic conditions. It is this latter phenomenon that the AfDB has evidenced in the economic vision it outlined, with significant empirical data, to show growing middle-income categories emerging in Africa, as the flip side to former acute poverty partially alleviated via economic growth, which is selectively shaping consumer patterns.

The AfDB has defined its "middle class" as those found between the 20th and 80th percentiles of consumption distribution, or at 0.75–1.25 times the median per-head income level. This equates to an annual income of around $3,900, or within this broader group defined by the AfDB as those with $2–4 and $8–10 daily per head income outlays, or more. While difficulties exist in definition, the AfDB reports this rather elastic "middle class" at around 300–500 million people, an imprecise and diffused category, sitting between the vast poor and the small elites. Those at its bottom at $2–4 per day are considered as "floating", vulnerable to slipping back into poverty, especially from exogenous shocks (I would add endogenous ones too, often far more damaging). Then come the "lower-middle class" with around $4–10 per day, living just above subsistence (this, like beauty, in the eye of the beholder), who can save and hold some discretionary income. The "upper-middle class" is depicted as the $10–20 per day category.

Between 1980 and 2010 Africa is found to have produced a wider "middle class". The floating category rose from 49.3 million to 190.5 million, the lower from 39.9 million to 79.7 million, and the upper from 21.9 million to 42.9 million over the period (rather precise numbers, but that is what the data do). In total, there was a numeric rise from 111.2 million to 313.2 million over 20 years, the share in Africa rising from 26.2% to 34.3%. Growth brought its benefits, but others in the "poor class" remained in large numbers, moving down from 69% in 1980 to 61% of all so in 2010. At poverty incomes of under $1.25 per day, 44.15% were recorded (down from 49.9% in 1980) and in the $1.25–2.00 per day category there were 16.7% in 2010 (down from 19.1% in 1980).

Though welcome news, these data do not show us anything about "middle-class" Africa. It is to be remembered that over the period 1980–2010 Africa's population grew from 478 million to 1,005 million. On equivalent global estimates of the actual middle class existing across the world, sub-Saharan Africa had only 32 million in 2010 (2% of the worldwide number). While these numbers will grow (an estimated 107 million foreseen by 2030), Africa's share of the middle class in the world will remain the same.

We must take care not to confuse this middle class with the AfDB's categories based merely on domestic income measures. The very poor with income under $1.25 per day rose from 238 million in 1980 to 445 million in 2010, and in the $1.25–2.00 per day category from 91 million to 167 million; their combined numbers grew from 329 million in 1980 to 612 million in 2010. At the end of the next 40 years more people will live in Africa than ever before – double the number living there now.

Many in the West wonder how people in Africa can live on extremely low incomes of around $1–2 daily. The reality is that these monies do not always come in daily, and people rarely consume all the income once it is received. Strategies for survival vary and are highly complex. The poor take loans, become indebted, make savings, trade on income/benefits, buy and sell small assets, make micro-purchases, incur periodic payments arrears, sometimes pool incomes, rely on monies from *stokvels* (in South Africa and elsewhere, groups that meet to share combined revenue benefits from joint activities), and derive part sustenance from income-in-kind as well. The subsistence value in kind can vary significantly. In effect Africa's *povo* juggle and jive their way through time, often waiting for some break, perhaps some windfall, and in the interim manage their meagre resources as if optimising their portfolio. Critically, many rely on older modes of dependence and sociocultural networks for survival and continuity. It is tough and typically gruelling.

In countries like Ethiopia – deemed by all today as one of Africa's fast-growth "transforming economies" – over 86% are living at under the $1.25 per day poverty datum line. The corresponding figure for Tanzania is 82%, with at least 15 countries (ten were not assessed, including

Sudan and Zimbabwe) over the 80% mark, Nigeria included at 82%. These large countries illustrate the depth and spread of income impoverishment in Africa. Many among the poor remain linked to the agrarian or informal modes of subsistence and survival. In Liberia this segment of the poor constitutes 94.8% of the population, and over 70% in 23 of the 44 countries measured, with South Africa at 44.7% and Nigeria at 76.3%, both mooted "champions" of the continent's success. Naturally, the distribution of the middle-income category as actually measured varies enormously across Africa's states: North Africa is well ahead.

The struggle for over 30 years to dent Africa's poverty has brought some success, but only very slowly. The growth record is largely to blame. In 2010 those with per head income below $10 per day amounted to 81.5% of Africa's total population. Though the emerging trends may be good news, they cannot yet be said to represent more than a modest middle class in conventional or global terms. Those with incomes above $20 per day ($600 per month or $7,200 per year), not exactly all in the "rich class", so described, were only 4.48% of the continent's population. If the Lorenz curve for Africa, measuring income differentiation, is examined for 2010 the cumulative share of income indicates large variances: the rich typically hold more income proportionately than the poor.

With increased incomes in Africa and falling product prices for many local consumer items (though often second-hand or of poor quality), more of Africa's households have acquired the trappings of modernist consumer culture – apparel, radios and televisions, mobile phones, fridges, electrical goods, motorcycles and vehicles. Yet this still leaves Africa a long way from any general or even predominant modernity. The idea that mobile telephony could, as some suggest, "transform the continent" is to me the "economics of wishful thinking", amounting to distraction from more fundamental matters like unlocking natural capital and enhancing productive wealth accumulation. It is like observing the commercial cart placed ahead of the economic horse. Enhanced income above subsistence allows for the purchase of more discretionary items as well, but income derives ultimately from the construction and exploitation of the productive base: there is no "money tree". At current levels

Africa's middle class today might approximate to the working class poor of Europe a century ago.

Since 1970 the income distribution curve has shifted only slowly – growth has been too anaemic to make a serious difference across the continent. Those under the $1 per day baseline in 1970 were 40%; this proportion rose over 1980–2000, then started to fall.[16] Variations exist all over Africa's economic map – by country and time period and according to whether a region is landlocked or coastal, resource poor or rich, conflict ridden or otherwise, has a high or low savings propensity, or did or did not have colonial origins.

The Gini coefficient measure of "inequality" for Africa rose from 0.63 in 1970 to reach around 0.66 in the mid-1980s; it then crept down, but is now back around the same level it was 40 years ago. It is a measure that needs to be treated with extreme caution in Africa's circumstances.[17] Weak growth induced more inequality while welfare later improved. Many more statistics on these lines can be constructed. None tells the entire economic story or captures the coexistent realities found: the medieval alongside the trappings of modernity.

There probably will be a larger middle class in future in Africa, but emerging from a modest base. Consumerism has attracted more to the cities and lifestyles of the rich and famous – celebrity culture is as strong in Africa as anywhere else. The managerial models of understanding Africa from "commercial think-tanks" like McKinsey and Ernst & Young (one advocate speaking of the "African phoenix") make serious play of this consumer-driven image of the continent on the move, even as a recipe for its future economic strategy; yet this amounts to nothing like the economic advancement built around an actual or dominant "middle-class" milieu as so commonly and quite wrongly suggested.[18] Informalised and subsistence Africa, with swathes of survivalist pockets of existence, remains the overriding economic reality.

Rich and infamous

We must not leave out of the picture Africa's wealthy. It was Gunnar

Myrdal who posited that "poverty created poverty" and in essence produced pessimism about income gaps and a global divide between rich and poor: "to he that hath shall be given, and to he that hath not shall be taken away" was the view (echoing the original biblical prophecy). For Africa, unbeknown to Myrdal (who died in 1987), this has indeed been prophetic.

According to the AfDB's estimate of the so-called rich, 4.48% of Africa's incomes exceed $20 per day. Yet this does not describe the "rich" as commonly understood. On this count, around 50 million would fit into this category in Africa (roughly equal to the population of South Africa). Clearly Africa's rich are smaller in number, their incomes and wealth larger by wide margins. Known rich individuals are found all over Africa, and wealth concentrations exist in several countries, notably Egypt, South Africa and Nigeria. All countries have some rich. A few even manage to make the rich lists compiled elsewhere in the world.

Capgemini-Merrill Lynch measures of high net worth individuals (HNWI) and ultra-HNWI, based on Lorenz curve analysis, are perhaps our best guide to the rich on a global scale.[19] Africa is not the locus for most of the world's rich. In 2010 Africa accounted for only 0.1% of the 11 million so-classified rich in the world, though this class in Africa had reportedly grown 11% over 2009–10. It would put HNWI in Africa at around 11,000 people. In Africa the rich are getting richer and their wealth amounts to 1.2% of HNWI numbers worldwide. Of the estimated $44 trillion owned by this measured world rich, Africa's HNWI hold collective wealth of $528 billion. This averages (though inequality exists among the rich as well) around $48 million each. The profile is no doubt incomplete and rather rudimentary, but it indicates the scale of wealth differentiation that exists.

Typically, wealth of great magnitude is not accumulated overnight. Most of the wealthy have built assets over decades, even if some managed to "get rich quick". Some have inherited family wealth. Many are found in the corporate world but also among Africa's political classes. Ultra-HNWI or billionaires in Africa identified on the *Forbes* Rich List 2011 included 14 individuals (up from ten the year before): two Nigerians, four South Africans and eight Egyptians. With an estimated $10 billion

Nigerian Aliko Dangote (51st in the world) was richest, followed by South African Nicky Oppenheimer and family at $7 billion, Egyptian Nassef Sawiris at $5.6 billion (his brothers are also rich with $3.5 billion and $1.4 billion, and the family patriarch holds $2.9 billion) and South African Johann Rupert and family at $4.8 billion. The 14 on the *Forbes* list held assets of about $50 billion between them.

In South Africa, state-mandated policies of empowerment produced privileged deal flows that have augmented the wealth of numerous now-rich post-1994 captains of industry. One thinks of Tokyo Sexwale, Cyril Ramaphosa, Patrice Motsepe (with wealth estimated at $3.3 billion), Bridgette Radebe and Saki Macozoma, all with personal control over conglomerates, equity stakes in listed and private companies, or commercial and mineral interests. The combined wealth of the country's top 100 richest people could now almost cover the country's budget deficit. Indeed, the 71,000 dollar millionaires in South Africa are expected to triple to 242,000 by 2016. The top 1% of households owns 38.5% of wealth.

In a number of countries in Africa wealth is shielded by tradition and undocumented records, making it near-impossible to obtain accurate data on the ultra-rich. Corruption in Africa has likewise distorted the veracity of information on the rich in both politics and the corporate world. Many who are known to hold significant wealth rarely disclose their scope of assets to public sources.

Africa's rich include traditional rulers (for example, Otumfua Ashanti-Hene in Ghana) and royal houses. King Mohammed VI of Morocco is the richest person in that country, with estimated net worth at $2.5 billion. Then there is King Mswati III of Swaziland, for whose royal house the provision in the 2011–12 state budget was $60 million, and where investment funds are held outside government control in the form of the Tibiyo Taka Ngwane (Wealth of the Nation) trust, which has shares in many Swazi firms, along with Tisuka Taka Ngwane (Pillars of Swaziland), which holds a large portfolio of assets and property. Parliament does not get to see their accounts, and they are widely regarded in Swaziland as a "black box", their boards appointed by the king. Opposition groups regard these funds as "feedlots for the king and the inner circle", so the *Mail & Guardian* reported.[20] South Africa's R2.4 billion putative bail-out of the Swazi state in 2011 received considerable local criticism as it came with no serious requirement for reform or conditionalities and many saw it as support for profligate monarchic continuity. Libya's Qaddafi family interests have not been found wanting either, the treasure chest of the former leader's monies and assets with access to holdings via the state (partly subjected to sanctions by Western powers) exposed during the 2011 Libyan revolution, estimated in the billions.

Meanwhile, many politicians in government or in one-party states often have access to or control over holding companies set up "by and for the party". An example is Press Holdings in Malawi, established in 1961 under President Hastings Kamuzu Banda and later reconstructed as the Press Corporation. In South Africa, Chancellor House acts as a corporate vehicle with extensive assets held on behalf of the ANC. Many other countries have similar corporate entities closely linked to parties, presidents and the political class.

While some of the wealthy have grown rich from assets accumulated while in politics, others with large wealth develop political (even presidential) ambitions. Many rich have been in politics within Africa, and many are still in power with reportedly large wealth: both presidents and ministers, including family members. Africa's political rich have generally not acquired wealth from high savings rates secured from their formal or official salaries, which are often modest. Allies and political acolytes typically join this parade of the powerful and enriched.

Crony capitalism is closely connected to Africa's intertwined corporate and political cultures. Quasi-privatisation of the state and many assets, and sometimes formal privatisation, has assisted this process. Among past African presidents the names of the rich are legendary: Omar Bongo in Gabon, Emperor Bokassa in the Central African Republic, Daniel Arap Moi in Kenya, Hosni Mubarak in Egypt, Ben Ali in Tunisia, and many more indicated or indicted over the years in the public media. Contemporary presidents do not escape this epithet, including José Eduardo Dos Santos in Angola, Robert Mugabe in Zimbabwe and Teodoro Obiang Nguema Mbasogo in Equatorial Guinea.

In 2010 the *Mail & Guardian* in Johannesburg cited numerous companies found on the public record to be affiliated with or under the ownership or control of the South African president, Jacob Zuma, and an entourage of wives, fiancées, connected women, children, close relatives and family associates.[21] The list is so extensive that the rubric "Zuma Inc" has been thought applicable. Some wonder how any president could manage this conglomerate of corporate interests that includes well over 100 companies and subsidiaries while attending to the affairs of state. An extended, and in this case polygamous, family structure has enhanced this commercial spectrum, and the vast majority of these companies and assets, spreading across many industries and activities, have been accumulated within the past few years.

In Africa it is not uncommon for family enrichment to surround presidential or ministerial power. Equally, many presidents and ministers in office in Africa make liberal and often blatantly excessive use of the resources of the state for personal benefit – luxury cars, property, national airlines and corporate jets – as well as assorted services and funding to augment their lifestyles. The division of private and state funds is not always respected. Few African presidents – they might be counted on one hand – have left office poorer in wealth than when they assumed power. It is likewise not uncommon for officials to operate private businesses while in office and as state salary earners. Many have used these vehicles for transactions with government and even ministries which they control or in which they work nominally. In Africa, many are employed by government, but fewer work for the state.

Beneath the HNWI and ultra-HNWI can be found growing classes of the well-off, the actual middle class *per se*, many with significant assets and property, whom the poor would consider as rich but the HNWI do not. Several billionaires can be found as well as many more millionaires. This is a growing segment of Africa's shifting demographic. It is reflected in the spread of business, corporate holdings, equity markets and assets found in high-quality and expensive property, including second homes, rural lodges and retreats, wine farms, and the accoutrements and bling that are increasingly part of Africa's social and celebrity landscape. It is not always feasible to find accurate numbers for such groups, and measures of net asset value held do not always equate with the value of assets within their control owing to unknown debt encumbrances.

Not all the wealth of Africa's HNWI is held in the continent. It is often spread in cash, equities and instruments both at home and abroad, on stock markets and in bonds or assets under management, or in trusts, with an unknown amount in overseas markets and in a mix of private or luxury assets (boats, cars, property and collectibles, jewellery, art). Typically, this class of rich will employ wealth advisers and management teams to guard, protect and enhance their wealth, secure capital value and provide income streams. Some assets will be dedicated to corporate investments and the funding of ventures owned or held in Africa. Data on the distribution of income and wealth among Africa's rich are hard to come by and mostly anecdotal. It is equally difficult to identify locations of wealth and how largesse is deployed for similar reasons. In Africa the wealthy include nationals and expatriates, private individuals and state officials. Many hold offshore investments making use of tailored financial products.

Economic growth in Africa has raised the fortunes of the rich and ultra-rich. State egalitarian policies, taxes and leadership codes will probably never ameliorate this deeply rooted condition, which looks to be embedded for the century ahead. While the numbers of poor will grow, so will those of the rich.

Roots and fruits of wealth

Africa has far more latent and inherent natural wealth than it has exploited to date, and indeed more bounty than it has unlocked in the last 1,000 years from the natural capital resource. Could this be the foundation for higher growth rates in the coming decades? Potentially yes, though there is the historic paradox that most of these resources have been in place for years and have not always been the only roots that have enabled the fruits of wealth to flower.

The creation of wealth is complex, usually requiring long time spans in its realisation, while economic growth is the flow linking the stock of wealth today and its accumulation in future. The economic transformations in long-cycle growth favour the modernising economies as the non-traditional modes cede ground and produced assets and intangibles become more significant in the wealth mix, while natural capital is converted to productive capital.

Wealth in sub-Saharan Africa for natural, produced and intangible capital was measured for 2000 by the World Bank.[22] The bottom ten countries in the global wealth stakes, apart from Nepal, were all from Africa. Wealth per head then was $10,730 compared with world wealth per head of $90,210. Here Africa was worse off than all areas except South Asia. The underdevelopment and poor monetisation of natural capital is indicated by the fact that 24% of wealth was found in this form, 13% as produced capital and the rest in intangible assets. Natural capital – made up of subsoil assets, timber, crops, and pasture land and forest resources – has yet to be fully unlocked and monetised at maximal value, to create more produced capital and productive capacity that could generate higher economic growth rates.

From 1995 to 2005 sub-Saharan Africa recorded almost zero real net savings. Due to population dilution effects some countries in Africa experienced falling net wealth per head, although 27 countries increased wealth per head. Overall gains from wealth accumulation from 1995 to 2005 were modest.[23] In the World Bank's view, sub-Saharan Africa consumed more than it produced in income from 1990 onwards, reflecting some destruction of its capital asset base; this limited the expansion of produced capital, with implications for economic growth in future.

From 1995 to 2005 total sub-Saharan Africa wealth per head rose by only 4.4% to $13,888. This equates to 11% of the world average. It might for 2010 be estimated at $14,500 per head. With the population at 856 million in 2010, total wealth would have been $12.4 trillion. On this basis, with GDP at, say, $1 trillion for these states, the "yield" on capital base would have been at around 8%. Of course there are huge variances in the wealth distribution profile in Africa, across states and in the composition of natural, intangible and produced capital, given the mix of economic modes and their relationships.

If the wealth accumulation trajectory of the recent past (ie, 4.4% per year) applied consistently over the period to 2050, wealth in sub-Saharan Africa might then total $69.4 trillion. One caveat applies. By then there would be around 1.6 billion sub-Saharan inhabitants, making wealth per head $43,375. On current yield at 8%, GDP might reflect an economy of $5.5 trillion. This would be a long way behind the optimistic forecasts made for Africa's GDP of around $13 trillion, even allowing for the inclusion of North Africa. Equally, achievement of this level would require no future wealth destruction, unrestrained investment over the years and a steady path for long-cycle capital-asset accumulation.

There exist many constraints to investment in the industries that are central to unlocking Africa's natural capital – in mineral-energy complexes, like oil and gas, as well as both capitalist and pre-modern agrarian development. What is critical in future for economic growth is to sustain not just long-cycle GDP expansion but also improvements in the exploitation of natural capital and the wider capital base; to convert the composition of capital assets; to grow the produced capital complex for productive investment; and to maintain higher yields for assets over the coming decades. It will be a tough task.

Who then will exploit this wealth to create the foundations for growth and lead Africa's economic future? The older economic modes will still be important in the social and economic fabric, but capitalist Africa is expected to be the prime driver for most domestic investments. Foreign investors will form part of that corporate initiative. Funding from governments in Africa will be increasingly constrained. Many could improve their positions but will need to hive off and restructure their overburdened parastatals. But will they? On the evidence to date, it will probably be a patchy record.

Africa will need to tap the global capital markets for funding, while there will be increased interest and competition for resources and markets coming from the BRICs and other foreign states seeking to access Africa's natural capital. All will need to compete in the market domains commanded by the companies existing inside the productive capital base. In broad terms this will define the "corporate scramble for

Africa", in motion for some years, which is expected to play out further in the coming decades.

Exploiting Africa

There has arisen a veritable industry of texts, reports, analyses and books on the 21st century scramble for Africa's economy.[24] I have explained this paradigm on the oil and gas industry in *Crude Continent: The Struggle for Africa's Oil Prize*. It is a complex economic and commercial competition, a game of corporate and state geopolitics, played among thousands of asset-holders, governments, state firms, investors from around the world and the *nouveaux arrivistes*. It includes companies from abroad, many state-owned firms, and investment funds, once never engaged in Africa but now with the continent – its resources and markets – in their portfolio sights. In this competitive lunge, the older economic modes within Africa have little leverage and stand at a potential disadvantage, except maybe through access to politics and the state.

Several observations are germane to the new commercial lunge for Africa. First, this continent is not the sole investment destination open to corporate and state players. Some with "Africa-blinkers" appear to operate this way. Then there are formidable challenges that must be overcome, including Africa's state policies and commercial terms, and a rising degree of resource nationalism. It is equally the case that all firms compete for the same prize on differential terms with varied competitive advantage. The shifting tides of state/corporate preference are often difficult to navigate. While there has been heavy focus on China's incursions into Africa over the past decade, this has obscured the many competitors from elsewhere that have targeted Africa, not only from the traditional North Atlantic powers but also from India, East Asia (Japan and South Korea), South-East Asia, Russia, eastern Europe, Turkey, Brazil and the Middle East.

Here the intent is to envision the competitive field as a whole. The primary consequence of the changed investment and corporate environment is that it has become more competitive, in some instances ultra-competitive. In this milieu Africa stands as a fragmented set of states vis-à-vis any investment suitor or state interest from abroad. It is likely to remain that way. The desire of the political class to shape an "Africa strategy" towards the outside world is doomed: national interests will typically predominate. Moreover, that is likely to apply even towards the corporate and investor interests from Africa's own rising states, as local players around Africa extend their portfolios outside their countries of origin.

The view that Africa is now beholden to emerging-market powers (China, India, and so on) that have "discovered" its potential is likely to be disproved by future history. There could be more localised instances of capture in cases of selected opportunities and industries, but the wider picture will be more along the lines of enhanced competition within and between the capitalist and proto-capitalist modes that seek a position for profit and benefit within Africa's economic game.

Many segments of Africa's economy are in play in this wider dimension of companies and interests seeking to exploit Africa. The number of companies engaged in oil and gas exceeded 750 firms in 2011 and more enter each year. The mineral base is largely underexploited and more companies have acquired assets and lined up investment for the future. Companies from Africa and abroad seek to take on investments in many other industries: forestry, fisheries, agro-allied industry, land assets, secondary industry, trading, armaments, manufacturing, and services over the entire economic value chain across the continent. This set of corporate interests will augment the "modern" within Africa at an accelerated pace, add to capital accumulation and strengthen capitalist Africa, including its own local corporate domains. In this rush, South Africa has emerged as the prevailing corporate giant on the continent, its many companies having taken to new pastures across the Limpopo through increased effort and investment over the past few years. This trend will accelerate.

With more suitors, Africa's states have taken to triage, with strategies to play off parties one against the other. This game is played by all. The contemporary model of *Chinafrique*, central-managed success versus unorganised diffusion, based on evident mercantilist, market capture and asset lunge, may not always be to Africa's advantage, though no one can simply predict all outcomes in this complex interface. For China, Africa represents the economic weight of a mid-sized province or two. The continent is convenient as the dumping ground for surplus *zhing zhong* (the pejorative term for cheap Chinese products). Yet China must contend with rivals, including India. China's interest in including South Africa in the BRICSA alignment should be viewed in this context, as · an economic briquette among the temporary convenience of bric-a-brac alignments that it holds spanning the globe. South Africa serves as the "eyes and ears" in Africa for China's stomach, to meet its growing continental appetite. One day it may not be so needed, courted or considered relevant.

In this global, multiphased, many-pronged investor lunge towards Africa, some Sinophiles advance an argument that Africa's economic growth rate is somehow hooked, in some uniquely correlated growth equation, to the cyclicity and growth rate of China.[25] Of course, correlation has no bearing on causality, which in this case is wholly unproven, and would be exceptionally surprising to anyone with knowledge of the multiple drivers and determinants of economic growth in Africa's past or present. None of this is to dispute the size of the China/Africa trade nexus, which is approximately $120 billion per year (about the same as China/Australia), while the investment inflows from China to Africa are at around 15% of Chinese outward investment. As "red capitalists", the Chinese are hedging. These funds are heavily predicated on negotiated commercial *quid pro quo*, and the impact of China on infrastructure and resource development in selected zones within Africa. It does not make Africa's economic future one directed by and hinging only on China.

While future growth rates for China – and hence part demand for Africa's assets, commodities and markets – are not known, the expectation is that its growth rate will in time decline. This is almost inevitable. Moreover, there are more states with companies abroad entering this competition for Africa. Old players such as France have not "gone away", certainly not in the 31 francophone states in Africa with markets of around 350 million people. Meanwhile, initiatives to hold and

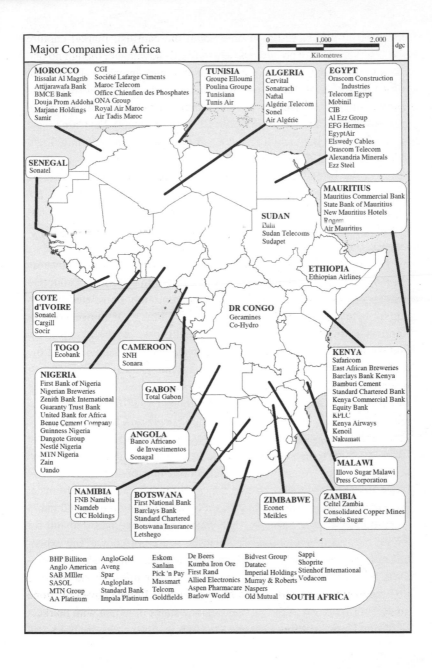

Major Companies in Africa

0   1,000   2,000
Kilometres
dgc

MOROCCO
Itissalat Al Magrib
Attijarawafa Bank
BMCE Bank
Douja Prom Addoha
Marjane Holdings
Samir
CGI
Société Lafarge Ciments
Maroc Telecom
Office Chienfien des Phosphates
ONA Group
Royal Air Maroc
Air Tadis Maroc

TUNISIA
Groupe Elloumi
Poulina Groupe
Tunisiana
Tunis Air

ALGERIA
Cervital
Sonatrach
Naftal
Algérie Telecom
Sonel
Air Algérie

EGYPT
Orascom Construction
    Industries
Telecom Egypt
Mobinil
CIB
Al Ezz Group
EFG Hermes
EgyptAir
Elswedy Cables
Orascom Telecom
Alexandria Minerals
Ezz Steel

SENEGAL
Sonatel

SUDAN
Bula
Sudan Telecoms
Sudapet

MAURITIUS
Mauritius Commercial Bank
State Bank of Mauritius
New Mauritius Hotels
Rogers
Air Mauritius

ETHIOPIA
Ethiopian Airlines

COTE d'IVOIRE
Sonatel
Cargill
Socir

DR CONGO
Gecamines
Co-Hydro

TOGO
Ecobank

CAMEROON
SNH
Sonara

KENYA
Safaricom
East African Breweries
Barclays Bank Kenya
Bamburi Cement
Standard Chartered Bank
Kenya Commercial Bank
Equity Bank
KPLC
Kenya Airways
Kenoil
Nakumatt

NIGERIA
First Bank of Nigeria
Nigerian Breweries
Zenith Bank International
Guaranty Trust Bank
United Bank for Africa
Benue Cement Company
Guinness Nigeria
Dangote Group
Nestlé Nigeria
MTN Nigeria
Zain
Oando

GABON
Total Gabon

ANGOLA
Banco Africano
    de Investimentos
Sonagal

MALAWI
Illovo Sugar Malawi
Press Corporation

NAMIBIA
FNB Namibia
Namdeb
CIC Holdings

BOTSWANA
First National Bank
Barclays Bank
Standard Chartered
Botswana Insurance
Letshego

ZIMBABWE
Econet
Meikles

ZAMBIA
Celtel Zambia
Consolidated Copper Mines
Zambia Sugar

BHP Billiton
Anglo American
SAB MIller
SASOL
MTN Group
AA Platinum
AngloGold
Aveng
Spar
Angloplats
Standard Bank
Impala Platinum
Eskom
Sanlam
Pick 'n Pay
Massmart
Telcom
Goldfields
De Beers
Kumba Iron Ore
First Rand
Allied Electronics
Aspen Pharmacare
Barlow World
Bidvest Group
Datatec
Imperial Holdings
Murray & Roberts
Naspers
Old Mutual
Sappi
Shoprite
Stienhof International
Vodacom
SOUTH AFRICA

improve economic stakes can be seen, and more are expected, from the UK, Germany, Spain, Portugal and the United States. One-way bets on China would be folly for Africa. Binary ideas about Africa – *Chinafrique* or other – need to be eschewed: they add little to our fuller economic understanding of this complex continent.

Though foreign trade and investment are important, they do not comprise the whole economic story. Africa is not a single market. Its borders, even if realigning or open to trade-bloc initiatives, provide modern-day impediments to unitary economic arrangements. Africa is far less globalised than most imagine and its economies are not all open in the classic sense. Regulations and barriers to entry and operation abound. Many economic modes in Africa have no direct linkages either with the outside world or with many economies outside their immediate environs inside nation-states, let alone countries next door. Cross-border connections are exceptional rather than general. For large swathes of Africa there has been little reduction in the tyranny of distance caused by economic geography, frontiers, infrastructure or language – despite the wonders of mobile telephony so lauded by the business gurus. Africa is not "flat".

Dynamic Africa

Within Africa changes are taking place in its modern economies and the capital base driven by its own companies. They are growing their corporate portfolio and commercial footprints in Africa. What difference will they make in future?

It will not necessarily be foreign companies that dominate in Africa for ever. Even now many local companies hold prominent positions. Some are household and global brands, not just from South Africa but also Egypt, Morocco, Nigeria and East Africa. They have grown in scale, reach, market capitalisation, intra-Africa market penetration and indeed on the world stage. Sasol in South Africa is one world-class, globally expanding player, which will enhance its corporate footprint further out of Africa in future. Corporate Africa is a growing animal.

This economic beast commands large and important industries, from mining and resources to consumer goods and services. In many senses this corporate mode represents a significant driver in Africa's future quest for modernity.

Several thousand African companies are quoted on the 19 local stock exchanges now established on the continent, and the number of significant unlisted companies is huge; no known figure exists, but I would hazard a guess of several hundred thousand. To these should be added smaller family firms running into the millions.

World-class players abound within corporate Africa, including Sasol, Anglo American, SAB Miller, Orascom, Standard Bank, Vodacom, Ecobank, Absa, Dangote and many more that are well known in Africa and abroad. Boston Consulting Group recently depicted the 40 top players and corporate challengers as the "African Lions".[26] These lions cross all industries and have recorded significant growth, making them targets for deals and partnerships with many foreign companies, some with equity holdings. Many have turnovers the size of the GDP of several of Africa's states (with corporate capitalisation ranging from $500 million to $80 billion), although this measure provides false comparison in reality. Nonetheless, corporate Africa is an important source of investment and FDI in Africa as a whole. Most have strategies to penetrate further into Africa's growing markets, and some have executed merger and acquisition deals to enhance their position both in Africa and abroad.

Among them, South Africa looms large. Its corporate footprint is expanding across sub-Saharan Africa, less so in the Maghreb. But this model is being replicated elsewhere by Nigerian companies in the Gulf of Guinea, Egyptian companies in North Africa and several East African companies (including KenolKobil) stretching outside their traditional domains. As the corporate lunge towards Africa from abroad from all quarters of the globe gathers pace, the continent is moving further down the modernised corporate value chain. Inside this company world, competition for survival and edge is becoming fiercer. All will stand in one way or another beholden to the guardians and gatekeepers of economic opportunity or fortune: the states and parastatals from which they must seek permits, procurement, deals or acquiescence.

In large measure the success of many states will depend on their ability to establish and retain competitive terms of engagement with the corporate world and their capacity to solicit corporate investment. Even though African corporates are significant, they too ride the roller coaster of difficulties that have impeded Africa's past and present. Yet most have the benefit of more intimate knowledge of Africa's political woodwork, commercial networks and *savoir-faire* than their foreign competitors.

African corporates hold some competitive advantages that should ensure a rising business presence and economic influence in the future. This will augur well for Africa in its quest for modernity and economic growth. But Africa's lions (or, if you like, corporate animals in the shape of elephants, buffalos, leopards or rhinos – many "big five" labels could be applied) will not alone inherit Africa's economic earth. By 2050 there will still be large economic remnants of pre-modern Africa in place, many more urban poor and a mix of subsistence or survivalist economies still prevailing across the continent.

Future diversity

The diversity of Africa's economic and social configurations can be confusing. Nigeria's 150 million-plus populace dwarfs tiny Seychelles (100,000). South Africa and Nigeria together command over 50% of sub-Saharan GDP. Equatorial Guinea's GDP per head at over $15,000 appears rich in relation to the $140 per head found in Burundi (both tiny states). The GDP of Africa's ten richest economies stands 25 times higher than in the ten poorest. South Africa has around 4,809 kW per head electric power, Ethiopia only 38.3 kW per head. In Seychelles, 92% of women are literate, in Chad barely 13%. Seychelles has 130 times more internet users per 1,000 people than Sierra Leone. Guinea-Bissau's GDP just crosses the $200 million mark, South Africa's stands at around $290 billion. Over 75% of firms in Congo expect to give gifts to secure contracts, only 8% in Mauritius. Djibouti is 85% urban, Burundi 10%. Zimbabwe has a 92% literacy rate, Burkina Faso and Mali only 29%. I could go on.

The comparison of economies is often bedevilled by the chalk and cheese problem. The difficulties are more pronounced when countries are lumped into categories of convenience. The problem compounds even more when their individual conditions and disparate economic cycles are measured to fit aggregated econometric models or regression coefficients of abstraction. The greater the level of abstraction in the economics of Africa, the less is the generic insight of applicability.

The socioeconomic condition of Africa is not as rosy as many would presume, with the deprived and poor within the economic underclass often lost in the macroeconomic jungle of aggregated data and corporate spin.

Let us consider some demographic facts. The number of young will grow much more rapidly than the doubling of total population projected to 2050; cities will by then be home to 1.3 billion, with over 500 million moving there before 2030, so substantially augmenting slum dwellers and the urban underclass (today 600,000 or 20% of the inhabitants of Nairobi are found in one slum, Kibera). There will still be 700 million rural dwellers, mostly in low-income subsistence circumstances. Today there are 15 million orphans across Africa and 150,000 children are tied up in armed conflicts (50% of civil conflict casualties are children). About 50% of Africans suffer from water-borne diseases (cholera, bilharzia, dysentery, river blindness). There are nearly 1 million deaths annually from malaria and 30 million encounter HIV-AIDS in the sub-Sahara region. Around 33% face malnutrition and 300 million have no access to safe water. More than 20% have no access to electricity. Around 200,000 child slaves are sold each year and the number of beggars exceeds 1 million. In a nutshell, this presents huge economic and social challenges for the future, ones that demography will make no easier.

The "demographic demand" – to satisfy another billion people, most joining the lower-income classes – will perhaps emerge as Africa's greatest challenge. The doubling of population in the coming 40 years is inevitable. Given the past poor record in employment growth, this will provoke rampant informalisation. It cannot be presumed as some naively do that this unstoppable expansion in numbers represents an unmitigated "economic dividend". In itself, it does not.

Several limits exist to potentially constrain the "natural economic growth rate" or to place a ceiling on expected expansion. The long-cycle growth rates of the past have taken decades to crawl into positive territory and slowly climb upwards. Interrupted economic cycles have wreaked material damage on many countries and even continental growth trajectories. With the drive to modernity, infrastructure and power deficiencies are huge and critical constraints going forward, while high growth will strain the old and creaking infrastructure.

For long-term socio-political stability, it will be essential to generate the inflows and levels of investment required for wealth accumulation to improve in value, composition and yield. The process of post-colony decay has taken a heavy toll on the hard-wired economic fabrics that mould and stitch Africa's economies together. Their unravelling may not yet be at its bottom if account is taken of several still-failing states and failed ones yet to turn any economic corner. New disasters would magnify this problem.

The economic imbalances are large, political discord often unresolved, and state fragmentation and balkanisation may be on the cards in several places. Africa's nation-states have a long road to reach statehood and modernity in terms of growth and efficiency in the provision of public goods. Most have yet to address the parasitic burdens of inherited and self-augmented parastatal dominance and economic blight that marked the state economic models adopted years ago. Some state entities remain as economic throwbacks to flawed thinking and models crafted generations before.

Many states have been captured by narrowly based, quasi-predatory elites. They could face the threat of local discontent. Often when there is a change of the political guard, it represents only the rotation of elites or the reconfiguration of contemporary elite interests. The propensity for conflicts to come could be seen as high in economies that have ossified and remain as one-party entities or commercial and family dynasties, out of tune with wider popular demands. The gerontocratic nature of Africa's political leadership and the longevity of so many in high office mean that there will be many unpredictable transitions in the near and medium term.

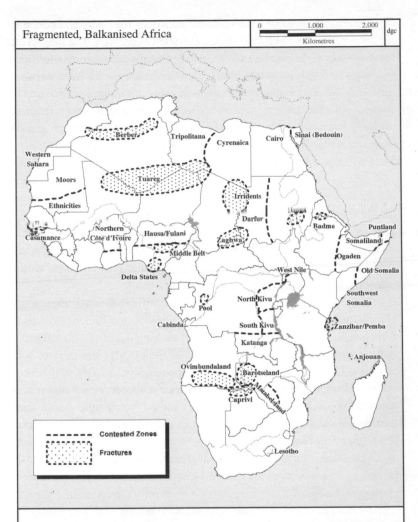

Fragmented, Balkanised Africa

0   1,000   2,000
Kilometres

dgc

Berber · Tripolitana · Cyrenaica · Cairo · Sinai (Bedouin)

Western Sahara

Moors · Tuareg

Ethnicities · Irridents · Darfur · Badme · Puntland

Casamance · Northern Côte d'Ivoire · Hausa/Fulani · Zaghwa · Somaliland

Middle Belt · Ogaden

Delta States · West Nile · Old Somalia

Pool · North Kivu · Southwest Somalia

Cabinda · South Kivu · Zanzibar/Pemba

Katanga · Anjouan

Ovimbundaland · Barotseland

Caprivi · Matabeleland

Lesotho

- - - - - Contested Zones

··········· Fractures

Multiple zones within and around the continent's nation-state boundaries reflect social fractures and potentially balkanising entities, some with long histories of irredentism, others seeking autonomy, with separatists established out of the remnants of failing or failed states. The potential for fragmentation remains significant, the nation-states only recently constructed on top of old socioeconomic realities. Both Eritrea and South Sudan are new states. More fissures might emerge in decades to come.

Recidivism and the repetition of past failed economic strategies remain a part of the landscape in Africa's political economy. If not in the hands of narrow interests, state bureaucracies remain expansionist and lack the basic ethos of productivity growth. Some states remain imprisoned in kleptocratic mode, and there are many pretenders to Africa's political thrones, such as opposition groups, rich businessmen, rebels, warlords, ethnically defined enemies and conflicting ideologies. These forces have been precursors of many false economic dawns before. They will not simply disappear from the stage.

Several curses on Africa's economic house remain to be dealt with over the decades to come: its politics, the poor productivity of land and agrarian assets, anaemic long-term growth rates, periodic or unexpected cyclical downsides, uneven and unbalanced economies, uncertain climates for foreign investment and the problem of how to ensure long-run wealth accumulation. The likelihood in future is for more continental diffusion and differentiation inside and among Africa's states, not any inner convergence.

Images old and new

Sometimes a photograph captures a thousand words. For this there is no better recommendation than the lens and eye on Africa, depicted in a collection of portraits of war, famine, disease, poverty and tragedy produced in the photojournalism, of Sebastiao Salgado.[27] This Brazilian photojournalist travelled extensively for decades in the byways and recesses of the continent during multiple, serial and extensive crises amid great drama.

The images cast by Salgado – from the Sahel, Moçambique, Angola and elsewhere – are haunting and daunting. They offer no political explanation, no economic theory – just bare essence, and sometimes merely the bare bones of the camera's subjects. Human tragedy encapsulated within raw beauty marks these black-and-white pictures of a recent past and present to tell of the dire conditions faced by many, just to survive.

We should not forget this reality, for it is there today in unwanted abundance and these images are likely to be found in Africa's future. In all these instances the moulding of the continent's image and maybe even parts of its future rests on these recurrent themes. Other collections of contemporary photography show the prevalence of Africa's ancient economic fabrics. These images reflect realities that have been deeply rooted in myriad social formations and their interfaces with adulterated local power. Some are wholly indifferent to the modern worlds encountered at large.

These are not the only images of Africa to be found. Dynamic Africa is widely reported in the journals and press of the continent, and in its broadcast media. In 2010 I crafted the TV/film documentary *Africa: Crude Continent (Quest for the Oil Prize)*, which was produced by CNBC-Africa. The film reflects modernity in many countries across Africa that have developed or begun exploration for oil and gas, the energy that will power Africa's economic future. Elsewhere on this channel you can witness daily the multiple images of the corporate world at work in Africa and its relative optimism on the economies and outlook. Its interlocutors have yet to encounter the drama of any long-term cyclical economic downside.

There are many visions of Africa to be accommodated in the mind's eye – no one image is enough to encompass the vast heterogeneity, past and present that is Africa. There will be more to be captured by the lenses and prisms of optical image and reality in the future.

✳

If you traverse the vast Kalahari sands in Southern Africa, and the small *dorps* in and around them, you will find many disparate and often broken communities of once-nomadic Khoisan existing frugally and often miserably on the fringes of the modern world. In the past their distant ancestors had roamed far and wide, over much of Africa, as hunter-gatherers. The intruders in their world, of all types, transformed the San's mode of existence, pushing them further and further into the bushveld and the Kalahari Desert.

Few knowledgeable hunters remain to practise their art. These once formidable kinship-based societies living off the animals and plants of the interior have become primarily modern "gatherers", in the view of some scavengers, collecting money and detritus from the consumer world to which they have had to adapt and of which they may never really become part. The old arts of tracking linger, desire for hunting too, but both will be lost more and more as the generations adjust from old worlds that have largely disappeared.

Some forage among the throwaway flotsam and second-hand products left before them. Others seek temporary refuge in alcohol while the Khoisan culture faces the forbidding onslaught of modernity, tourism in game parks that were once their natural hunting grounds, dislocation from edicts crafted by their governments, enduring xenophobia and hostility from adjacent societies, and threats from a shrunken economic base, the essence of which has already slid into the mists of time. It is a telling image and reality amid all the talk and progress on modernity that Africa has achieved, and not the only one of desperation in Africa.

Elsewhere, others may face an even worst fate. In Mogadishu, where the Mad Max world has come to town, rival clans contest the pock-marked buildings and streets that have endured 30 years of vicious internecine warfare. Families hide in buildings by day and night that once reflected certain charms of Italian architectural splendour. Theirs is a desperate struggle to find food, get through the day and, for many, just to stay alive. The "state" has all but disappeared. In its place are decayed economic structures – once of colonial modernity – held together in apocalyptic form by those who today wield the means of violence. The adherents to diverse clans are commanded by militia, armed insurgents, ideologies or a mix of ethnic affinities. Even the African Union's armed forces sent there to establish control on behalf of a fragile pseudo-state often cower inside their barricades, with temporary shattered buildings used as fire posts for battles with al-Shabaab, an al-Qaeda affiliate. The recognised "government" from time to time controls a fraction here and there of Mogadishu, buttressed by foreign forces, which have often commanded only a few streets, sometimes more, in a "capital" (barely recognisable today as such) where authority has regularly changed hands at the end of the barrel of a gun in a conflict of bewildering brutality, factionalism and shifting complexity.

Meanwhile, in southern Somalia and over the Horn of Africa is played out another apocalyptic drama of humans' and nature's making: the famine and helplessness that have afflicted millions. This predicament has been etched into the economic landscape without the deliberate intervention of the human hand. Except that there are obvious antecedents to this saga, in a Somalia that for 30 years has not taken heed of any sound economic policy or sage advice. More critically, famine has been at extreme levels. Much devastation has been caused by relentless wars and in the battlefields of southern Somalia, with many of the victims drawn from the minority or weaker clans preyed upon by nomadic militia and the ruthlessness of al-Shabaab.[28]

At the same time, surrounding these dramas, we find "dynamic Africa", with a wide variety of industries, companies and firms – economic modes, and inside them expanding numbers of competitive nodes – which seek to build the edifices of modernity in a race against the tides of history. Africa has many more independent elements like this than formal states or enduring political entities. As before and despite conflicted histories, the economic modes in Africa will, I believe, trump the curse of continental politics and obscurantism, as in the past, to enable economic continuity and growth to be realised. Even though there will be no early end to Africa's convoluted histories, this forward movement is likely to be the mark of the next 50 years as well.

Yet the fundamental schism in Africa between its rising capitalist modernity and older economic forms of subsistence with contemporary means of survival will remain and will continue to shape the economic drama for decades to come, perhaps even the entire century and beyond. It took over three centuries for the most modern piece of Africa's economic architecture, South Africa, to reach its current pinnacle. This holds signal lessons for the rest of the continent about the time it may take to match even this imperfect and still-hybrid construction. Most of Africa's economies began their modern journey much more recently, many with lesser resources at hand.

These are images of both the old and the new – Africa's extremities, if you like. In between is found the rest of Africa, often as a world apart. The trek from Olduvai to Africa's modernity has been an extraordinarily long one. It continues as a tale of the continent's economic evolution.

Acknowledgements

Over time one accumulates numerous intellectual debts. Here I think of several economists who shaped my understanding of economics in Africa and from whom I benefited over the course of decades.

It was one of South Africa's renowned economists, a former economics adviser to Jan Christian Smuts and author of standard texts studied by all undergraduates at South African universities, Professor Desmond Hobart Houghton, who taught me at Rhodes University (1966–69). He also recommended St Andrews, Scotland, as the place to do research.[1] Thereafter followed sojourns at the University of St Andrews, notably with Professor Peter Robson, the leading light on East Africa and an architect of world-class analysis on Africa's economies and economic development.[2] It is with grateful thanks to these life-long and Africa-savvy economists that I happily dedicate this work.

At home my research engaged analysis of mining economies, commercial farms and plantations, rural-urban migrancy, rural household economics and survival, the informal trading domain, Southern Africa's contract labour mechanisms, poverty datum line measurement, labour-market and union economics in the urban-industrial complex, local and foreign investment, and the economics of "masters and servants" in domestic households. A fair amount of this work was published by Mambo Press, and other studies in diverse journals in Africa and abroad.[3] Further research on economics done in Southern Africa was conducted during time spent with the Development Studies Research Group at the University of Natal in Pietermaritzburg under the tutelage of Professor R.T. Bell.[4]

Thanks are due to my former colleagues in economics and friends who have helped significantly – Rob J. Davies in Harare for spending time with me on this tome and its ideas, adding many useful insights and observations, and Peter Harris for clarifications and critical advice offered from afar in Wellington, New Zealand. I am greatly indebted to them both for the many views explicitly or inadvertently provided.

It was sitting in the Café Lion d'Or in Geneva that I encountered ideas about non-linear dynamics and chaos theories, from an unexpected source: post-atomic nuclear physicists at CERN (Organisation Européenne pour la Recherche Nucléaire) – their advice accompanied by *vin ordinaire*. They led me to rethink notions on the theory and practice of economics and how contemporary economies often reflect many seeds long planted.[5]

✳

It would have been impossible to tackle this task without enormous support from various colleagues and a cast of many who assisted in one way or another.

Special thanks go to Babette van Gessel (vice-chairman and member of the board of Global Pacific & Partners), the key player in our firm, for persevering with undiminished support to bring this work to realisation.[6]

My appreciation goes to Ian Games in Harare who most ably shaped the cartography, to reflect key themes, and created the original maps drawn. Thanks are likewise due to Graham Sadler and Lydia Thevanayagam at Deloitte in London for allowing usage of maps on Africa's exploration acreage in operated oil blocks across the continent at the end of 2011.

Once more much appreciation is due to my publisher, Profile Books. After my earlier book, *Africa: Crude Continent: The Struggle for Africa's Oil Prize* (2010), Andrew Franklin (publisher and managing director) and Daniel Crewe (editorial director) committed to forging ahead with this endeavour. The skilled team at Profile Books in London, notably Paul Forty, crafted the final outcome, and my thanks go to them all.

My personal acknowledgement is due to Anthony Haynes in England who provided early ideas, and ably shaped this text, deploying his usual sharp insight with dedicated editing, to provide greater clarity in this narrative seeking to "see Africa".

Another with my utmost appreciation is Charmaine, who has been willing to tolerate many inconveniences before and during the writing of this tome.

To rethink or reinterpret Africa's past, present and future economies is a huge, maybe impossible task. I am well aware this text will have shortcomings and even errors, which, while perhaps inevitable, remain those of the author.

Duncan Clarke
Johannesburg, October 2011
duncan@glopac.com

Abbreviations

AfDB	African Development Bank
AQIM	Al-Qaeda in the Islamic Maghreb
AU	African Union
BBC	British Broadcasting Corporation
BCE	Before Common Era
BRIC	Brazil, Russia, India, China
BRICSA	Brazil, Russia, India, China, South Africa
CE	Common Era
COMESA	Common Market of Eastern and Southern Africa
DRC	Democratic Republic of the Congo
EAC	East African Community
ECA	Economic Commission for Africa
EU	European Union
FDI	Foreign Direct Investment
GDP	Gross Domestic Product
G7	Group of Seven industrialised nations (Canada, France, Germany, Italy, Japan, UK, US)
G8	Group of Eight major economies (Canada, France, Germany, Italy, Japan, Russia, UK, US)
HDI	Human Development Index
HIPC	Highly Indebted Poor Countries
HNWI	High Net Worth Individuals
IMF	International Monetary Fund
IPO	Initial Public Offering
kW	kilowatt
NGO	Non-Governmental Organisation
Noczim	National Oil Corporation of Zimbabwe
SADC	Southern African Development Community
UN	United Nations

UNCTAD   United Nations Conference on Trade and Development
Zesa   Zimbabwe Electricity Supply Authority

Notes

Preface

1 There are numerous works now written on Darwin and related natural sciences, even on the application of Darwinian ideas to non-scientific domains. One of the best treatises on the life and thoughts of Darwin I have found is David Quammen, *The Reluctant Mr Darwin: An Intimate Portrait of Charles Darwin and the Making of His Theory of Evolution*, Atlas Books, 2006.

1   Finding Africa

1 See Louis Liebenberg, *The Art of Tracking: The origin of science*, David Philip, 1990.

2 For a riveting account of this saga over the epochs, and on the long quest to understand human prehistory, as well as its discovery, see Martin Meredith, *Born in Africa: The Quest For The Origins Of Human Life*, Simon & Schuster, 2011.

3 For a masterpiece on Africa's cartobibliography, with allied interpretation on many mapmakers and the intellectual influences behind their acquired knowledge, see Richard L. Betz, *The Mapping Of Africa: A Cartobibliography of Printed Maps of the African Continent to 1700*, Hes & De Hraaf Publishers BV, 2007. Another with equally valid knowledge is Dr Jeffrey Stone (editor), *Norwich's Maps Of Africa: An illustrated and annotated carto-bibliography*, Terra Nova Press, 2nd edition, 1997. For more modern versions of maps in a world context, indicating the many social and economic changes across Africa over the millennia in around 60 maps, see Ludwig Konemann (editor-in chief), *Historical Atlas Of The World*, Paragon, 2010. On mapping history's technologies and the origin of Africa in nomenclature, see "The Fall and Rise of Development Economics", found on Paul Krugman's website at http://web.mit.edu/krugman/www/dishpan.html, in an essay written in 1994.

4 See the magisterial and path-breaking work of Malvern van Wyk Smith, *The First Ethiopians: The Image of Africa and Africans in the Early Mediterranean World*, Wits University Press, 2009.

5 Ibid.

2 Imagined Africa

1 I have coined the term *Chinafrique* to refer to the widening complex of China's modern demarche into Africa, reflected in diplomatic forays, commercial engagements, military endeavours, intelligence networks, political strategies and security initiatives, direct financings, company intrusions and high-level links to Africa's presidents, ministers, political entities and corporate players. In the 21st century, it has come to dominate in ways that were common in the past to *Francafrique*.

2 Professor Francis Wilson, *South Africa: Past, Present and Future*, 5th Africa Economic Forum 2011, Cape Town, Global Pacific & Partners.

3 The thesis is held in the Library of the University of St Andrews (Scotland): Duncan Godfrey Clarke, *The Political Economy of Discrimination and Underdevelopment in Rhodesia with Special Reference to African Workers 1940–1973*, unpublished, 1975,

4 Gary S. Becker, *The Economics of Discrimination, University of Chicago Press*, 1971, Lester C. Thurow, *Poverty and Discrimination, Studies in Social Economics*, The Brookings Institutions, Washington, 1969; Kenneth J. Arrow, *Economic Theory and Racial Discrimination*, Marshall Lectures, University of Cambridge, 1970.

5 For Becker, discrimination was akin to a restrictive practice only and operated at the behavioural level, as individual consumer preference. There was no appreciation of historical specificity or structural dynamics in the economy. Arrow augmented this theory to examine discriminatory behaviour in terms of utility functions, allowing for positive or negative impacts in consumer exercised preferences. At the heart of such theory lay a binary division between the economic and non-economic, as if they could be divorced in reality. Thurow's approach allowed for imperfect and monopolistic systems with connections to poverty and income distribution, but could not explain the evident historic realities of underdevelopment.

6 Stephen Enke, "Western Development of a Sparsely Populated Country: The Rhodeslas", *American Economic Review*, Volume L, 1960; and J.H. Boeke, *Economics and Economic Policy of Dual Societies*, New York, 1953.

7 W. Arthur Lewis, *Economic Development with Unlimited Supplies of Labour*, Manchester School, 1954, along with other works; also J.C. Fei and C. Ranis, *The Development of the Labour Surplus Economy*, Irwin, Homewood, Illinois, 1964; and in the neoclassical tradition, D.W. Jorgensen, "The Development of the Dual Economy", *Economic Journal*, June, 1961; and W.J. Barber, *The Economy of British Central Africa: A Case Study of Economic Development in a Dualistic Society*, Oxford University Press, 1961.

8 See notably, Giovanni Arrighi, *The Political Economy of Rhodesia*, Mouton, The Hague, 1967 and "Labour Supplies in Historical Perspective: A Study of the Proletarianisation of the African Peasantry in Rhodesia", *Journal of Development Studies*, No. 6, Vol. 3, 1979, among many subsequent works, some in conjunction with other authors. It is striking how this theoretical debate, centred in and on Rhodesia and

Central Africa, became the formative work done in Africa for theorists and research conducted by many well-known names in subsequent economic analyses of Africa and elsewhere in the developing world. I will not cite them all but merely a few authors, including *inter alia* John Saul, Samir Amin, Arghiri Emmanuel, Harold Wolpe and John Weeks, as well as historians and social scientists inside and outside Central Africa such as Charles van Onselen, Ian Phimister, Terence Ranger, Julian Cobbing and many others. An account of the authors, issues, theory, debates and empirical work is found in I.R. Phimister, "Zimbabwean Economic and Social Historiography Since 1970", *African Affairs*, Royal African Society, 1979.

9   A review of this is found in Gilbert Rist, *The History of Development: From Western Origins to Global Faith*, 3rd edition, Zed Books, London & New York, 2008, where many of the economists involved in development economics over the last 50 years are commented upon.

10 For a theoretical discussion on economics over time and a critique of its many practitioners, see Ben Fine and Dimiris Milonakis, *From Economics Imperialism to Freakonomics: The shifting boundaries between economics and other social sciences*, Routledge, 2009, and *From Political Economy to Economics: Method, the social and the historical in the evolution of economic theory*, Routledge, 2009. From an institutionalist viewpoint, see Geoffrey M. Hodgson, *How Economics Forgot History: The problem of historical specificity in social science*, Routledge, 2001, and *Economics in the Shadows of Darwin and Marx: Essays on Institutional and Evolutionary Themes*, Edward Elgar, 2006.

3   Economic modes

1   J. Bradford DeLong, "Estimating World GDP, One Million B.C.–Present", University of California, Berkeley, found on DeLong's website at www.j-bradford-delong.net and reported in Eric D. Beinhocker, *The Origin of Wealth: Evolution, Complexity, and the Radical Remaking of Economics*, page 9, the data cited in dollars as of 1990.

2   See the epic story in David Landes, *The Wealth and Poverty of Nations: Why Some Are So Rich and Some So Poor*, Abacus, 1999.

3   Significant economists argued for the adoption of evolution in economics, including Thorstein Veblen, Alfred Marshall, Joseph Schumpeter and Friedrich Hayek; and lately Richard R. Nelson and Sidney G. Winter, *An Evolutionary Theory of Economic Change*, The Belknap Press of Harvard University Press, 1982.

4   John Sender and Sheila Smith (editors), *The Development of Capitalism in Africa*, Methuen, 1986. Also Henry Bernstein and Bonny K. Campbell (editors), *Contradiction of Accumulation in Africa: Studies in Economy and State*, Sage Publications, 1985. For other insights see Giovanni Andrea Cornia, Rolf van der Hoven and

Thandika Mkandawira (editors), *Africa's Recovery in the 1990s*, Palgrave Macmillan, 1992.

5   This notion of nodes is set at a more micro-level than the economic mode, as if like neutrons within the atom, as a deeper-level component of the economic universe. Typically, many nodes constitute any discrete mode. They tend to expand significantly in number with time, possibly with partial exceptions as found in pure monopoly (usual selective state-driven industries). Or they may possibly wilt in preponderance under competitive market pressure, even perhaps inside modes controlled by large oligopolies. Competitive threats to survival or subsistence may emerge equally inside any mode, and between nodes that search for their own survival edge. All are competing for the best advantage. The economic survival of the fittest often implies attrition for others. Vulnerability extends to the forces shaping the continuity of economic modes and their relative status. Transitions whether along the value chain or into another *modus vivendi* might be forced by the advent of competitive pressures, market shifts or even state interventions.

6   It would be a difficult task to place accurate numbers on the evolution of economic modes in Africa today, and a gargantuan effort would be required to identify all their inner nodes. But with 1 billion people found on the continent, if only 100,000 were somehow primarily linked to any one identifiable mode – say an industry, corporate system, state body, or self-sufficient entity (village, subsistence household or collections thereof) – the economic fabric would comprise thousands of modes of survival. These elements make up the economic base. Today there exist 55 African states, plus some statelets or zones outside the effective remit of central government edict. All hold their own complexities and economic composites making up Africa's modes of existence. The archetype economy might have, say, 50 separate "sectors" in modern or pre-modern form – maybe with half-a-dozen more modern or large countries like South Africa or Nigeria having many more. Each sector probably has a minimum on average of, say, 50 firms, entities or companies competing for the economic space. In the informal economies of Africa, these numbers would be far larger, in the millions. On this calculus, there are most probably several million units of subsistence and survival in Africa, in the form of entities that operate, act and see their own economic interests as primordial, and on which many more inhabitants depend for their basic livelihood.

7   It is worth here noting, albeit in the jargon of the discipline, some of the evident variances from the conventional supply-demand model of standard economics. In orthodox models the constituents shaping outcomes are atomistic, equilibrium is the outcome, prior histories are unimportant or neglected and uninfluential, simplicity is of the essence, static and linear parameters normally perform the magic (while the use of dynamic or constrained boundaries amount to more of the same), the maximisation of utility is sought, the entities involved in supply or on the demand side exhibit

general anonymity and continue through the process without hindrance, as the models exhibit uniformity of application irrespective of circumstance.

8   More technically, the economic evolution implied here stresses connectivities between and within these highly imperfect worlds, with disjunctions not uncommon, competitive selection processes dominant in shaping outcomes, while the economic histories are germane to this model of complexity, where change is non-linear as the various economic modes struggle for accumulation as a means for survival, potentially with zero-sum outcomes, while a process of creative destruction shapes the interfaces, and the modes involved speciate as well, to encounter internodal competition and even nodal exits from one mode to another.

9   A case in point is the Congo Basin. There economic and social fragmentation is legendary. Many conflicted zones operate as appendages unharnessed in reality to the "nation-state" as nominally accepted, whatever the fiction, as the primary unit of analysis. There are many micro-studies done in economics and other universes may be used for data and interpretation, but it is the macro that typically engages the main reference point for analysis of the state of Africa, its economies and their performance. In the case of the DRC, during the last decade there have been around 40–50 economic wars and separatist enclaves established or dissolved within its cartographic boundaries. Many instances in Africa exhibit significant economic fragmentation, perhaps of a lesser degree, on the same lines. National accounts are weak tools for understanding any of this drama. For insights on state collapse, fragmentation and economic medievalism see Gerard Prunier, *Africa's Great War: Congo, the Rwandan Genocide, and the Making of a Continental Catastrophe*, Oxford University Press, 2009, and Jason K. Stearns, *Dancing in the Glory Of Monsters: The Collapse of the Congo and the Great War of Africa*, Public Affairs, 2011; in a different context see Tim Butcher, *Blood River: A Journey In Africa's Broken Heart*, Chatto & Windus, 2007, and *Chasing The Devil: The Search for Africa's Fighting Spirit*, Chatto & Windus, 2010, depicting conditions in Sierra Leone and Liberia.

4   Africa's evolution

1   John Reader, Africa: *A Biography of the Continent*, Hamish Hamilton, 1997, for appreciation of this, in an account of the deep natural forces that have shaped Africa over thousands of years.

2   The complex adaptive process over time typically leads to many mutations and competition between modes, and even within them. It equally provides the option, chance and opportunity for an economic mode to move ahead in the struggle, leading beyond mere survival towards enhanced success. Africa's evolutionary pathways can be highly diverse, random even, and are unlikely to be subject uniquely to any calculated economic plan set in stone by policymakers in the nation-state or governments,

let alone those proclaimed by edict. Economic modes and nodes search for survival within constraints set before them.

3   In the Pareto rule, for example, a company may derive 80% of its revenues from 20% of its ventures or products.

4   For the process affecting the San coming from the settlers in the Cape, see Mohamed Adhikari, *The Anatomy of a South African Genocide: The extermination of the Cape San peoples*, UCT Press, 2010. Adhikari fails, however, to address the much earlier displacement over a much longer era that flowed from initial Bantu incursions and presence in Southern Africa.

5   For evaluations of economic growth, policy and multiple country case studies, see the compendium of analyses on Africa shown in Benno J. Ndulu, Stephen A. O'Connell, Robert H. Bates, Paul Collier and Chukwuma C. Soludo (editors), *The Political Economy of Economic Growth in Africa 1960–2000*, Vol. I, and Vol. II (Country Case Studies), Cambridge University Press, 2008. Another magnum opus of this type is awaited and could not be consulted here as it was due for publication in January 2012: see Ernest Aryeetey, Shantayanan Devarajan, Ravi Kanbur and Louis Kasekende (editors), *The Oxford Companion to the Economics of Africa*, Oxford University Press, 2012.

6   There is a mini-industry of texts on Robert Mugabe and the regime's kleptocracy. Few know it better from the inside than Michael Auret, *From Liberator to Dictator*, New Africa Books, 2009.

7   For detailed instances of this slide in fortunes and the extent of corruption in government, see R.W. Johnson, *South Africa's Brave New World: The Beloved Country Since the End of Apartheid*, Allen Lane, 2009. Also John Pottinger, *The Mbeki Legacy*, Zebra Press, 2008. The details of flawed empowerment deals, state indulgence, cadre exploitation of the public service, and much more, can be read daily in the local press. It is almost impossible to keep up with the shenanigans recorded, and it all seems like an unstoppable gravy train on the railway to ruin.

8   A simple calculation can show the cost for, say, an economy of $10 billion, in which the normal real compound growth rate might have been 4% for 20 years, yielding GDP of $21.19 billion. With the loss of, say, half that growth (the economy growing at 2% annually), the outcome would yield GDP of only $14.86 billion, a loss of over 25%. Some African economies actually went into negative growth over significant periods of time, others slashed their growth rates by much more, and in many cases recovery trajectories have been slow and arduous.

9   The evidence can be found in Africa's multiple and complex shifting economic ecologies, in the widely varied histories of the continent's socioeconomic matrices, and along the intertemporal pathways that economies have grown in size and differentiation (even as some have fossilised or atrophied). It may be seen within the morphology of almost any of Africa's nation-states, and in the sometimes repetitive design of economic structures from one era to another. Growth likewise brings to the

fore the class of more modernised economies while others, or zones within, follow economic paths that have locked them into destinies that may not survive the competitive evolutionary path before them.

5 Subsistence pathways

1   The most acknowledged historian on the *prazos* must be Allen F. Isaacman, *The Africanization of a Portuguese Institution, the Zambezi Prazos 1710–1902*, Madison: University of Wisconsin Press, 1972; also see by the same author, *The Tradition of Resistance in Mozambique: Anti-Colonial Activity in the Zambezi Valley 1850–1921*, Heinemann, 1976.

2   Described in detail in *The Life and Explorations of David Livingstone, LL.D., Carefully Compiled from Reliable Sources*, J.R. Halsam, Nottingham, undated, but printed following his death, with the references cited on the page entitled "Mode of Elephant Hunting".

3   For an instance of this hustle and bustle around rising and ubiquitous border trading complexes, see Terence McNamee, "The rise of the African border town", *Mail & Guardian*, 23 December 2010, which aptly describes Kasumbalesa, 90km south of Lubumbashi.

4   It is well worth consulting many older texts on Africa's transitions to the modern era for insights on the medieval and on shifts towards its current juncture over the last 100–500 years, providing a stock of knowledge that most contemporary economists seldom appear to read. See Melville J. Herskovits and Mitchell Harwits, *Economic Transition in Africa*, Routledge & Kegan Paul, 1964, and Peter Wickens, *An Economic History of Africa from the Earliest Times to Partition*, Oxford University Press, 1981, as well as John Gunther, *Inside Africa*, Hamish Hamilton, London, undated, Calvin W. Stillman (editor), *Africa in the Modern World*, University of Chicago Press, 1955, and Nigel Heseltine, *Remaking Africa*, Museum Press Limited, 1961. See also Walter W. Bishop & J. Desmond Clark (editors), *Background to Evolution in Africa*, University of Chicago Press, 1967, on old historiography and anthropology. Likewise of interest is Frank Vincent, *Actual Africa; or, the coming continent*, William Heinemann, 1895, which captures realities at the time; and Arthur Silva White, *The Development of Africa*, George Philip & Son, 1890, which recounts much on Africa's natural obstacles encountered in the 19th century. Robin Hallett, *Africa to 1875: A Modern History*, University of Michigan Press, 1970, looks at the continent in the 19th century, as does Edgar Sanderson, *Africa in the Nineteenth Century*, Charles Scribner's Sons, 1898. These are just a few that tell parts of the story I recount.

5   See various studies by Angus Maddison, *Contours of the World Economy, 1–2030 AD: Essays in Macro-Economic History*, Oxford University Press, 2007, and *The*

World Economy: Volume 1: A Millennial Perspective, Volume 2: Historical Statistics, OECD, Development Centre Studies, 2006. See also the analysis and data compiled by the late Angus Maddison found at www.ggdc.net/maddison.

6   In the booming Africa oil and gas industry there are found far-flung nodal points around operating centres, oil towns, gas facilities, pipelines, LNG plants, offshore bases, inland and desert exploration facilities, oil camps and rig locations, expatriate complexes, refineries, and the like. These structures created new impetus in many parts of the continent, which, without them, would probably have been condemned to economic backwardness. Africa's many hundreds of different oil and gas units are loosely interfaced with perhaps thousands of disparate economic modes, at the centre and in the peripheries, on the coasts and in many interiors. The existence of one and all has sometimes had an impact on the others. No automatic predetermined offset in the form of a zero-sum game should be expected (though many accounts assume such). It is the entirety of the continent that constitutes the complexity of Africa, the oil locomotive being only one part of this economic collage.

7   See notably statistics found at www.ggdc.net/maddison. Updates for 2009–10 have been made on IMF and World Bank data.

8   Ian Morris, *Why The West Rules – For Now: The patterns of history and what they reveal about the future*, Profile Books, 2010.

9   Vijay Mahajan, *Africa Rising: How 900 Million African Consumers Offer More Than You Think*, Wharton School Publishing, 2009.

6   Natural Africa

1   Eric Halladay, *Africa: The Emergent Continent in the 19th Century*, St Martin's Press, 1972.

2   For details on African mythologies and relationships to hunters, cattle-herders and diverse African kingdoms across the continent, see Stephen Belcher, *African Myths of Origin*, Penguin Books, 2005.

3   For insights on these issues in natural order, see "Africa: Whatever you thought, think again", *National Geographic*, September 2006.

4   For insights on geography in contemporary Africa, see *World Development Report, Reshaping Economic Geography*, The World Bank, 2009.

5   A depiction of African river cultures and their economic significance can be found in Molefi Kete Asante, *The History of Africa: The Quest for Eternal Harmony*, Routledge, 2007.

6   For a sense of this economic world, see Mike Boon's journal of his 3,000km journey by canoe from the headwaters of the Zambezi to the Indian Ocean: *Zambezi: The First Solo Journey down Africa's Mighty River*, Struik Publishers, 2007.

7   See world review on this issue and related aspects in Felipe Fernandez-Armesto, *Pathfinders: A Global History of Exploration*, Oxford University Press, 2006.

8   Stephen Belcher, op. cit.

7   Stone Age triumph and beyond

1   Roland Oliver, *The African Experience: From Olduvai Gorge to the 21st Century*, Westview, 1999.

2   Thomas N. Huffman, *Handbook to the Iron Age: The Archaeology of Pre-Colonial Farming Societies in Southern Africa*, University of Kwa-Zulu Natal Press, 2007.

3   H. Ellert, *The Material Culture of Zimbabwe*, Longman, 1984.

4   See "The Prehistoric Wealth of Nations", *Foreign Policy*, March/April 2007, page 23.

5   For details see Alastair Hazell, *The Last Slave Market: Dr John Kirk and the Struggle to End the African Slave Trade*, Constable, 2011.

6   Ralph A. Austen, *Trans-Saharan Africa in World History*, Oxford University Press, 2010.

7   This is well depicted in David Eltis and David Richardson, *Atlas of the Transatlantic Slave Trade*, Yale University Press, 2010, which provides excellent maps of the slave traffic from source to destination with a deep analysis of its patterns and volumes of slavery conducted over time.

8   See studies contained in Henri Medard and Shane Doyle (editors), *Slavery in the Great Lakes of East Africa*, James Currey, 2007.

9   See the historical study of the era by Bill Freund, *The Making of Contemporary Africa: The Development of African Society since 1800*, Indiana University Press, 1984.

10   For details on the consequences of the Mfecane, see Carolyn Hamilton (editor), *The Mfecane Aftermath: Reconstructive Debates in Southern African History*, Witwatersrand University Press, 1995.

11   R.N. Hall, *Pre-Historic Rhodesia: An Examination of the Historical, Ethnological and Archaeological Evidences as to the Origins and Age of the Rock Mines and Stone Buildings, With a Gazetteer of Medieval South-East Africa, 915 A.D. to 1760 A.D. and the Countries of the Monomotapa, Manica, Sabia, Quiteve, Sofala and Mozambique*, T. Fisher Unwin, 1909; and S.I.G. Mudenge, *A Political History of Munhumutapa c.1400–1902*, African Publishing Group, 2011.

12   See social and economic research done on central Africa and Rhodesia/Zimbabwe over the 20th century and after, including by I.R. Phimister, op. cit., where numerous historical works and sources are cited for this issue including works by Terence Ranger, Charles van Onselen, David Beach, Julian Cobbing, Ngwabe Bhebe, Robin Palmer and others.

13　These difficulties in world exploration have been portrayed by Felipe Fernandez-Armesto, op. cit.

14　Ryszard Kapuscinski, *The Cobra's Heart*, Penguin Books, 1998. One of the most prolific and widely acknowledged writers, Ryszard Kapuscinski, a Polish journalist, arrived in Africa in 1957, at the time of Ghana's independence, and wrote on the continent for over 40 years. See Ryszard Kapuscinski, *The Shadow of the Sun: My African Life*, Allen Lane, 2001. There are many related texts from this scribe, and in recent times this writing has come in for some criticism from Africans following the author's death in January 2007.

15　While there is an enormous literature on South Africa's history, for an excellent synoptic overview see Francis Wilson, *Dinosaurs, Diamonds And Democracy: A short, short history of South Africa*, Umuzi, 2009.

16　See Martin Legassick, *The Struggle for the Eastern Cape 1800–1854: Subjugation and the roots of South African Democracy*, KMM 2010, and on the San peoples see Mohamed Adhikari, *The Anatomy of a South African Genocide: The extermination of the Cape San peoples*, UCT Press, 2010.

17　On Tippu Tip's significance in Central Africa, see Leda Farrant, *Tippu Tip and the East African Slave Trade*, Hamish Hamilton, 1975.

18　Gerald L'Ange, *The White Africans: From Colonisation to Liberation*, Jonathan Ball Publishers, 2005.

8　"Modern" Africa

1　Thomas K. McCraw, *Prophet of Innovation: Joseph Schumpeter and Creative Destruction*, The Belknap Press of Harvard University Press, 2007. The quotation is taken from Schumpeter's review of Keynes's *General Theory of Employment, Interest and Money*, in *Journal of the American Statistical Association*, Vol. 31, (December 1936), page 791.

2　Alec Russell, *Big Men, Little People: Encounters in Africa*, Macmillan, 1999, for examples drawn from Mobutu Sese Seko, Hastings Banda, Kenneth Kaunda, Daniel Arap Moi, Jonas Savimbi, King Mswati III and some leaders from South Africa where I believe this complex, owing to its peculiar history, is less a feature. A riveting account of African dictators is found in Riccardo Orizio, *Talk of the Devil: Encounters with Seven Dictators*, Walker & Company, New York, 2003. On Africa, it deals with Idi Amin, Jean-Bédel Bokassa and Mengistu Haile Mariam.

3　*Shamwari* is a word much used in Zimbabwe and Central Africa for "friends", those with a special place in the heart but as an obligation towards "one's own", for ethnic, familial or related reasons.

4   This interview with V.S. Naipaul took place on 13 May 1979, during a dire time across Africa. See details at www.nytimes.com/books/98/06/07/specials/naipaul-meeting.html

5   V.S. Naipaul, *A Bend in the River*, Random House, 1980.

6   Paul Theroux, "Colonial Times", *New York Times*, 1 July 1979.

7   Paul Theroux, *Dark Star Safari: Overland from Cairo to Cape Town*, Hamish Hamilton (Penguin), 2002. In a more recent piece, "Continent Adrift", *Vanity Fair*, April 2008 (pages 129–30), Theroux notes that "nothing will change as long as the Governments are corrupt, indifferent or posturing".

8   Chinua Achebe, *Things Fall Apart*, Penguin Books, 1958.

9   I have here brought together references to the authors cited. For background on Ngugi and the many works written, see www.kirjasto.sci.fi/ngugiw.htm. Also see Wole Soyinka, *The Open Sore of a Continent: A Personal Narrative of the Nigerian Crisis*, Oxford University Press, 1996, and an autobiography, *You Must Set Forth at Dawn: A Memoir*, Methuen, 2006. As well as Patrick Wilmot, *Seeing Double*, Jonathan Cape, London, 2005, and Franz Fanon, *The Wretched of the Earth*, Grove Press, 1986.

10 Apart from maybe Nelson Mandela, and I am excluding Leopold Senghor, a poet and cultural theorist, who represented established order in Senegal (as president from 1960 to 1980).

11 Bob Geldof, *Geldof in Africa*, Arrow Books, 2006.

12 See *The Week*, 9 July 2011.

9   Post-colony aftermath

1   For this global phenomenon and on Africa, see Mike Davis, *Planet of Slums*, Verso, 2006.

2   On Malthusian economics, see Gregory Clark, *A Farewell to Alms: A Brief Economic History of the World*, Princeton University Press, 2007, and for arguments on why the shift from hunter-gatherer societies has often meant a decrease in living standards around a new Malthusian equilibrium.

3   Gregory Clark, op. cit., Table 3–3, page 46.

4   Jean-Marc Balencie, *Les nouveaux mondes rebelles: Conflicts, terrorisme et contestations*, Editions Michalon, 2005.

5   For an excellent exposition of this desert world across Africa west to east, see Paul Salopek, "The Sahel", *National Geographic*, April 2008, page 49.

6   Tim Butcher, *Chasing the Devil*, op. cit.

7   V.S. Naipaul, *The Masque of Africa: Glimpses of African Belief*, Picador, 2010.

10 State complexities

1 Francis Fukuyama, *The Origins of Political Order: From Prehuman Times to the French Revolution*, Profile Books, 2011.

2 Jean-François Bayart, *The State in Africa: The Politics of the Belly*, 2nd edition, Polity, 2010, the French original published in 1989.

3 The view is put by Adekeye Adebajo, *The Curse of Berlin: Africa After the Cold War*, University of KwaZulu-Natal Press, 2010.

4 Olufemi Taiwo, *How Colonialism Preempted Modernity in Africa*, Indiana University Press, 2010.

5 John Reader, op. cit.

6 Guy Arnold, *Africa: A Modern History*, Atlantic Books, 2005.

7 Ibid.

8 Martin Meredith, *The State of Africa. A History of Fifty Years of Independence*, Free Press, 2005.

9 I have dealt in depth elsewhere with the economic fallacies, arguments, theory and logic when confronted with actualities related to the "oil curse" syndrome in Africa, in Duncan Clarke, *Africa: Crude Continent: The Struggle for Africa's Oil Prize*, Profile Books, 2010.

10 Paul Nugent, *Africa Since Independence: A Comparative History*, Palgrave Macmillan, 2004.

11 Christopher Clapham, Jeffrey Herbst and Greg Mills, *Big African States*, Wits University Press, 2001.

12 See Norrie MacQueen, *The Decolonization of Portuguese Africa: Metropolitan Revolution and the Dissolution of Empire*, Longman, 1997.

13 See collected writings in Maxim Matusevich (editor), *Africa in Russia, Russia in Africa: Three Centuries of Encounters*, Africa World Press Inc., 2007.

14 Howard W. French, *A Continent for the Taking: The Tragedy and Hope of Africa*, Alfred A. Knopf, 2004.

15 Patrick Chabal and Jean-Pascal Daloz, *Africa Works, Disorder as Political Instrument*, James Currey & Indiana University Press, 1999.

16 Jean-Francois Bayart, Stephen Ellis and Beatrice Hibou, *The Criminalisation of the State in Africa*, James Currey & Indiana University Press, 1999

17 Tim Butcher, *Blood River*, op. cit. Another in a similar genre, with travel by river from Kinshasa to Kisangani on river boats then back again in a hand-carved pirogue, tells a similar tale: see Jeffrey Tayler, *Facing The Congo*, Little, Brown and Company, 2000. On the travels and travails of Stanley, see Henry M. Stanley, *Through the Dark Continent* (2 volumes), Dover Publications, Inc., New York, 1988, and for a biography read Frank McLynn, *Stanley: Dark Genius of African Exploration*, Pimlico, 2004.

18 Ibid, page 286.

19   The best work on Stanley and a correction to myth is found in Tim Jeal, *Stanley: The Impossible Life of Africa's Greatest Explorer*, Faber and Faber, 2007. It speaks of the wars raging around the Congo (these continue today), the pointlessness of "preaching to Africans", the disparaging views held (by Stanley) of "easy chair geographers" (think here contemporary rock stars, economists and foreign-policy wonks), the many myths held on Africa (still highly apposite today), how slavery was a precursor to the migrant labour systems across the continent (common in the 21st century too), the many modes of subsistence survival encountered (that remain in place), the criticality of traditional leaders in rural Africa, multiple inter-ethnic wars (an echo of the modern saga in many countries), the impacts of warlords (that still command economic and political space inside Africa), cannibalism (found around the Great Lakes), the importance of riverine Africa and ecology to socioeconomic conditions, the pre-scramble roles of Great Powers (this mirrors the post-independence 21st-century scramble by states and private companies for African resource patrimony), the disconnected fiefdoms scattered across vast terrains, continuous instances of wanton brutality (a condition the continent seeks to escape), the claims made for nationhood amid ethnic separatism, and the extensive Western interest in "redeeming Africa" (a practice found in NGO efforts and modern literature on Africa).

20   Michela Wrong, *In the Footsteps of Mr Kurtz: Living on the Brink of Disaster in the Congo*, Fourth Estate, 2000. Wrong followed up this work with one on Eritrea and then another on corruption in Kenya: *It's Our Turn to Eat: The Story of a Kenyan Whistle-Blower*, Fourth Estate, 2009, which examines the scale of corruption in Kenya, where many leading politicians had their snouts in the trough. On King Leopold, see Neal Ascherson, *The King Incorporated: Leopold the Second and the Congo*, George Allen & Unwin, 1963.

21   Thomas Turner, *The Congo Wars: Conflict, Myth and Reality*, Zed Books, 2007.

22   Gerard Prunier, op. cit. See also for another angle John F. Clark (editor), *The African Stakes of the Congo War*, Fountain Publishers, 2003.

11 Economic tracks

1   S. Herbert Frankel, *Capital Investment in Africa: Its Course and Effects*, Oxford University Press, 1938. Another old economics text on Africa worth reading is René Dumont, *False Start in Africa*, Andre Deutsch, 1966, which lamented on what had gone wrong, mostly in francophone Africa, even at that early stage in a work and with advice that went mostly unheeded. See also the long interview with Dumont in 1981, reprinted again in *New African*, November 2010.

2   Robert Calderisi, *The Trouble with Africa: Why Foreign Aid Isn't Working*, Yale University Press, 2007. Another former World Bank economist, William Easterly, provides a critique directed at the world aid game, of which Africa is a major

consumer and the most recalcitrant, sometimes recidivist client. He chastises the West for its aid strategies, knocks the big push theses behind many development attempts, and sees the failure of foreign and state planning as a cause of poor market structures that ill-serve the poor, Africa's included. See William Easterly, *The White Man's Burden*, Oxford University Press, 2006.

3   There are innumerable economic reports available, issued annually, and much research, with one of the latest, African Development Bank, *Africa Economic Outlook, 2011*, done in partnership with the ECA, OECD and UNDP, while the World Bank has issued many documents, research and reports on Africa's economies and its own strategy.

4   Benno J. Ndulu (editor), op. cit.

5   Vishnu Padayachee (editor), *The Political Economy of Africa*, Routledge, 2010.

6   Paul Collier, *The Bottom Billion: Why the Poorest Countries are Failing and What Can Be Done About It*, Oxford University Press, 2007.

7   See Edward Miguel, *Africa's Turn?* (A Boston Review Book), MIT Press, 2009.

8   For more details on the views of this political scientist, see Robert H. Bates, *When Things Fell Apart*, Cambridge University Press, 2008, where an analysis is offered based on game theory. I find it wholly uncompelling, especially the use of cross-country regressions based on the use of vague and subjective political variables.

9   *Vanity Fair*, July 2007, page 106.

10 Jeffrey Sachs, *Common Wealth: Economics for a Crowded Planet*, Allen Lane, 2008. The aid game has recently come in for severe criticism from divergent sides. See notably in regard to Africa Dambisa Moyo, *Dead Aid*, Allen Lane, 2009, where the argument is made that the aid taps should be turned off, as Africa is being "killed with kindness". For one review of Moyo, see Jagdish Bhagwati, *Foreign Affairs*, January/February 2010.

11 Paul Theroux, "Lies and Daring: Revealing Stanley", *International Herald Tribune*, 29–30 September 2007, page 9 (a review of Tim Jeal, *Stanley: The Impossible Life of Africa's Greatest Explorer*, Yale University Press, 2007).

12 Patrick Bond, *Looting Africa: The Economics of Exploitation*, University of KwaZulu-Natal Press and Zed Books, 2006. In a similar vein, as a critique of modern economic policies, see Graham Harrison, *Neoliberal Africa: The Impact of Global Social Engineering*, Zed Books, 2010. Much of the economics literature from the left over the past three decades can be found in the *Review of African Political Economy*.

13 Robert Guest, *The Shackled Continent: Africa's Past, Present and Future*, Pan Books, 2004.

14 Greg Mills, *Why Africa is Poor: And What Africans Can Do About It*, Penguin Books, 2010

15 Moeletsi Mbeki, *Architects of Poverty: Why African Capitalism Needs Changing*, Picador Africa, 2009. See also Moeletsi Mbeki (editor), *Advocates For Change: How to Overcome Africa's Challenges*, Picador Africa, 2011. Mbeki has remarked

elsewhere that Africa's elites have used the economy as an "eating option" of sorts: see "In the end it's all about having the economy for dinner", *The Star*, 30 August 2010, Johannesburg. Recently, South Africans have begun, after a long winter of enclosure in the laager and post-apartheid introspection, to take more interest in Africa's economic world north of the Limpopo. This has in part been driven by the corporate lunge into the continent, the *comme ci, comme ça* economic diplomacy of Pretoria and the erosion of Johannesburg's presumptive "gateway" status into Africa (with many competitor hubs, entry conduits and launch pads threatening this once-presumed primacy: Mauritius, Nairobi, Lagos, Singapore, Dubai, even Cyprus and Cape Verde) – most oil or mineral companies from abroad go straight to their resource target destinations, and Johannesburg makes little sense for those with any Maghreb portfolio to cultivate.

16 Moeletsi Mbeki has even suggested that there is "nothing mysterious" about why Africa is the least-developed continent and Africans the poorest. Plunder seems to be the answer, an eternal fascination of political scientists with the bogey of the dominant elites that "determine" development or not. If only Africa's policymakers would heed the policy wonks. Clearly they often do not. Should this be the case, why then would the contemporary elite-nationalists, found in all states, heed any such advice? The idea that a few policies of reform alone, of state machines or deformed capitalism, might turn Africa's economic ship around is one beloved by all policy advocates. It is in a sense hope over expectation, and neglect of the embedded and many complex economic structures built in multiple histories and transitions that underlie both modern Africa and its economies.

17 Let me here merely refer to historians and works already mentioned in I.R. Phimister, op. cit. See also Kwame Anthony Appiah, "Africa: The Hidden History", *New York Review of Books*, Vol. 45, No. 20, 17 December 1998, and Neal Ascherson, "Africa's Lost History", *New York Review of Books*, Vol. 29, No. 11, 11 June 1992.

18 Albert Camus, *Le Mythe de Sisyphe*, 1942, in http://en.wikipedia.org/wiki/The_Myth_of_Sisyphus

12 Future imperfect

1 The quotation is from Stephen Ellis, *Season of Rains: Africa in the World*, Jacana Media, page 29.

2 See Justin Lin's remarks in "Transformation without tears", *African Business*, July 2011, pages 13–16.

3 McKinsey Global Institute, *Lions on the Move: Progress and Potential of African economies*, June 2010,

4 Rises had been recorded in the probability of surviving to 40 years in many countries, although doctor densities varied enormously across Africa, health workers had

emigrated and malaria ravaged the sub-Saharan environs. Famines too had come and gone, but come again, the hand of nature apparently untamed, although most failed to distinguish the reality that while nature induced drought, it was typically the hand of mankind that led to famine. Indicators of water access, sanitation and social measures on the HDI front remained stubbornly high. Unemployment was a continuing and rising scourge on the economic front, the future dilemma expected in fast-rising populaces glossed over by those that converted this malaise into some fictional and future demographic dividend.

5 Details are reported in Malcolm Ray, "Tipping Point: How South Africa Lost its Way", *Business Times Magazine*, Vol. 03, August 2011, an edited extract from his forthcoming book to be published by Random House Struik in spring 2012.

6 I have made these rough guesstimates for Africa from adjustments to data provided on world demography based on estimates by Carl Haub in "How Many People Have Ever Lived on Earth?", found at www.prb.org/Articles/2002/HowManyPeople-HaveEverLivedonEarth.aspx

7 Jakkie Cilliers, Barry Hughes and Jonathan Meyer, *African Futures 2050*, Institute for Security Studies, Pretoria, 2011

8 Reported in the Johannesburg *Sunday Times*, 21 November 2010, and drawn from an excerpt of the second Anton Rupert Memorial lecture at the University of Pretoria.

9 World Bank, *Africa's Future and the World Bank's Role in it*, Washington, 2010. See also World Bank, *Africa's Future and the World Bank's Support to It*, March 2011.

10 Steven Radelet, *Emerging Africa: How 17 Countries are Leading the Way*, Center For Global Development, 2010.

11 African Development Bank, *Africa in 50 Years' Time: The Road Towards Inclusive Growth*, Tunis, September 2011.

12 Mastercard Worldwide, *Africa 10/21: The Ten Markets in Sub-Sahara Africa That Will Lead the Transformation of the Continent in the 21st Century*, Mastercard Worldwide Insights, 2010.

13 Renaissance Capital, *Africa: The Bottom Billion Becomes the Fastest Billion*, 18 July 2011.

14 See details in Vivien Foster and Cecilia Briceno-Garmendia (editors), *Africa's Infrastructure: A Time for Transformation*, Agence Française de Développement and World Bank, 2010.

15 African Development Bank, *The Middle of the Pyramid: Dynamics of the Middle Class in Africa*, Market Brief, April 2011.

16 See Xavier Sala-i-Martin and Maxim Pinkovskiy, *African Poverty Is Falling ... Much Faster Than You Think*, NBER Working Paper Series, Working Paper 15775, February 2010.

17 Care should be exercised with these Gini measures, however, since often they rely on incomplete and imperfect data while typically they are based on pre-tax incomes and do not account for subsidies and benefits distributed to lower income groups.

Equally, with intertemporal measures the same people are not necessarily covered in the same income class from one time to another, while in places such as Africa the large demographic shifts make for non-standardisation in measures shown for any specific group. Moreover, measures are shown typically on individual income and may not therefore reflect household incomes, so providing additional inaccuracies for certain purposes of interpretation.

18   See McKinsey Global Institute, op. cit.
19   Capgemini-Merrill Lynch Global Wealth Management, *World Wealth Report*, 2011.
20   See "Call to open Mswati's 'feedlot'", *Mail & Guardian*, 29 July–4 August 2011.
21   See *Mail & Guardian Online*, 26 July 2011, for an update found in http://mg.co.za/article/2010–03–19-zuma-incorporated
22   The World Bank, *Where is the Wealth of Nations: Measuring Capital for the 21st Century*, Washington, 2006.
23   The World Bank, *The Changing Wealth of Nations: Measuring Sustainable Development in the New Millennium*, Washington, 2011.
24   Among these works, see Roger Southall and Henning Melber (editors), *A New Scramble for Africa? Imperialism, Investment and Development*, University of KwaZulu-Natal Press, 2009, Padraig Carmody, *The New Scramble for Africa*, Polity, 2011, Guy Arnold, *The New Scramble for Africa*, North South Books, 2009, and with a more historical bent, Paul Southern, *Portugal: The Scramble for Africa*, Galago Books, 2010.
25   Martyn Davies, Frontier Advisory, 5th Africa Economic Forum 2011, Global Pacific & Partners, in *China's Work in Progress in Africa*, where the regression coefficient for the growth rates of Africa/China over the years 1999–2008 is given at 0.919972.
26   See *The African Challengers: Global Competitors Emerge from the Overlooked Continent*, Boston Consulting Group, 2010.
27   Sebastiao Salgado, *Sahel: The End of the Road*, University of California Press, 2004, and *Africa*, Taschen, 2007.
28   This drama and the man-made extremities of famine have been well portrayed by Aidan Hartley, "The famine myth", *The Spectator*, 6 August 2011.

Acknowledgements

1   D. Hobart Houghton, *The South African Economy*, Oxford University Press, 1967.
2   For works by Professor Peter Robson, see *inter alia*: Peter Robson, *Economic Integration in Africa*, Routledge, 2010 (reprinted: first published 1968), and Peter Robson and D.A. Lury (editors), *The Economies of Africa*, Routledge, 2010 (reprinted).
3   The main works were the following: *Domestic Workers in Rhodesia: The Economics of Masters and Servants*, Mambo Press, Gwelo, 1974; *Contract Workers and Underdevelopment in Rhodesia*, Mambo Press, Gwelo, 1974; *Unemployment and*

Economic Structure in Rhodesia, Mambo Press, Gwelo, 1976; *The Economics of African Old Age Subsistence in Rhodesia*, Mambo Press, Gwelo, 1977; *The Distribution of Income and Wealth in Rhodesia*, Mambo Press, Gwelo 1977; *Agricultural and Plantation Workers in Rhodesia*, Mambo Press, Gwelo, 1977; *Labour conditions and discrimination in Southern Rhodesia (Zimbabwe)*, ILO, 1978; *International Labour Supply Trends and Economic Structure in Southern Rhodesia/Zimbabwe in the 1970s*, ILO, World Employment Programme, Working Paper No. 20, Geneva, 1978; *Foreign Migrant Labour in Southern Africa: Studies on Accumulation in the Labour Reserves, Demand Determinants and Supply Relationships*, ILO, World Employment Programme, Working Paper No. 16, 1977; *International Aid and Debt in Migrant Labour Exporting Economies in Southern Africa*, Economic Commission for Africa, Addis Ababa, 1978; *The Employment Impact of Altered Trade Relations on Migrant Labour Exporting Countries in Southern Africa*, Economic Commission for Africa, Addis Ababa, 1978; *Structural Economic Conditions in Least Developed Countries*, UNCTAD, 1979; *The Agriculture, Forestry & Fisheries Sectors in Southern Africa*, SADCC, Arusha Conference, 1979; *The Monetary, Banking and Financial System in Zimbabwe*, UNCTAD, 1979; *Review of Skills Problems & Policies in Zimbabwe*, UNCTAD, 1979; *Agricultural Sector Investments in Least Developed Countries in the 1980s*, UNCTAD, 1979; *Foreign Companies & International Investments in Zimbabwe*, IIR/Joseph Rowntree, London, 1980; *Money and Finance in Zimbabwe*, Whitsun Foundation (with RAL Merchant Bank), Harare, 1983; *Southern Africa Intra-Regional Trade Financing Facility*, Feasibility Appraisal, USAID/IFC, Washington, 1983. In addition, through the 1980s numerous private client studies on Africa were done for companies, institutions, banks and multilateral agencies on, *inter alia*: money and finance, telecommunications and satellite systems, energy and electronic infrastructure, oil and gas industries, exploration in resources including mining, risk and investments, balance of payments, rural development, Africa's landlocked and least-developed countries, agribusiness and agro-allied industries, OECD investments in Southern Africa, minerals and rare metals, the Preferential Trade Area in Eastern and Southern Africa, and a range of macroeconomic questions in Western, Eastern and Southern Africa. Since then many advisory and research reports have been done, under the aegis of our firm, for private clients on the upstream and downstream oil and gas industries in Africa and worldwide.

4 Research done then included: *Foreign African Labour Supply in South Africa 1960–1977*, DSRG Working Paper No. I, University of Natal 1977; Charles Simkins and Duncan Clarke, *Structural Unemployment in Southern Africa*, Development Studies Research Group, University of Natal Press, 1978.

5 My initial application of notions on chaology and complexity under uncertainty was conducted on the world oil industry, found in *Strategic Petroleum Insights*, published by Petroconsultants, Geneva. The study examined the notions of reserve dynamics and world oil endowment. This thinking was further enhanced in our Global Pacific & Partners report published under the same title in the early 1990s.

6   Core ideas in *Africa's Future* originated in our Sub-Saharan Africa strategy briefings conducted worldwide (in Cape Town, Johannesburg, Marrakech, Tunis, Dakar, Houston and London) over the last two decades, and in presentations on Africa conducted elsewhere (Nairobi, Entebbe, Arusha, Abuja, Luanda, Windhoek, Maputo, Accra).

Index

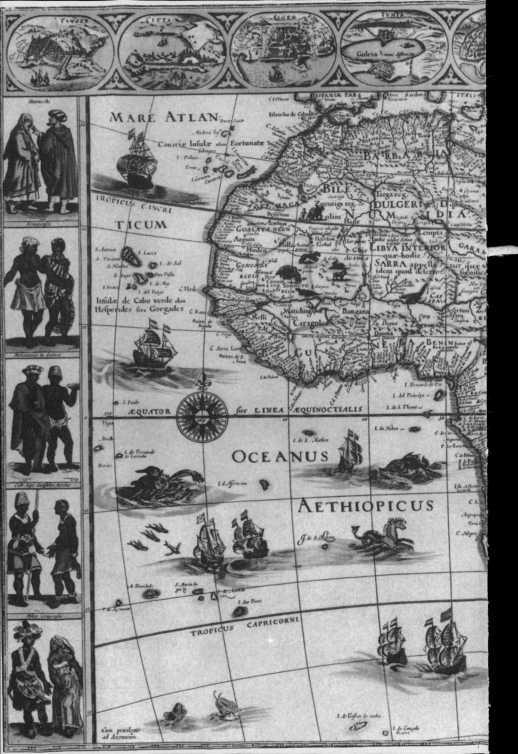